A HISTORY OF WOMEN IN 100 OBJECTS

A HISTORY

OF WOMEN

IN 100

OBJECTS

MAGGIE ANDREWS & JANIS LOMAS

The
History
Press

First published 2018

The History Press
The Mill, Brimscombe Port
Stroud, Gloucestershire, GL5 2QG
www.thehistorypress.co.uk

British Library Cataloguing in Publication Data.
A catalogue record for this book is available from the British
Library.

ISBN 978 0 7509 6714 3

Typesetting and origination by The History Press
Printed in Turkey

Contents

Introduction

Women's history is multifarious, women's experiences infinitely varied, too wide-ranging to be summarised by 100 objects in 100,000 words. The objects we have included provide a starting point for exploring and discussing women's past. They provide a sense of the rich heritage of women, stories of how women were encouraged to conform to ideas of femininity and how feminist forebears challenged any such pressures; the objects are indications of women's oppression, women's heroism, women's ingenuity, and their skill and expertise.

The journey to select the 100 objects for this volume is littered with objects that were going to be included and were then sidelined in favour of others. The choices we have made will not, and should not, be those that others would have made. Historians are not neutral or impartial; they start from where they are at, their own experiences and knowledge, values and interests, their concerns and politics. This is a history written by and with the priorities of social and cultural historians of England in the nineteenth and twentieth centuries, but we have attempted to look beyond this to explore some of the communalities in women's experience across time and space. Written for publication in the year that Britain celebrates the ʾary of suffrage being granted to some women, maybe suffrage and the steps way from women's domestic focus to their increasing engagement in the ʾ loom larger than they otherwise might. This book is however *a* history ʾt *the* history of women; our choices are intended to provide a starting discussions, debate and some discord about women's history, about what, ʾnd why women's lives have been changed, shaped and redefined.

Women's history has perhaps inevitably charted many of the constraints, controls and restrictions placed on women in the past and the present. But women are not passive nor merely victims; they have agency, they find ways of taking control even if the conditions of their lives are far from ideal. In 1852 Marx argued that 'men make their own history, but they do not make it as they please; they do not make it under self-selected circumstances, but under circumstances existing already, given and transmitted from the past'. His analysis could perhaps very usefully have discussed women, who also make their own history, and as rulers, scientists and creative talents they have also made everyone's history although this has all too frequently been forgotten. The objects in this volume celebrate women's skills and resourcefulness, their tenacity and creativity, their sense of fun and freedom in the face of constraints and criticism.

The significance of individual objects discussed sprawls across borders and boundaries although we have arranged them thematically, in sections, to make it easier for readers to navigate their way around the topics. Some of the objects could have been placed in a different sections; the electric refrigerator, which was invented by New Jersey housewife Florence Parpart in 1914, could have come under 'Wives and Homemakers', but is included in the section on 'Science, Technology and Medicine', because it serves as a reminder that domestic technology is not something that is invented for women but something that women have taken a role in inventing themselves.

This is not a book we have written on our own: so many people have been involved in discussion about it and made suggestions for inclusions. We have had the benefit of a considerable number of professionals with relevant expertise. Our special thanks therefore go to Paula Bartley, Dickie James, Sallie McNamara, Lesley Spiers and Gill Thorn. Research and specific chapters have been written by past and present postgraduate and undergraduate history students at the University of Worcester: thanks are due to Hayley Carter, Nicola Connelly, Amy Dale, Lisa Davies, Richard Dhillon, Scott Eeles, Jade Gilks, Elspeth King, Rose Miller, Anna Muggeridge, Linda Pike, Charlotte Sendall and Leah Susans, who have all contributed to making this a more richer and more varied text. The research in this book relies upon the explosion of women's history that has occurred in the last fifty years; it draws upon the academic research of countless historians, who are too numerous to mention or reference. It is not a book intended to sit on the shelves of university libraries but rather to enter the homes of those who had not realised how fascinating women's history can be. We hope you will get excited by women's history and explore it further in the hundreds of books, films, blogs, events and websites dedicated to women's history, perhaps beginning with the Women's History Network, which since its formation in 1991 has been promoting and encouraging women's history in Britain. This book is therefore dedicated to historians of women, past, present and future, with grateful thanks.

Part I
The Body, Motherhood and Sexuality

For some it is the body that defines what it is to be a woman – the experience of menstruation, pregnancy and giving birth – but although these may seem to be unifying biological experiences, they are given many varied meanings in different cultures at different historical moments. There have been, for example, shifting attitudes to the pain women experience in childbirth; thankfully the idea that it was something that women needed to experience in order to love their babies has now been abandoned, thanks to objects such as the Lucy Baldwin apparatus for obstetric analgesia.

Recent debates about gender have shifted away from the idea of a binary opposition between men and women, emphasising the fluidity between the genders, and the degree to which people exert agency in shaping their own gender identity. Objects such as baby feeders have separated the degree to which biology predetermines women's experience.

Nevertheless, many religions have placed taboos on the natural functions of women's bodies, forbidding women to undertake various tasks or enter holy places during menstruation and insisting on the ritual purification of women after giving birth. Similarly, the pleasure that women can enjoy from their own bodies and masturbation remains a topic that may elicit social disapproval. While medieval historians have debunked the myth of metal chastity belts as humorous fantasy objects, there are a range of social and physical ways in which power has been exerted over women's sexuality. Female genital mutilation (FGM) is still practised and is the subject of contemporary feminist campaigns across the world.

For some women who transgress social expectations in relation to sexuality, there has often been a heavy price to pay: they may be considered mad or bad. The tokens left by mothers who had to part with their illegitimate children at the London Foundling Hospital provide an insight into the ways in which women have suffered because they are, so to speak, 'left holding the baby'.

The objects explored in this section also have some upbeat stories to tell: the fun to be had from the introduction of the dual-action vibrator, the Rabbit, in 1984; the freedom women obtained when the Maclaren baby buggy was introduced in the 1960s; and the role grandmothers take in passing on women's history to the next generation.

1 | The Bones of Lucy

The Grandmother of Humanity

MAGGIE ANDREWS

In July 2015, President Obama visited the National Museum of Ethiopia in Addis Ababa to see several hundred pieces of bone fossils representing 40 per cent of the skeleton of a female of the hominin species from some 3.2 million years ago, known as Lucy.

She was discovered by a team of palaeontologists, led by Donald Johanson and Tom Gray, digging in the Afar region of Ethiopia in November 1974; as the team celebrated their discovery over supper, the Beatles album *Sergeant Pepper's Lonely Hearts Club Band* played on the stereo. Someone hearing the song 'Lucy in the Sky with Diamonds' suggested calling this collection of bones, which had most of its skull missing but contained portions of the jaw, vertebral column, pelvis and limbs, Lucy. President Obama referred to his visit to the museum at a state dinner with the Ethiopian Prime Minister, Hailemariam Desalegn, saying:

> We honour Ethiopia as the birthplace of humankind. In fact, I just met Lucy, our oldest ancestor. As your great poet laureate wrote: 'Here is the land where the first harmony in the rainbow was born ... Here is the root of the Genesis of Life; the human family was first planted here'.

He pointed out that Lucy is 'a reminder that the world's people are part of the same human family' and referred to Lucy as the 'grandmother of humanity'.

Scientific evidence suggests that the physical traits shared by all people originated from apelike ancestors slowly evolving over 6 million years. A range of archaeological finds provides indications of significant steps along this evolutionary path. Lucy has attributes of both man and ape; in a sense she is a halfway house between the two species. Most importantly, scientists studying the structure of Lucy's knee and spine curvature have ascertained that she spent most of her time walking on two legs – a distinctly human trait. Furthermore, evidence of tool making has been identified in the East Turkana district of Kenya, believed to be from over 2.5 million years ago. Evidence of this has also been located in East Africa and estimated to date from 2 million years ago. All the fossils of early humans who lived between 6 and 2 million years ago have been found in Africa. The first migration from Africa into Asia is considered to have occurred between 2 million and 1.8 million years ago, and migration to Europe between 1.5 million and 1 million years ago.

The history of women in the millions of years since Lucy lived rests upon snippets of the past, incomplete traces and fragments of women's lives that historians struggle to understand and interpret. As the 1970s feminist Sheila Rowbotham astutely

In 2012, women comprised 64.2 percent of grandparents who lived with their grandchildren in the USA.

pointed out, women have been 'hidden from history'. Their history is often about the private and domestic spheres, intimate relationships, heroic struggles to survive; women's stories are rarely considered important enough to be written down and recorded. Instead women's history is often passed down by stories told by mothers to daughters, and perhaps even more importantly, told and retold by grandmothers. As Angela Cavender Wilson explained in the *American Indian Quarterly* in 1996:

> As I listened to my grandmother telling the last words spoken by her great-great-grandmother, and my grandmother's interpretation, I understood that our most important role as women is making sure our young ones are taken care of so that our future as Dakota people is assured ... It also was clear, through this story and others, that although these were and continue to be hard memories to deal with, always there is pride and dignity in the actions of our women.

Histories and traditions are often handed down in the many hours grandmothers spend caring for their grandchildren. In Britain, women working in the Lancashire factories in the nineteenth and early twentieth centuries often relied on grandmothers for childcare, as did women who worked in the Portsmouth dockyards in the Second World War. In many contemporary societies marital breakdown and the need to combine paid work and motherhood ensures grandmothers continue to play a role in providing physical, practical and emotional support to their daughters and daughters-in-law. Furthermore, the Helping Hands study of 3,000 over-55s carried out in Britain in 2010 discovered that 65 per cent of what is now being referred to as the 'sandwich generation' in Britain struggle to care for both the elderly parents and grandchildren of their family. One in four working families depends on grandparents for childcare in the UK; in Holland the figure is nearer to one in two. In many African communities grandmothers are caring for children orphaned by AIDS. In 2006 the Grandmothers to Grandmothers campaign was launched in Toronto to 'raise awareness, build solidarity and mobilize funds for community-based organisations that support African grandmothers and the children in their care'.

Has the important role played by grandmothers in conveying women's history to their grandchildren been overlooked?

Many women it seems are now continuing Lucy's role as grandmothers of humanity, and indeed proponents of the Grandmother Theory suggest humans' longevity evolved because grandmothers played a crucial role in taking care of children: 'Grandmothers', according to Kristen Hawkes in an interview with the *Daily Mail* in 2015, 'are what make us human'.

2 | Venus of Willendorf
Women and Fertility

MAGGIE ANDREWS

The 'Venus of Willendorf' is a small female figurine thought to date from the old Stone Age, between 28,000 and 22,000 BCE. Johann Veran found the figurine during excavations led by the archaeologist Joseph Szombathy, near the town of Willendorf in Austria in 1908. It is made from oolitic limestone, measures 110mm in height and is tinted with red ochre; it is now kept in the Naturhistorisches Museum in Vienna.

This is perhaps the most well known of several hundred stone figurines of somewhat curvaceous women found in the area between the Russian Steppes and the Pyrenees, which are collectively known as Venus figurines. This name, which links the figurines to Venus, is perhaps a little confusing as they pre-date by millennia the Roman period, to which the mythical figure of Venus belongs. Venus was the goddess of love, beauty and fertility; and such a name has led to an assumption that these earlier figurines were also fertility goddesses, which were perhaps appealed to by women in order to bring about conception. Certainly the statue is female, and the parts of body associated with childbearing are emphasised: the enlarged stomach, breasts and pubic area, and absence of facial features seem to define this woman by her role in procreation. Furthermore it has been suggested that the red ochre pigment symbolises menstrual blood.

Certainly time and effort were invested in constructing these figurines, but by whom, or how they were used, is hard to gauge. The figures themselves and their feet were particularly small; they seem constructed to be carried or placed on display lying down. They may have been good luck charms, which accompanied nomadic tribes in their search for food – such ample, even obese, proportions are sometimes venerated by groups facing food shortages. While some have suggested they could be cave porn with exaggerated features to appeal to men, others see them as fertility charms given by women to other women as examples of the great fecund mother goddess, perhaps even indicating a matriarchal culture. Emblems of fertility, goddesses, fruits and even animals that appear to reproduce prolifically have a place in many cultures; for example, mistletoe, hazelnuts, pomegranates, and lotus flowers. Indeed in Hindu culture the lotus flower is perceived to grow untouched by the impurity of the muddy waters in which it grows, whereas the abundant reproduction of frogs and rabbits have carried sexual symbolism, and the Easter bunny is an emblem of both rebirth and fertility. Nature and particularly women's ability to reproduce is a potent and powerful symbol, something to be both revered and feared. When the magazine *Vanity Fair* displayed in 1991 the heavily pregnant actress Demi Moore on its cover a media controversy ensued. Some news-stands refused to sell the magazine; others enfolded it in brown paper, suggesting such an image was pornographic.

The Venus of Willendorf may be a fertility charm or a great fecund mother goddess.

Arguably for women the 'sacred call of motherhood' can be a double-edged sword. Women who do not, or cannot, bear children, historically, have been more likely to be abandoned or divorced – whether infertility was their 'fault' or not. In contemporary society, women unable to conceive naturally continue to feel inadequate, isolated by the numerous images of 'perfect motherhood' that circulate on various media platforms. In wealthier Western countries, a range of treatments for infertility has become more readily available. In 1978 the birth of the world's first test-tube baby, Louise Brown, was considered a landmark. In vitro fertilisation (IVF) gave hope to many women struggling to conceive, and is now used alongside surrogate motherhood, ova donation and adoption to enable women to become mothers. But in developing countries such as sub-Saharan Africa infertility is also common but medical assistance is hard to obtain, as health programmes are geared towards controlling the population and containing high fertility.

Are women, even in the twenty-first century, defined by their fertility?

Women encounter social and health challenges when going through IVF treatment which involves being injected with powerful drugs that can lead to excruciating headaches, mood swings and spots in front of the eyes. But perhaps it is the emotional rollercoaster of IVF that is most challenging. One woman recalled her experience:

> Those years of trying for a baby were hands-down the most difficult in my life. They really changed me. Gradually I became someone I didn't recognize or even like any more: a baby-obsessed, crazy, tearful nightmare. Never mind crying over newborn photos on Facebook, I once lost it while watching *Shrek* when it turned out Fiona was pregnant!

Medical and social interventions to enable women to become mothers are not problem free, or value free. Controversy now rages over the practice of women from wealthy Western countries adopting children from Africa or using surrogate mothers in India. As Carole Joffe has pointed out, 'Adoption, by its very nature, typically brings some combination of pain and loss as well as joy and peace to all involved in the "adoption triangle" of birthmother, child and adoptive parents'. Little wonder, then, that some have begun to question why so many women define themselves by their reproductive capabilities, and have sought to challenge the social pressures on women to have children, arguing there is a need to monitor medical intervention in women's fertility carefully. It is thousands of years since the Venus of Willendorf was carved but many women still define themselves by their fertility.

3 | London Foundling Hospital Token

Having Illegitimate Children

JANIS LOMAS

The collection of tokens left at the London Foundling Hospital by mothers, mostly unmarried or abandoned, who were unable to keep their babies is a poignant reminder of the difficulties single mothers faced in eighteenth- and nineteenth-century Britain.

Every child admitted to the hospital was baptised with a new name, so mothers left tokens in the hope of being able to identify their child if they were reunited at some point in the future. 18,000 of these tokens can be seen at the Foundling Museum in London. Sadly, records show that only two children were ever reclaimed by their mothers.

Prior to the hospital being established, children were left at the doors of Poor Law institutions, hospitals or in public places. By the early 1700s the growing population in the cities meant the situation was acute. Thomas Coram, a sea captain arriving in London in 1720, was shocked to see babies and children dying abandoned in the streets. It took Coram nineteen years to overcome prejudice against unmarried mothers and secure a Royal Charter from George II, enabling the London Foundling Hospital to be opened in 1741. Mothers sought to hand over their babies themselves; but this hospital's acceptance of the baby was not automatic. Women had to appear before a panel of men who questioned them about their respectability; only mothers who 'proved' to the panel that they were truly penitent, and were victims rather than deliberate sinners, were allowed to leave their infant.

The care of abandoned children and their unmarried mothers has vexed societies for centuries. In Italy from 1198, to stop desperate women throwing their infants into the River Tiber, the pope decreed babies could be left at the entrance to a foundling hospital – a practice gradually adopted all over Italy, Sicily and many other Catholic countries. In Paris, foundling wheels were introduced in 1638 for mothers to leave their babies anonymously. A revolving door was installed and the baby could be placed on the platform, which rotated. When the infant was inside the building, the mother rang a bell and left. There were 251 wheels in France when the system closed in 1863. Ireland operated a similar scheme from 1730 until 1825, when the Dublin Foundling Hospital was closed due to the high infant mortality rates. Foundling wheels have reappeared since the 1950s in countries seeking to avoid infanticide or child abandonment.

In the United States informal arrangements were virtually the only help for abandoned babies and children prior to the founding of the Children's Aid Society in the 1850s. From 1854 until 1929, an estimated 200,000 babies and children found

There are approximately 2 million single parents in Britain, 90 per cent of whom are mothers.

on the streets of New York and other large eastern cities were shipped westwards, on so-called 'orphan trains' which took them out of the cities to be brought up on farms for a healthier, more wholesome life. Britain operated similar schemes whereby orphans, or those from children's homes or workhouses, were transported to Australia and Canada up until the 1970s. Those who organised these schemes may have had good intentions, but many children found themselves working without wages and stigmatised within communities as ruffians and potential thieves. The suffering of the mothers who were temporarily unable to care for their children and discovered they had been sent abroad is unimaginable. Aswini Weereratne QC, for the Child Migrant Trust, explained:

> From their evidence, a number of common themes emerge. They and their families were lied to, many parents were told that their children had been adopted by loving families, some children were told their parents were dead. Some have learnt after years of searching for their records that their parents tried to get them back. One foster mother campaigned to have her foster daughter returned to her from Australia.

The Catholic and Protestant Churches, who were active in setting up schemes to deal with the children's homes, 'wayward' girls and unmarried mothers, tended to see illegitimacy as a problem that needed to be punished to deter others. The best-known and longest lasting of such institutions were the Magdalene Laundries, which existed in many countries but are mostly commonly associated with Ireland where the regime was widespread. Their name derived from the biblical Mary Magdalene, thought to be a reformed prostitute. Parish priests or families who sought to avoid the shame and expense of a girl having an illegitimate child precipitated this by sending women to the laundries. Mentally unwell girls, those who had committed petty crimes or who had sexually transgressed were also sent there as a punishment. Over 2,000 babies born in Magdalene Laundries were illegally adopted by wealthy American families in return for a donation, while their mothers were forced to work, unpaid, in silence, for gruelling twelve-hour shifts, with little medical care, poor food and no way of leaving. Many women lived and died in the laundries and the child mortality rate was high, as the graves of as many as 800 children at Tuam near Galway testify. The laundries existed for over 200 years with the last only closing in 1996 as home washing machines meant that they had become uneconomic.

With a quarter of children brought up in single-parent families in the UK, has disapproval and judgement of non-traditional families finally ended?

From the 1950s onwards, mother and baby homes were seen as a solution to unwanted pregnancies in the UK; there were 172 in 1968, mostly run by church organisations. The only option available to the majority of mothers who gave birth in these homes was to have their child adopted after breastfeeding and caring for it for only six weeks; 16,164 babies were adopted in 1968 alone. Girls or women were then expected to resume their previous life as if nothing had happened. Families often made up a cover story to explain the absence of the young mother from home and the subject was never mentioned again. Girls and young mothers subsequently had no one to talk to about the loss of their child and often suffered a lifetime of regret and suffering. A common theme in the attitudes towards illegitimate children and their mothers over the centuries is the lack of sympathy or counselling for mothers dealing with an unplanned pregnancy, the trauma of birth and the loss of their child.

4 | Terracotta Baby Feeder

Infant Feeding and Formula Baby Milk

MAGGIE ANDREWS

The 4,000-year-old terracotta baby feeder provided archaeologists with evidence that, although breast milk is ideal for babies, for thousands of years women have needed or wanted to find substitutes.

Babies require nurturing even when their mothers are unavailable due to any number of reasons, such as illness, death, domestic and paid labour, social expectations, looking after farms or other members of their families. Besides wet nurses, animal milk and other substances have been used to feed babies. Cow's milk and boiled wheat kernels were suggested to sustain babies in Egypt in the fifteenth century BCE. In later times advice books provided recipes for pap, made of flour or breadcrumbs cooked in water sometimes with milk added, gruel and thin porridge as sustenance for the very young. In 1867, the first factory-made formula milk for babies made its appearance and soon became popular in Europe and the USA.

Evidence of the use of wet nurses has been identified as early as eighteenth-century BCE Babylon and also in ancient Egypt, Greece and Rome, where it was most common among royalty or the wealthy. Predictably, the process of selecting an ideal wet nurse provoked much debate, with the quality and supply of milk not being the only concern. In ancient Greece, it was thought that, ideally, wet nurses should have brown hair, a calm temperament and not be pregnant or menstruating. In the medieval and early modern periods, when wet nurses were usually selected by fathers, there was a preference for those who had previously had a male child, although temperament was still important. Wet nurses were required to be of good character, neither vicious nor 'sluttish', and according to Thomas Phaire, writing in 1545: 'sober, honest and chaste, well formed, amiable and cheerful, so that she may accustom the infant to mirth. No drunkard, vicious or sluttish [women], for they corrupt the nature of the child.'

Should formula baby milk, like cigarettes, carry a health warning?

Puritan theology during the Reformation suggested that non-breastfeeding mothers who employed wet nurses were selfish and lacking in love for both their child and God. Breastfeeding became almost a religious duty. Nevertheless the practice of using black women slaves as wet nurses became common throughout all American slave-owning societies in the eighteenth and nineteenth centuries. To take on the role of wet nurse, a woman had usually either lost her child or was compelled to neglect or abandon them. The image of the black 'mammy' holding a thriving white child, which has become a

sentimental, softer image of slavery, often masks a more complex history. The use of black women's bodies allowed white women to recover after childbirth and return to what some saw as a frivolous lifestyle.

Many countries, such as Brazil, abandoned using slaves as wet nurses when ideas of scientific motherhood became popular at the end of the nineteenth century. At this time other alternatives to breastfeeding also came under criticism. In early twentieth-century Britain, with one in five children not living to reach their fifth birthday, attention turned to maternal care and the welfare of babies. The discovery that there was lower infant mortality among breastfed babies led not only to disapproval of mothers who went out to work, but assertions of neglect by them from middle-class observers with little understanding of the pressures and the poverty that working-class women endured. Few working-class women could afford formula; struggling with domestic or paid labour, many instead used the cheapest available condensed milk diluted with hot water to feed their infants, which unfortunately had little nutritional value. Unscrupulous manufacturers marketed a brand of skimmed cow's milk as 'Goat', exploiting the belief that goat's milk was the best substitute for breast milk, even though the product had little to recommend it. The lack of knowledge and means to sterilise feeding bottles was a particular problem for poor families, especially as feeding bottles could be made from pewter, tin plate, earthenware or porcelain; some were even attached to long tubes with a form of teat on the end, enabling babies to suckle on demand, almost feeding themselves. The tubes were difficult to clean and became a breeding ground for bacteria. Little wonder such baby feeders became nicknamed the 'Murderer' or the 'Killer'.

In 1974, the charity War on Want published a report entitled 'The Baby Killer', written by Mike Muller; he argued that what was becoming a worldwide trend away from breastfeeding was significantly influenced by the marketing of the baby food industry. For those living in poverty, with poor housing and sanitation and impure water, bottle-feeding led to infection and diarrhoea which can kill babies, especially if they have not had the initial dose of antibodies in the colostrum (the milk-like substance produced in the first few days after birth). Furthermore 'stretching' or over-dilution of milk powder can cause malnutrition. Consequently, in developing countries:

> Babies are dying because their mothers bottle-feed them with western-style infant milk. Many that do not die are drawn into a vicious cycle of malnutrition and disease that will leave them physically and intellectually stunted for life.

When Muller's pamphlet was translated into Swedish with the title 'Nestlé Kill Babies', the company successfully sued, but the bad publicity led to a widespread boycott of the company's products. Across the world, 7 million children under 5 years of age die each year, many from preventable causes, and nearly half are newborns whose chances of survival would be drastically improved by breastfeeding. Consequently the charity Save the Children has recently suggested formula baby milk should carry health warning messages, as cigarettes do. Other campaigners point out this will only add to the guilt experienced by women who want to breastfeed but find they cannot. The World Health Organisation now recommends exclusive breastfeeding of infants for the first six months of life, but many women cannot afford to give up work for this long, especially if, as in the USA, there is no statutory right to paid maternity leave. Many mothers, seeking to maintain their families' financial survival, their health or sanity, continue to choose the age-old tradition of using bottles and baby feeders, modern equivalents of 4,000-year-old terracotta feeders.

5 | Postcard of Hottentot Venus

Pornography and Objectifying Women

MAGGIE ANDREWS

Saartje Baartman, a South African woman referred to as the Hottentot Venus, was brought to England in 1810. Baartman, born among the Khoikhoi (Hottentot) or Khoisan (Bushmen) people, was displayed semi-naked with African beads and ostrich feathers as a sideshow attraction, first in Piccadilly, Bartholomew Fair and Haymarket, and then throughout London, the provinces and Ireland. She was then sold to an animal trainer in France, where she died in 1815.

One sympathetic onlooker noted how this spectacle of otherness was 'ordered to move backwards and forwards and come out and go into her cage, more like a bear on a chain than a human being'.

Her subjugation and objectification served to legitimise racist and imperialist oppression, and her degradation is symbolic of the treatment of black women, both at that time and often since. Press coverage and public responses to Baartman, whether on display in carnivals or the private homes of the wealthy, obsessed on the size of her buttocks. Her body was referred to, reproduced, commented on and observed in cartoons, ballads, vaudeville plays and numerous illustrations. In these Baartman was sexualised, reproducing and reinforcing nineteenth-century attitudes to black women in medical and scientific literature, and in paintings and cartoons; postcards of Baartman's body were produced for men to leer at.

Nineteenth-century culture, in many ways, suppressed and was anxious about sexuality. Black women like Baartman were portrayed as eroticised, animalistic, lustful and depraved, regarded as less than human, a source of fear and fascination. The scientific community of naturalists and ethnologists wrote learned treatises on Baartman, measuring, drawing and scrutinising her body when she was alive and dead. Three scientists inspected her in Paris in 1815 and considered Baartman to be more similar to an orang-utan than 'a Negro', and concluded Hottentots 'were barely human'. Hottentot women were reputed to have elongated labia; during her lifetime Baartman did not permit inspection of her genitals, but after her death her body was investigated by Napoleon's surgeon general, Georges Cuvier, the chair of anatomy of animals at the Museum of Natural History in France. Following Cuvier's scientific exploration and writing on Baartman, images of her genitalia and buttocks appeared in anatomy textbooks; a jar containing her genitals, a skeleton and cast of her were on display in the Musée de l'Homme until 1976. When Nelson Mandela became President of South Africa in 1994 he urged François Mitterand to return the remains; this did not happen until 2002, when Baartman was finally buried in South Africa. As journalist Chris McGreal asked at this time: 'This young

LOVE and BEAUTY -- SARTJEE the HOTTENTOT VENUS.

woman was treated as if she was something monstrous. But where in this affair is the true monstrosity?'

The models and images of Baartman conserved in museums and reproduced in textbooks symbolically dismantled her, dissecting her into parts, turning her body into objects and licensing unregulated voyeurism, as pornography has arguably done since. While there are examples of images and materials created for sexual stimulation in the seventeenth century, well before Baartman's arrival in Britain, even in the middle of the nineteenth century they were too expensive for mass consumption. Pornographic postcards became more affordable towards the end of the nineteenth century, and in the second half of the twentieth century glossy porn magazines appeared. Shifting attitudes to sexuality, censorship and new publishing techniques enabled *Playboy* to be launched in the USA in 1953, and the British magazine *Mayfair* was first published in 1965. New media technologies have continued to increase the platforms through which pornography has spread problematic images of women for the male gaze.

There were objections to Baartman being exhibited for others' interest and amusement in the early nineteenth century; similarly more recent pornography has its critics. Some of the most vociferous of these critics were the radical feminists of the 1970s and '80s, when the American feminist and activist Robin Morgan proclaimed that 'pornography is the theory, and rape is the practice', suggesting that pornography not only degraded women but encouraged violence against them.

A number of women campaigned against pornography, for example in Minneapolis, where they demonstrated and visited porn stores once a week in the 1980s. Protestors stood behind customers and one, Jacqui Thompson, explained: 'It makes the people in the stores uncomfortable, and that's the point.' On 30 December 1983 the city council voted to ban pornography – a decision later vetoed by Mayor Don Fraser, causing women to protest against him. Andrea Dworkin and Catherine MacKinnon's attempt to introduce civil rights anti-pornography legislation in 1988 in the USA was also unsuccessful.

A number of feminists have, however, argued against censorship, and pointed out it contains a complex and contradictory range of representations of women while evidence that pornography is linked to violence against women is inconclusive. Others have sought to celebrate and explore 'fantasies' and their ability to dislodge traditional notions of women as sexually passive. The American singer Madonna's popularity has at times rested on her ability to re-appropriate the iconography of pornography in pop videos such as 'Justify my Love' (1990) and her coffee-table book *Sex* (1992). More recently the novel *Fifty Shades of Grey* (2011) topped bestseller lists around the world and led to the genre of 'mummy porn'. Like Baartman, *Fifty Shades of Grey* embodies many of the anxieties and preoccupations of its era. The exploration of bondage, dominance and submission exaggerates and explores some of the uncertainties around sexuality and relationships in an age of self-governance, individualism and self-gratification. Unlike those who made money out of selling postcards of the Hottentot Venus, the process of producing mummy porn does not degrade actual women, as happened to Saartje Baartman in the nineteenth century.

Does the sexualisation and objectification of women in pornography have an impact on attitudes and behaviour towards women in general?

6 | Early Twentieth-Century Medical Vibrator

Masturbation

MAGGIE ANDREWS

Vibrators produced at the beginning of the twentieth century were initially intended for medical purposes; their ability to massage muscles and relieve tension apparently had health benefits for men and women. The medical profession's enthusiasm for vibrators was, however, limited and the product was quickly rebranded for the consumer market.

More than sixty vibrator patents were issued in the years 1905–20 in the USA, and by 1909 there were more than twenty companies producing vibrators there, including the Eureka Vibrator Co.; all advertised the health and beauty benefits of their devices in newspapers. These included removing wrinkles and curing nervous headaches, but people found other uses for the little devices, which the advertising 'acknowledged'. Although any newspaper being too open about the use of vibrators for masturbation would have risked prosecution, in 1902 one advert suggested that the vibrator would ensure that 'All the pleasure of youth will throb within you'.

There were forerunners to these electric vibrators: the steam-fired manipulator invented by the American physician George Taylor in 1869 has been seen as the prototype of the modern vibrator. His patented designs, which, according to historian Rachael Maines, 'included a table with a cutout for the lower abdomen, in which a vibrating sphere, driven by a steam engine, massaged the pelvic area', were for products intended to be purchased by doctors and spas.

The first electromechanical vibrator did not appear until 1882 – an invention credited to the British physician J. Mortimer Granville. He used it to treat nervous problems in men and women, believing that disease could result from what were supposed to be healthy vibrations in the body's nerves being out of balance. The credibility of his theories was called into question in a letter from a physician to the editor of *Medical News* in 1898, pointing out:

Is women's sexuality too often seen in terms of what pleases men?

After many years of vibratory therapy I am now convinced that its value is greatly exaggerated, and depends more on the creation of suggestion than anything else ... This form of therapy has become so popular with hypochondriacs that a few years ago a company with a large capital was formed here to exploit the 'household' vibrator.

It has been suggested that the vibrator was invented to administer vulva massage to women with hysteria. A common myth in the Victorian era was that women with symptoms ranging from loss of sexual appetite, fatigue and anxiety to mild depression were suffering from female hysteria, which could apparently be cured by pelvic massage leading to hysterical paroxysm (orgasm). Despite the absence of any evidence to support this myth about the practices of Victorian doctors, it remains tenacious. In 2012 the film *Hysteria* suggested that a doctor dealing with numerous women suffering from hysteria invented the vibrator to alleviate carpal tunnel syndrome.

Vibrators and female masturbation remained shrouded in euphemism and shame for much of the twentieth century but the work of sexologists in the period following the Second World War began to change this. The Hite Report (1976) drew upon over 3,000 questionnaires completed by women to argue that for many women heterosexual penetrative sex was less than satisfactory. The survey suggested that 8 per cent of women preferred sexual activity with other women, 53 per cent preferred sexual activity with themselves and 17 per cent preferred no sexual activity at all. Simultaneously the slogan of the feminist movement – 'the personal is political' – made sexuality, orgasm and masturbation deeply political issues. There was discussion within women's groups, magazines and feminist novels about the pressure many women felt to fake orgasm. In her seminal article 'The Myth of the Vaginal Orgasm' (1970), Anne Koedt argued that 'women have been defined sexually in terms of what pleases men; our own biology has not been properly analysed'.

Some feminists, such as Betty Dodson, encouraged women's exploration of their own bodies; her bestseller *Sex for One* (1973) and women-only masturbation classes called 'Bodysex' made her one of the leaders of pro-sex feminism. She argued many women were 'afraid of sex because they say it's too controversial. But I feel it's because they're personally too conflicted. They don't want to masturbate, they want Prince Charming. It's Walt Disney. Puke.'

Notwithstanding Betty Dodson's comments, popular culture, particularly in the USA, embraced female masturbation by the end of the twentieth century. The Eurythmics' popular feminist anthem in 1985 included the chorus:

Sisters are doing it for themselves,
Standing on their own two feet,
And ringing on their own bells.
Sisters are doing it for themselves.

It was the introduction of the dual-action vibrator, the Rabbit, in 1984, which made vibrators and female masturbation mainstream. It has been described as 'one of the most visible contemporary signs of active female sexuality' and featured in the HBO hit series *Sex and the City* (1998), in which heroine Charlotte becomes addicted to the pleasures of her Rabbit. A further indication of shifting attitudes can be seen in *Desperate Housewives* (2004) star Eva Longoria's statement: 'I give Rabbit vibrators to all my girlfriends … They scream when they unwrap it. The best gift I can give them is an orgasm.' However, women's enjoyment and expression of their sexuality still remains framed by both experiences and legal and cultural restraints.

Many religious groups still oppose masturbation, and selling sex toys was illegal in Texas until 2008. Mandy Van Deven pointed out in *Bitch* magazine (2010):

I think there's an expectation for feminists to be all sexually liberated and uninhibited, but sex is complicated, even when it's solo. And masturbation isn't intuitive for everyone, particularly those of us who have been victims of sexual abuse. I wish the conversation about feminism and masturbation was broader and made more room for complex and uncomfortable truths about sexuality.

7 | Sanitary Towels
Female Hygiene Products

JANIS LOMAS

The invention of the sanitary towel transformed the difficulties and potential embarrassment of menstruation for millions of women. The first towels were produced in the UK by Southall's in 1888. In the USA, Lister's produced the first commercial disposable sanitary towel in 1896. However, the cost of these products meant that in both countries they were beyond the means of the majority of women; it was to be decades before they were in common use for most women in Europe and the USA. In many parts of the developing world they are still not available and women are still subjected to real difficulties and worry every month of their reproductive lives.

Before sanitary towels, women had no option but to use initially leaves and grass, or whatever scraps of material or rags were available, which were boil washed and reused after use. Women also fashioned their own reusable towels from wadding used for quilting with an outer layer of cheesecloth or cotton rags. At times in rural areas, rabbit's fur or sheep's fleece was cut into strips with the skin side of the fleece serving as the outer layer, which was sometimes rubbed with tallow to make it more leak proof. When away from home women had to produce a quantity of homemade sanitary towels or cotton strips to take with them and it was one of the selling points of the commercially made towels that they were convenient for travelling. By the end of the nineteenth century, American women could also buy rubber bloomers to ensure there was no leakage. Sold for $13.50 per dozen, they were advertised as reversible and with side openings for ventilation.

When factory-made sanitary towels were finally introduced, they created an advertising problem for manufacturers, as it was not acceptable for such intimate products to be mentioned openly. This British advertisement from 1894 shows the discretion that had to be used in advertising and selling these items:

> For private parcels of Southall's Sanitary Towels by post securely packed – with private address labels, quite free from anything to attract observation; write to – The Lady Manager, 17, Bull Street, Birmingham – this department being entirely managed by Ladies.

Some stores even had a moneybox where women could place the correct money and take a packet of sanitary towels without having to ask the shopkeeper for the item. Similar discretion can be seen in this letter sent to Herbert Gladstone, the British Home Secretary, in August 1908. R.C. Wyatt, the husband of a suffragette, wrote to him about the failure of the prison authorities to provide suffragette prisoners

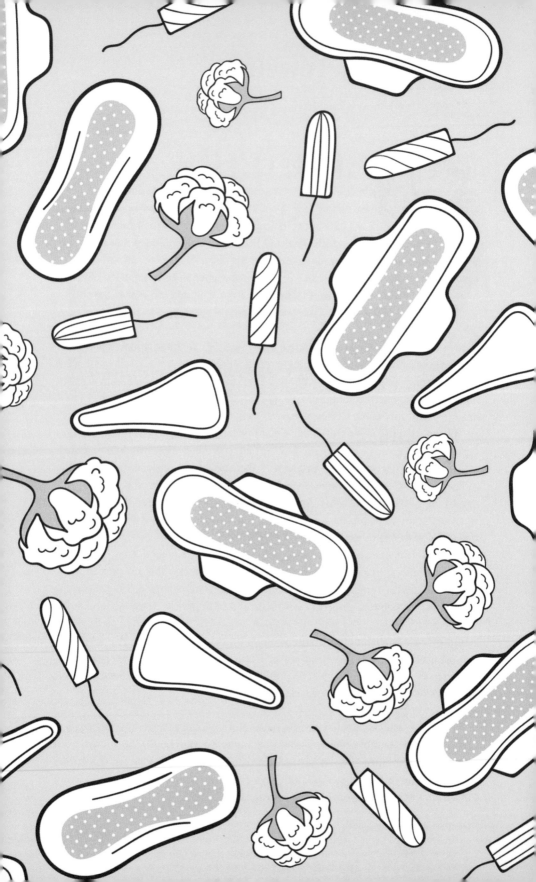

Made entirely of White Absorbent Wool.

Southalls' 'Sanitary

ABSORBENT, ANTISEPTIC. **Towels.'**

(IMPROVED).

1/-, 1/6, & 2/- per doz.

FREE SAMPLE on application to the Lady Manager, 17, Bull St., Birmingham.

ALSO A CHEAPER MAKE AT 6d. PER DOZEN.

Superior to any Halfpenny "Towel" on the market.

Mixed Sample Packets (three of Size O, one each 1, 2, & 4) post free from the Lady Manager for 8 stamps.

Sold by all Drapers, Outfitters, and Chemists throughout the world.

with sanitary towels. With typical Edwardian reticence, he attempted to make his complaint clear without being explicit. He asked why 'at certain times, certain indispensable clothing is not provided ... an outrage on decency and health'. He requested the Home Secretary to stop this 'filthy punishment'; however, it is not known if he received a reply, or even if Gladstone understood what his complaint was about.

A survey commissioned by the Indian government in 2011 found that only 12 per cent of women used sanitary towels, and in much of the Indian sub-continent women are still not allowed to prepare food or attend religious festivals when menstruating. In Nepal, despite the practice having been officially banned since 2005, some women in rural areas are still exiled from their home and forced to live in the forest, caves or in crude huts while menstruating, as they are thought to be unclean and that if allowed to remain in the home others will get sick or the house will catch fire. Similarly in the Hollywood horror movie *Carrie* (1976) the title character has a complete freak-out in the showers when she starts menstruating, fearing she is bleeding to death. Instead she is given supernatural powers to enact evil deeds and revenge her enemies. Such superstition and the continuing taboo and embarrassment continue to cause shame and untold misery around a natural bodily function for hundreds of thousands of women and girls.

The earliest historical record of tampon use is in ancient Egypt, where medical records describe tampons fashioned from papyrus. The physician Hippocrates, in ancient Greece, described women using tampons of lint wrapped around a small piece of wood, while the Romans used wool. At a later point, sheep's wool, cotton wool balls and sponges also had a role to play as homemade tampons. It wasn't until 1929 that tampons with a cardboard applicator were invented, while Tampax came on to the market in the mid-1930s.

The history of the sanitary towel and tampon represents a turning point in women's lives. Before sanitary towels women were often afraid to travel or play sports during their period, and menstruation was seen as something to be embarrassed about and never mentioned. It was often referred to as 'the curse'. This has gradually changed and now sanitary towels and tampons are advertised openly in many countries, and shame and embarrassment are becoming much less commonplace. The introduction of the sanitary towel provided a hygienic, convenient and disposable way of dealing with menstruation, and it relegated what was a major obstacle to women taking a full active role in all aspects of life to a mere inconvenience. Its introduction gave women more freedom; not simply physical freedom, but also freedom from awkwardness, embarrassment and prejudice.

Why is period pain often dismissed as normal?

8 | Powick Asylum Patients' Notes, Volume 19

The Treatment and Attitudes Towards Women and Madness

MAGGIE ANDREWS

Powick Asylum patients' notes, volume 19, records that 26-year-old farmer's wife Ellen Bullock was admitted to the asylum as a private patient on 8 August 1877. Married without children, she was not considered suicidal but she used obscene language, threw her supper and plate through a window, and apparently suffered with many delusions, which seemed to centre on a rejection of her marital status.

She removed her wedding ring and claimed she wanted to marry again into another family. Her 'irrationality' and eccentric behaviour improved dramatically when she was in the asylum; she was discharged in May 1879, only to be readmitted in September 1882 when she stated her husband ought to have been sent to the asylum instead of her, had cut up her clothes and threatened her husband with a pair of scissors. He ceased to pay her asylum fees in December 1882, declaring the marriage was over and from that moment on her health improved; when she left the asylum this time she never returned. It seems Ellen Bullock's mental health problems were a response to her tempestuous marriage and the circumstances of her life.

Women historically have been linked to insanity, seen as hysterical, irrational and over-emotional in comparison with men's apparently innate rationality. The records, which indicate that more men were admitted to mental institutions in Britain in the eighteenth century than women, do not, however, support this. Ellen Bullock fell foul of the assumptions about femininity when some husbands and medical practitioners conspired to use insanity and private medical institutions to sideline inconvenient women and curtail their actions and voices. Hannah Mackenzie, for example, was incarcerated in Peter Day's Paddington 'madhouse' at her husband's instigation as he sought to continue an adulterous affair with her niece in 1766.

Elizabeth Ware Packard was similarly detained in a mental institution, in Illinois, USA, for contravening the social conventions of appropriate female behaviour in 1860. She had expressed radical religious views, which her husband considered detrimental to his career as a minister. She was released three years later only to be imprisoned, in her home, by her husband. In the ensuing court battle leading to a divorce, she was financially ruined and lost custody of her six children. She wrote a memoir of her experiences, which played a role in campaigns to alter the process of committing women – and men – to asylums. Such campaigns were given a boost on both sides of the Atlantic by the publication of Wilkie Collins's sensational novel *The Woman in*

White, about two women incarcerated in a private medical asylum by an unscrupulous husband seeking to appropriate his wife's fortune. Initially serialised in Charles Dickens's magazine *All the Year Round*, beginning in November 1859, the book was turned into a play and translated into other languages. *The Woman in White* perfume, bonnets and clothes were sold in shops as the book became a publishing phenomenon.

It was not only the committal of women to asylums which was controversial in the nineteenth century, but, then as now, the efficacy of the treatments which were administered by the medical profession. In the 1860s, Dr Baker Brown gained some notoriety by undertaking operations to surgically remove the clitoris of women he considered to be suffering from insanity. He had been president of the Medical Society in London and helped found St Mary's Hospital in Paddington, but his actions are indicative of the era's fear and anxiety about the female body and sexuality. His rather troubling definition of symptoms of insanity in women included: epilepsy, masturbation, undertaking too much reading or expressing a desire to be a nurse. He asserted that the first signs of women's degeneration from masturbation, through to epilepsy and insanity to eventual death could be identified when a woman 'becomes restless and excited, or melancholy and retiring, listless and indifferent to the *social influences and domestic life*' (emphasis in original).

Is there still a tendency to see women as hysterical, irrational, mad and over-emotional compared with men and their apparently innate rationality?

Baker Brown was expelled from the Obstetrical Society in 1867, but women continued to be confined in mental institutions for what society considered aberrant sexuality, having an illegitimate child or sex before marriage well into the twentieth century.

While the practice of the medical profession and definitions of madness have been strongly gendered through the supposition that women are psychologically weaker, or assumptions of what constitutes 'normal' female behaviour, treatment of women who are suffering the genuine distress of mental illness has changed dramatically. Had Ellen Bullock entered Powick Asylum in the middle of the twentieth century, she might have been given electric shock treatment (ECT), while in the 1960s and '70s she would probably have taken tranquilisers such as Valium, promoted by drug companies for its capacity to enable women to embrace their duties as wives and mothers. Since 1987, selective serotonin-reuptake inhibitors (SSRIs) such as Prozac have often been used to help women adjust to their lives. In the twenty-first century, Ellen would also have had a range of alternative ways to escape a difficult marriage, but many women continue to suffer from depression and mental illness as a result of the circumstances of their lives and their inability to bring about a change in their personal situation.

Ellen Bullock at 26, Married (no child) Farmer's Wife Church of
England Good Education. Admitted 8th August 1877 from Pinchany nr Ledbury

No 125 Private (Case) Mania Hysteria	This is her first attack of about two months duration the supposed cause being a hereditary predisposition (mother's side). She is neither highly Epileptic nor suicidal but is dangerous to others. Her certificates state she got out into the fields in the middle of the night to get an offer of marriage, says she can hear gentlemen talking to her. She says she has taken off her wedding ring too now a single person & is going to get married as she wishes to get into another family. She has thrown a knife & a petroleum lamp at persons, has run about in the rain, threw a shawl over the hedge, & wanted to know where the booking office was. She is very thin in person, pale, anaemic, and apparently very violent, has never menstruated and abdominal organs appear to be acting normally. She is suffering from Mania, her appearance and demeanour are absurd and very eccentric, her conversation is irrational and confused, her mind is very deluded, then she declares she is a single woman and is about 40. Dressed her bearing and dress are ridiculous, at times she is very impulsive swears and uses obscene language and one night through her supper and plate thro' a window, is constantly asking for beer & brandy, refuses her food and is obstinate & troublesome.
August 30	Her mind still continues in a very confused, deluded & deluded state, & her language is from time to time persuaded. On the whole however

Sept	13	she is fairly tractable & quiet with us & is taking her food much better
Nov	8	Since last entry she has again become very troublesome, destroys her dresses, is inclined to refuse her food, & behaves in a very irrational manner
1878 Feb	18	She has considerably improved since last entry, has picked up in condition, takes her food & sleeps well, & her appearance is not so eccentric, though her dress is still peculiar & exaggerated, her ideas are confused, wandering & irrational. She is industrious & useful in her ward.
	18	The improvement mentioned in last entry still continues, though she is still very eccentric. She appears happy & contented, playing the piano making herself generally useful. She still however has delusions regarding her personal importance, her dress & actions are exaggerated.
May	14	Since last entry most if not all the delusions have left her. She continued to make herself useful & is in good bodily health
Oct	14	The improvement mentioned in last entry has not been maintained. She has been excited & quarrelsome & on one occasion had sleeping draught at night. Her bodily health & condition remain, easily fed, she eats very well & appears now happy & content
1879 Jany 15th May 15th		Continues much improved both in bodily health & mental condition. Discharged.

Ellen Bullock at 30, Married (widow?) Mania Chronic Church of England Admitted 1st September 1882 from Barton Regis Bristol

No 207 Private Case Mania Chronic	This is her second attack of about 2 years duration the supposed cause being Mania & previous attack [...] She is neither Epileptic nor suicidal but is dangerous to others. Her certificates state she is puzzled in behaviour having mind to suicide & that by general conversation & appearance nothing to remark, she says she was attacked by a London mob without any cause & says that when she went to a Lunatic Asylum before it was a mistake as her husband ought to have been not asked, she says her marriage is not legal. She cuts up her clothes, she threatened her husband with a pair of scissors & from fear & fire he was in another room with locked door. This patient has been in this Asylum before & was discharged in May 1879 (for particulars of last attack see Case Book No 125 p 231). She is a tall thin woman, spare but moderately well nourished. She was free from marks of bruise on admission, and to abdominal organs on prior appeal no active disease, her mind was healthy & was suffering from Chronic Mania: she is very spare and irritable in conversation and demeanour, resents being questioned, and is suspicious and defiant, she does in fact she says had too much to drink, but says that very policemen [mob] & follows, and mob her in the street, she does not know where she is, that her husband behaved badly & threatened to pull her & pieces. She is quiet & orderly, & gives no trouble.

Sept	23	She continues in much the same state, is reserved, taciturn & defiant in appearance & demeanour, gives no trouble & employs herself usefully in the various light occupations
Oct	14	She remains in the same quiet reserved condition & can not easily be drawn into conversation. She appears however to forget herself a little at the weekly entertainments which she apparently enjoys
Nov	7	She is quiet & well behaved though somewhat dull & confused, her general health is satisfactory
Dec	12	She is unchanged
Dec	4	Transferred from Private to Pauper class
1883 Jan	26	She is quiet & reserved & though answering civilly is not disposed to enter into conversation. She is employed as before & her general health is good
Feb	22	She remains as at the last note
March	19	She was today allowed to leave the Asylum on Trial
April	9	Discharged "Recovered"

9 | Chinese Baby Sling
Methods for Transporting Small Children

MAGGIE ANDREWS

The beautifully embroidered baby sling from the Bai region of south-west China is both a celebration of a young baby and a traditional, convenient method for mothers to carry their children while working.

Egyptian artwork from the era of the pharaohs depicts children being carried in slings, and since then women have continued to find ingenious ways of carrying their infants. A 4–5ft length of fabric is often used to secure babies on to their mothers' backs, front or side. Inuit mothers use a special Amauti coat wrapped around mother and baby to keep their infants warm, while in Peru brightly coloured woven shawls secure little ones to their mothers' backs. Carrying children in these ways has been particularly important for women undertaking domestic and agricultural work while also caring for a small baby. Traditionally many Bai women lived on farms, taking a role in harvesting and weeding crops such as tea, sugarcane, tobacco and wheat and working in rice fields. In recent years Chinese Bai women have also made and sold their embroidered handicraft items, like this sling, to tourists.

Fashions, fads and attitudes to child-rearing, as well as financial resources, have governed how mothers transport children. Wealthy women in Europe and the USA left the intimate tasks of bathing and dressing to domestic servants or slaves in the eighteenth, nineteenth and early twentieth centuries. The very first prams were designed for such wealthy families, which assumed most mothers would have limited close physical contact with their children. One of the earliest prams was invented by William Kent, at the request of the Duke of Devonshire, in 1733. It was pulled by a small pony or goat and took the children around the grounds of Chatsworth Park and Devonshire House. In the nineteenth century, large and expensive perambulators emerged which could be pushed by a maid or nanny taking their little charges out for air. It was not until the early twentieth century that it became common practice for many mothers in Western countries to borrow or buy a pram to enable them to transport their children. Pushing the pram, or even a pushchair, was often seen as a particularly female task. Even in mid-twentieth-century Britain, although some men proudly pushed their children in a pram or pushchair, many thought such a task compromised their masculinity.

Cumbersome prams and pushchairs may be ideal for the grounds of country estates and London parks, but they are not so perfect for mothers clambering on and off public transport or climbing stairs to flats when the lift is broken. Furthermore, they take up large amounts of space in many of the compact homes built in Britain and Europe since the Second World War. Consequently women responded

enthusiastically when in 1965 Owen Maclaren, a retired aeronautical engineer who had worked on the Spitfire, designed the first version of a 'baby buggy' in response to his daughter's complaints about how difficult it was to travel with a pram. This new lightweight pushchair could be folded up and carried like a large umbrella, lifted on to trains and put in the boot of cars. Its small size and easy manoeuvrability provided mothers of the women's liberation era with a mobility their grandmothers

Psychologists suggest carrying babies in a sling establishes a closer bond between mother and infant.

could only have dreamed of. Millions of buggies were sold worldwide and the iconic pushchair was displayed at the Museum of Modern Art in New York and the Design Centre in London.

As the twentieth century drew to a close and consumer culture dominated Western societies, manufacturers marketed multiple expensive products for parents to purchase as expressions of their love for their children. The Bugaboo, apparently 'game-changing', prams and pushchairs were the epitome of modern design and safety, making a lifestyle statement. Bugaboo mums were stylish, chic, go-getting and quite different from the harassed mothers pushing cheap buggies through the shops, overladen with parcels and worrying their pushchairs might tip over backwards. Maclaren buggies were no longer such a symbol of women's freedom when it was discovered, in 2009, that some children had their fingers cut off in the hazardous folding mechanism. Mothers and grandmothers responded with fury when they discovered safety kits to remedy the problem had only been provided in the USA. Rosemary Lacey, whose daughter used Maclaren buggies for her children, demanded to know: 'Why are American children more important than ours? If it's a dangerous product, it's a dangerous product and should be recalled.'

Is the way mothers transport their children just about fashion, fad and parental convenience?

Within years Bugaboo had also upset mothers. A publicity photograph with toned model Ymre Stiekema, dressed only in a bikini and pushing her daughter in a Bugaboo pram, created a storm of criticism on social media in 2017. While some commented that having spent £1,000 on the Bugaboo maybe she could not afford clothes, Christina Miskis remarked it was a 'totally ridiculous photo ... Give mums a break!' A journalist in the *Telegraph*, who recalled a period of eating chocolate digestives in weepy despair after her child was born, responded with the headline: 'Pram-pushing in a bikini? We mums are just busy trying not to wet ourselves.'

Psychologists' suggestion that carrying babies in a sling helped establish a closer bond between mother and baby has fuelled a new trend for slings recently – one that some fathers also embrace. Celebrity endorsements by Myleene Klass, Madonna and Nicole Kidman have made expensively produced designer slings a 'must-have' item for 'yummy mummies' in the Western world, aligning themselves with the millions of women who have no option but to strap their babies on to their bodies while they work. However, the childcare author Penelope Leach has drawn attention to the 'tendency to romanticise rural infancy in the developing world'. In 1997, she pointed out: 'If you have no crib or pushchair your baby must be carried to keep her physically safe [but] how babies are treated largely depends on what suits care-taking adults.'

10 | Lucy Baldwin Apparatus for Obstetric Analgesia

Painkillers for Childbirth

MAGGIE ANDREWS

The British Oxygen Company in London made the Lucy Baldwin apparatus for obstetric analgesia in the late 1950s. It provided a mixture of oxygen and nitrous oxide through a face mask to alleviate women's pain during childbirth.

The device was rather heavy but, as it had wheels, it could be moved around within hospitals; for district midwives attending home births it was however rather cumbersome. The apparatus's name was chosen as a tribute to a woman who had worked to improve women's experience of childbirth in the inter-war years. Lucy Baldwin was the wife of a British Conservative politician, Stanley Baldwin, who first became Prime Minister of Britain in 1923.

Lucy Baldwin's first child was stillborn but she went on to give birth to a further six healthy children and become vice chairman of the National Birthday Trust Fund in 1928, campaigning to improve maternity services and reduce maternal mortality rates. Evoking the horrors of the carnage of the First World War, she likened the uncertainty mothers faced when going into labour to men 'going into battle', arguing that 'our women daily, hourly, are "going over the top" risking death from childbirth as men did in the trenches'. Her key preoccupation was pain relief for mothers, which was only available to the wealthy who could afford to pay for it. She helped set up the Analgesics Appeal Fund in 1929, promoting the cause though public speaking and radio broadcasts. The organisation undertook significant fundraising activities, enabling them to purchase equipment for district hospitals and midwives to administer gas and air to mothers in labour. It also provided midwives with training so they could use the apparatus. When Lucy Baldwin died, newspapers reported that 'thousands of mothers owe a debt of gratitude to her for the wider use of analgesics in childbirth'.

Religious attitudes and social practices surrounding the pain women suffer during childbirth have varied between nations and across historical periods. In the biblical story of Adam and Eve, Eve transgresses by eating a forbidden apple and is told: 'In sorrow thou shalt bring forth children.' For some religious groups this pronouncement, directed at Eve and her descendants, justifies women's experience of pain during labour. Nevertheless, many have attempted to alleviate women's suffering with drugs, potions, massage, distraction and even the power of suggestion. The ancient Egyptians burned turpentine near the labouring woman and rubbed a vinegar and marble dust mixture on to the abdomen. The early Chinese used opium and alcohols to dull the pain, while in the Middle Ages herbal mixtures with poppy, mandrake, henbane or hemp were used. It has only been in the last

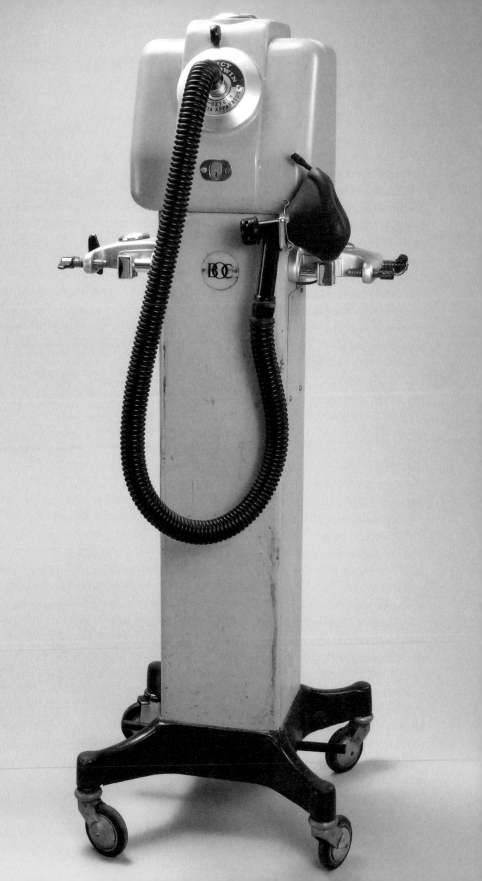

200 years, however, that there has been significant, if patchy, progress to alleviate women's labour pains.

In the nineteenth century in the USA and UK physicians, chemists and local doctors explored the use of nitrous oxide for pain relief, amputation and dentistry. By 1847 ether was being trialled to alleviate pain during childbirth. The wife of the American poet Henry Wadsworth Longfellow wrote of her experience of it: 'I did it for the good of women everywhere as no woman should have to suffer that much pain. I am very sorry you all thought me so rash and naughty in trying the ether.'

Queen Victoria's use of chloroform for the birth of her eighth child in the 1850s did much to make the practice of administering painkillers more socially acceptable – for those who could afford them. At the beginning of the twentieth century German doctors Bernhardt Kronig and Karl Gauss experimented with drugs to enable women to experience a pain-free labour while unconscious. A potentially toxic mixture of morphine and scopolamine was administered to ensure women were not even aware that they had given birth; instead they experienced what became known as a 'twilight sleep'. A fulsome account of this practice penned by two American women journalists in *McClure's Magazine* in 1914 led influential women, including many feminists, to form The National Twilight Sleep Association in the USA. They campaigned, with some success, for every woman's right to a pain-free labour. However, such powerful drugs were not without danger; women could become psychotic, screaming and hurting themselves and having to be restrained. The drugs could also have a detrimental, sometimes lethal, effect on the baby's breathing.

> Are women really able to exercise choice over pain relief in labour?

The high cost of analgesics and concerns over their side effects meant that in the inter-war years in both the USA and Europe the vast majority of women gave birth without painkillers. In the aftermath of the Second World War 68 per cent of women in Britain had no form of analgesic during labour, but following the introduction of the National Health Service and campaigns from women's organisations, the figure had halved within a decade. In the 1970s some feminists argued that childbirth should be seen as a natural process, and that pain relief could stifle women's experience of the birth and apparently the mother–child bonding process with it. More recently feminists have argued that women should exercise choice over their own use of pain relief during childbirth. However, many women across the world still do not have access to the facilities and drugs that would enable them to exercise such a choice.

11 | The Shoreditch Sisters' Vulva Quilt

Female Genital Mutilation

MAGGIE ANDREWS

The Vulva Quilt, created by the Shoreditch Sisters branch of the Women's Institute movement in 2011, contains numerous sumptuous depictions of vulvas, knitted, embroidered or crocheted into 8in by 8in colourful squares which have been sewn together to make a giant quilt.

This powerful celebration of the most intimate and hidden parts of women's bodies was the inspiration of Shoreditch Sisters campaign officer Tara Scott and has become a symbol of the struggle to eradicate female genital mutilation (FGM). As Tara explained: 'We want to raise awareness about the horrors of FGM through celebrating the positive, beautiful and powerful traits of women and their bodies.'

FGM is defined by the World Health Organisation as the total or partial removal of any part of the female genitalia for non-medical reasons; this may involve the removal of the clitoral hood, the whole of the clitoris or all external labia minora and much of the labia majora and then stitching the vulva together leaving a small hole for urinating. This stitching is sometimes referred to as embroidery. FGM carries health risks from complications such as excessive bleeding and infection. Psychological and physical scarring has long-term effects, sometimes making women infertile or increasing the likelihood of complications in childbirth. The practice of FGM varies between and within countries, with a high incidence in Djibouti, Egypt, Mali, Somalia and Sudan. It is not linked to or required by any religious group, and predates Christianity, Islam and Judaism, with some communities continuing to believe it will guarantee a girl's chastity and improve her marriage prospects.

Girls can be subjected to genital mutilation at any age, from newborn to adolescence. In some countries it is carried out in hospitals, elsewhere in back rooms or en masse as a 'celebration' of womanhood. Nimko Ali, a British Somali woman subjected to FGM at the age of 7 when on holiday in Djibouti, points out that the painful practice conveys a message to women:

> It's about fear, limiting aspirations and stopping girls from speaking out and challenging the status quo … FGM is not just about the cutting, it's everything that goes with it. FGM legitimises the forced marriage, the rape, the so-called 'honour' killings – all these things. It's another form of violence linked to the role of women and the value given to the girl child.

Worldwide 125 million women have suffered female genital mutilation; 30 million girls are considered to be at risk.

Worldwide 125 million women have suffered FGM and 30 million girls are considered to be at risk, although FGM is now illegal in a number of countries and is generally declining. It was outlawed in Indonesia in 2006 and in Nigeria in 2015. In many counties the enforcement of such laws has been patchy, hence the World Health Organisation and women's organisations like the Shoreditch Sisters and Soroptimist International continue campaigning.

The Vulva Quilt is one example of a tradition of what has been called 'stealth feminism' – women using traditionally feminine crafts to respond to political issues. In the USA, women created quilts when campaigning to abolish slavery and for temperance and women's suffrage. Quilts, in a range of mediums, continue to be used to express women's social concerns. The Association for Progressive Communications' Women's Rights Programme produced a collaborative digital quilt to campaign to 'reclaim information and communications technologies' and express solidarity with defenders of women's human rights. More traditional materials were employed by the World March of Women, an international network of 6,000 grassroots women's organisations which created a solidarity quilt in 2005 to promote their global charter with thirty-one goals, disseminated in sixty-four events held throughout the world. Each country's commitment to the charter and events was commemorated in a patch for the quilt. In São Paulo, Brazil, 30,000 women marched to demand salary increases, agrarian reform and abortion rights, represented on the quilt by a collage of feet, flowers and butterflies. World March of Women's International Secretariat Miriam Nobre explained: 'Each square has a story to tell and a meaning behind it … The quilt is our global charter for humanity expressed in a different way … It is our dreams, the different world we're struggling for, materialised.'

Is stealth feminism really the way to change women's lives?

In October 2013, Women for Refugee Women asked the Shoreditch Sisters to run craft workshops for refugee women. The women shared knitting and crochet skills at regular meetings, every other Saturday morning, creating squares that were patched into their very own solidarity quilt. As the women worked together, a community developed and the Shoreditch Sisters became increasingly aware of the plight of refugee women who had fled persecution in their own countries and sought refuge in Britain. Women and girls, sometimes pregnant, disabled or elderly, make up half of the millions of people worldwide who are forced to flee their homes due to conflict and violence. Many of the refugee women who became Saturday knitters had been in Yarl's Wood detention centre, where the quilted blanket of over 400 squares was later hung. Members of the public also had the opportunity to contribute squares and messages of support for the women in Yarl's Wood when the quilt was taken to the WOW Festival on International Women's Day in 2014. As Lauren Fuzi of the Shoreditch Sisters Women's Institute explained: 'We hope to continue using the blanket as a campaigning tool, raising awareness of women's experiences in Yarl's Wood and encouraging members of the public to take action against the detention of women asylum seekers.'

Who's watching your drink?

Drug Rape - Know the Risk

www.drugrapetrust.org

Working for a safer London

METROPOLITAN
POLICE

12 | Date Rape Warning Poster

Rape of Women

JANIS LOMAS

This poster warning to watch your drink emphasises that the use of substances make especially women susceptible to sexual assault. Rohypnol and GHB are powerful 'date rape' drugs; Rohypnol is about ten times more powerful than Valium and, when added to a woman's drink, can render her confused and drowsy – helpless to resist sexual assault.

Date rape drugs provide a new method of perpetrating rape with reduced chances of legal repercussion, as victims often have hazy recollections of events afterwards. Reportedly more than 1,000 UK women have been raped while drugged, yet there have been only four successful prosecutions. Rape has always been a notoriously difficult crime to prove; the court records for the Old Bailey in 1686 report that:

> A Person was Indicted for Committing a Rape upon the Body of a Young Woman on the 2d. of March last: The Evidence was heard at large on both sides; and upon a full hearing of the Matter, the Prosecution was looked upon in the Conclusion, as a Design to get money, and so the Prisoner was found Not Guilty.

An influential forensic textbook in the 1890s put forward the notion that working-class women were not susceptible to sexual assault, stating:

> Women of the lower classes were accustomed to rough play with individuals both of their own and of the opposite sex and had acquired the habit of defending themselves against sportive violence … Their capacity for defence rendered them capable of frustrating the attempts of any ravisher.

In recent years, with shifting attitudes to violence against women, reported rape in the UK has soared. Ministry of Justice statistics (2013) suggest nearly half a million adults are sexually assaulted in England and Wales each year, with one in five women between 16 and 59 having experienced some form of sexual violence. Of these only 15 per cent choose to report it to the police. In the USA the figures appear similar to the UK, with 18 per cent of all women reporting being sexually assaulted but only 16 per cent of these reporting it to the police. The average sentence for rape in the UK is eight and a half years but conviction rates remain stubbornly low. Professor Liz Kelly points out they should be calculated as 'a proportion of reports. The vast majority of cases are lost at the investigation stage. If you don't look at the whole process … then you get a skewed picture … 80% of cases don't get to prosecution'.

There have been attempts to make the court process less daunting for victims. Defence solicitors are no longer supposed to question a woman about previous sexual history and judges are more likely to intervene if the questioning becomes too vicious. But victims are still accused of being liars or fantasists. For some the trial is experienced as another assault.

The feminist movement in the 1970s argued that rape is an exercise of power, a personal invasion of a woman's body, sometimes as a way of bringing them into line, or of extracting revenge and dominance over individuals, and even over nations. Women historically have often been treated as 'spoils of war', raped during and immediately after many conflicts by military personnel. There are reports of widespread rapes by Soviet troops when they entered Berlin at the end of the Second World War; less well known are the incidences of rape by Allied troops. In 1945 in Okinawa a British marine reported:

> Marching south, men of the 4th Marines passed a group of some 10 American soldiers bunched together in a tight circle ... Then as we passed them I could see they were taking turns raping an oriental woman. I was furious, but our outfit kept marching by as though nothing unusual was going on.

Even those serving within the military are not safe; in a survey of 558 women who served in the American military during the Vietnam War and after, almost a third reported having been raped. In March 1977 a judge in Norwich passed a three-year sentence on a guardsman for attempting to rape a 17-year-old girl who was left with severe internal injuries and broken ribs, and was unable to work for four months. The Court of Appeal reduced his sentence to a suspended six-month sentence. The judge told him that 'the best thing you can do now is to go back to your unit and serve your country', justifying his decision by saying the guardsman's career would be destroyed if he was imprisoned and that the girl 'would probably have been less severely injured if she'd submitted to rape'.

Why is it now more dangerous to be a woman than to be a soldier in modern conflict?

More recently, International Criminal Tribunals have punished the perpetrators of rape; an estimated 25–50,000 Bosnian women and girls were raped during the Yugoslavia conflict between 1991 and 1995. Between a quarter and half a million women were purportedly raped in the Rwandan Civil War in 1994, the Special Rapporteur to the United Nations later reporting that 'rape was the rule and its absence the exception'. In 2008, Major General Patrick Cammaert, former Commander of the UN Peacekeeping operations in Democratic Republic of

Le vieux Séducteur.

Congo (DRC), declared that 'it is now more dangerous to be a woman than to be a soldier in modern conflict'.

Different cultures at different historical moments have viewed rape very differently, and the process of criminalising rape within marriage occurred comparatively recently – in the USA between the mid-1970s and 1993, and in England and Wales in 1991. In April 2017 a Malaysian MP caused an outcry from women's groups when he suggested that rapists and their victims should 'turn over a new leaf' and get married, adding:

> Perhaps through marriage they can lead a healthier, better life. And the person who was raped does not necessarily have a bleak future. She will have a husband, at least, and this could serve as a remedy to growing social problems.

Part II
Wives and Homemakers

It starts as you sink into his arms, ends with your arms in the sink.

Marriage and domesticity have been both desirable ideals and lived experiences for women throughout history. What it means to be a wife and a housewife has, however, shifted and changed over time, shaped by legal, economic and political constraints and interpreted in a multitude of different ways according to a woman's class, nationality and religion. The objects in this section provide a starting point for exploring this, indications of moments of change as with the Married Women's Property Acts which have been stepping stones on the way to the very different ideas of marriage and relationships that co-exist in the twenty-first century.

While, for many women, being a wife has been a career, a role to which they aspire, women's greater economic independence means that more is now expected of relationships. The ideals of romantic love and marriage articulated in fairy stories such as *Cinderella* are consumed by small children and embodied in objects like the Taj Mahal and many films and fictions. But for many women romantic love turns out to be less than ideal and escape routes are needed. Shakespeare reputedly suggested that 'many a good hanging prevents a bad marriage'; for some women, being sold, widowed or finding a women's refuge have been the only exit strategies available from unreliable relationships.

Women may find romance and ideals sink underneath more mundane domestic tasks and the effort to survive and to feed families. Their struggles are more acute in times of war, conflict, financial crisis or austerity, when support such as access to food banks is needed. Women, as wives, daughter, sisters or servants, have traditionally been allocated the majority of tasks related to home-making. In this section attention is drawn to how women have exercised creativity and resourcefulness to feed their families. Little wonder that domesticity is often an expression of women's expertise, skill and power, and nowadays, with the new turn to domesticity in Western countries, an escapist pleasure.

Marriage is both a personal relationship, an alliance between families, and an institution of the state; consequently the path into and out of marriage is not straightforward, and society and family place numerous expectations on women who are wives and housewives. Women and wives have been subject to a remarkable amount of advice, censure and criticism – their voices restrained in scold's bridles and their drinking condemned. Nevertheless women have found spaces and places of pleasure and power – a little spending supported by a credit card, for example, or the joys of a nice cup of tea and a chocolate biscuit.

13 | Terracotta Figures

Baking and Cooking

JANIS LOMAS

The figure, found in the Boeotia district of Central Greece and dating from 500 BCE, shows a woman busy in a domestic task to feed her family. She is seated in front of an oven holding a loaf of bread.

Different cultures at different historical moments have seen a range of styles of bread from flatbreads to baguettes, but as this figure portrays, in almost every civilisation since time immemorial, bread-making has been one of women's most common chores. Indeed, recent scholarship suggests people may have been eating a primitive version of bread 30,000 years ago and the cultivation of wheat to make bread led to the replacement of the nomadic life by settlements. The free-standing oven as shown here appears to have been first used in ancient Greece. The fire heated the oven and was then removed, enabling the bread to bake in the retained heat.

By the Middle Ages, women in European countries were using large cauldrons placed on an open fire to bake bread but by the early 1700s a cast-iron oven was beginning to become available although most houses still had limited means of cooking. In the early nineteenth century coal-fired ovens were developed alongside early gas stoves, the first of which was patented in 1826. Most women making bread had to light fires and warm the bread oven to the correct temperature. Undercooked or burned loaves could result in a horrendous waste of the family's scarce resources. Yet in William Cobbett's *Cottage Economy* (1821) he expressed his concern about women's bread-making skills:

Is baking more enjoyable now it is something women can choose to do rather than the daily chore it was?

As to the act of making bread, it would be shocking indeed if that had to be taught by means of books. Every woman high or low, ought to know how to make bread. If she does not, she is unworthy of trust and confidence: and indeed a mere burden on the community. Yet it is but too true, that many women, even those who get their living from their labour, know nothing of the making of bread.

Despite Cobbett's concerns, bakers and bakers' shops were well established; bread-making was one of the first of women's domestic tasks to be undertaken outside the home. In Greece, in the fifth century BCE, bread could be bought from bakers' shops. Cakes and breads sweetened with honey and topped with seeds were also

available. Greek bakers also ran bread and cake shops in ancient Rome. The Great Fire of London is said to have started in a baker's shop in Pudding Lane in 1666. In the nineteenth and early twentieth centuries it was common for housewives to take the roast to the bakery on a Sunday morning, where for a few pence it was cooked.

Nevertheless, at the end of the nineteenth century in Britain, the vast majority of bread was still baked by housewives in their homes. Bread was the staple food of the working classes, eaten several times a day; its production was therefore an onerous task, particularly for women with large families. When in 1908 Mrs Towler,

Women have been making bread for 30,000 years.

a suffragette from Preston, wanted to travel to join a rally in Hyde Park, she had to ensure she had left provisions for her husband and four sons. Before leaving for London, she made sure her house was immaculate, having spent the entire previous week cooking and baking enough bread to keep them going for a fortnight, in case she was imprisoned. By the 1930s most bread in Britain was shop bought, relieving housewives of a time-consuming domestic task. Many still disapproved of buying bread, and some considered housewives who resorted to shop-bought bread lazy. A popular radio broadcaster and domestic goddess of the era, Mrs Webb, singled out home baking for particular praise in her wireless series *Farmhouse Cookery* (1935). Her programmes praised the traditional home-cooking skills of the farmer's wife, who baked:

> Once a week, bread and such bread – plain, spiced, currant, wholemeal, Yorkshire teacakes, pies, cheese cakes, and great big useful fruit cakes, by magic from the work of that pair of capable and utterly efficient hands.

This farmer's wife cooked with a wood-fuelled fire. The AGA cooker, still a luxury item often desired by the upwardly mobile middle classes, had been introduced in 1922 and the design has remained a classic ever since.

The first machine to slice and wrap bread was installed in the Wonderloaf factory in Tottenham, London in 1937, having been developed in the USA in 1928, saving women yet another task. No wonder the phrase 'the best thing since sliced bread' entered common use. In 1961 bread-making on a commercial scale was revolutionised by the development of the Chorleywood bread process, which reduced the fermentation process so a loaf could be produced from start to finish in 3.5 hours; 80 per cent of British bread is still produced using this process today. By the end of the twentieth century, bread-making and baking had become a pastime in many Western countries, a relaxation and hobby rather than the chore it had been for almost all women for hundreds of years. In the present foodie culture of home baking, breads made by artisan producers using traditional methods such as slow fermenting sourdough, home bread-making machines and the popularity of the *Great British Bake-Off* (2010–) has made home baking easier and increasingly popular.

14 | Scold's Bridle
Silencing Women's Voices

RICHARD DHILLON

On 13 August 1546 Marion Ray was brought before the court in the city of Stirling in Scotland, charged with multiple counts of slander after she accused her neighbours of adultery, which she witnessed 'throe ane hole'. For her 'trublus wordis', Ray was ordered to beg the forgiveness of her accusers, before receiving her punishment: to be locked into 'the claspis and calvill of irne' for twenty-four hours 'without any relaxing'.

This case is one of the earliest recorded uses of the scold's bridle, or 'branks'. The device consisted of a heavy iron frame which was placed over the victim's head and worn as a collar; a protruding plate fixed to the front was projected into her mouth, immobilising her tongue, leaving her unable to drink, eat or talk.

The bridle was punishment for a 'scold' – a term overwhelmingly applied to women who exercised irreverent or unruly speech, defying patriarchal expectations, or who challenged accepted notions of womanhood. The device had complex social functions. It served to silence women's voices, and to suppress acts of expression that were considered unruly or disruptive, through pain and shame. The victim would have been subjected to ritualised humiliation as she was paraded through the streets of her parish, exhibited in a central location, such as the market cross, and subjected to ridicule, abuse – and sometimes sympathy – by her own community. This public ritual served to re-assert male authority by demonstrating the consequences of disorder, and to re-affirm accepted gendered structures of power in society; the bridle was as much a restorative and didactic tool as one of retribution.

Evidence for the use of the device is piecemeal, and while the bridle was never an officially sanctioned legal practice, a variety of surviving source material suggests that it was employed at the local level from at least the 1540s throughout Britain, and continued well into the eighteenth century. Early American sources suggest that the device was exported to the New World, and later repurposed for use on slaves. It is noteworthy that the crime of 'scold' was only removed from the British penal code in 1967. A fragment of the long history of the silencing of women, the bridle represents an enduring campaign to suppress female voices and exclude women from the public sphere. It also reflects a much broader cultural unease surrounding female speech, which continues to this day.

In January 2013, classicist Professor Mary Beard appeared on the BBC's political debate programme *Question Time*. Following her appearance, Beard was subject to horrific online abuse which, in her own words, would put many women off appearing in public. In the same year journalist and campaigner Caroline Criado-Perez received

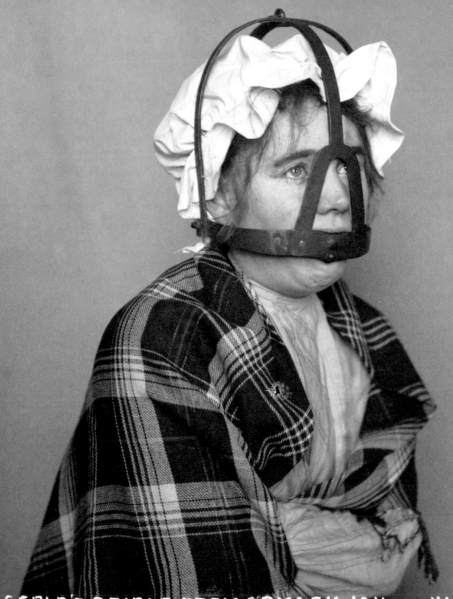

SCOLD'S BRIDLE FROM ARMAGH JAIL.   WAG 38

unprecedented abuse from trolls, threatening violence, rape and murder, following her successful campaign to maintain female representation on British banknotes. Criado-Perez has spoken of the psychological effects of her ordeal, and how the abuse impacted her ability to function and interact in society. Indeed, the trolling of women on social media has been described as a modern equivalent of the scold's bridle; in order to silence the women through the language of insult, trolling, as it is called, attempts to drown out their voices in a sea of constant abuse, personal attacks and warnings of violence, often sexual in nature, as well as threats of death.

The bridle speaks to other modern expressions of misogyny. Developed from a device traditionally used to control horses, the bridle reduced women to the status of an unruly animal, to be subjugated as chattel, controlled, and tamed. The language of abuse aimed at women does the same thing; 'bitch' – a female dog – for example, is a pejorative insult overwhelmingly applied to women. The term and its meaning is one which appears in cultures across the globe, and has appeared in the historical record for centuries. 'Scold' and 'bitch' have similar connotations; indeed, the verb 'to bitch', has itself evolved into common parlance as an activity which is allied to femininity, meaning to verbally critique in an unkind or spiteful way.

Even in the twenty-first century there seem to be numerous ways of silencing women's voices.

The scold's bridle is a remnant of the historical subjugation of women representing the concern with female voices, and unwittingly demonstrates their threat to male authority. Confined to the past, the device represents a barbaric device of torture in a very different world from today. However, the phenomenon of social media trolling, and the gendered language of insult, demonstrates twenty-first-century equivalents of the bridle, which attempt to shame and humiliate women who dare to assert themselves in public. These attacks are, however, also evidence of the strength of the women's voices trolls seek to suppress, and like the scold's bridle, show that women's voices have the power to shake the very foundations of society, and are therefore a source of great anxiety.

15 | Taj Mahal
Romance and Romantic Fiction

JANIS LOMAS

Maharajah Shah Jahan built the Taj Mahal in memory of his much-loved wife Mumtaz Mahal. She was his third wife but also his chief advisor and companion. She died in childbirth having her fourteenth child in 1631. He decided to build a lasting monument and mausoleum to honour her and employed the best designers; in return, for a large sum of money, he made them promise they would not work on anything that could rival its beauty.

Built in the city of Agra, of ivory-white marble with ornate carving and formal gardens on three sides, the tomb of Mumtaz Mahal is the centrepiece of the huge construction, which took 20,000 artisans twenty-one years to complete. It has been considered one of the most beautiful and significant buildings in the world ever since, visited by over 7 million people each year and considered an enduring symbol of romantic love. However, recent research has hinted that Shah Jahan was a womaniser, so perhaps the Taj love story is itself a myth.

Ideas of romantic love, the agony of separation, suffering and dying for love and narratives of star-crossed lovers have been reproduced thousands of times in fairy tales, fables, films and books. In the twelfth century the Celtic myth of Tristan and Iseult, tragic lovers who could never be parted even by death, became popular and has since been retold in many cultures. The marriage of Henry II to Eleanor of Aquitaine in the twelfth century is credited with both uniting the kingdoms and introducing writing about courtly love, troubadours and poets into the English court. Eleanor was at the centre of this passion for courtly love and enthralled by stories of King Arthur and his Knights of the Round Table, who were both warriors and lovers. In *Sir Gawain and the Green Knight*, Gawain explained that 'it is for love and for their lovers that men do gallant deeds'. Courtly love was seen as a game whereby a virtuous woman was placed on a pedestal, an object of male desire. For the duration of the game, at least, women had power over men and appeared to control the situation. Once the knight had won his lady, however, she was constrained, in his possession; the power she wielded was lost. The ideal of courtly love waned and was satirised in the popular novel *Don Quixote* in 1605. The author, Miguel de Cervantes, tells the adventures of an elderly country gentleman who is so obsessed with gallant deeds that he has been driven slightly mad and tries to recreate the heroes of the stories, with comic results.

Is romantic love just a fiction?

Many romantic narratives with an enduring appeal like that of Maharajah Shah Jahan and his wife have had more tragic endings. The Shakespearean tragedy of *Romeo and Juliet*, written in the late sixteenth century, ends with the couple's death and the famous words:

> For never was a story of more woe
> Than this of Juliet and her Romeo.

In the nineteenth century a number of literary novels such as *Madame Bovary* (1856), *Anna Karenina* (1877) and *Tess of the D'Urbervilles* (1891) which were written by men, portray romantic heroines who transgress the sexual codes of their era, and consequently meet untimely, early deaths. A plethora of films from *Brief Encounter* (1945) to *Love Story* (1970) have continued to suggest that romantic love ends in death or misery and that attempts to defy convention will end badly. Alternatively, widely read romantic novels, which became popular in the twentieth century, were predominantly written by women such as Georgette Heyer, Catherine Cookson and Danielle Steel. They portrayed heroines who were more active and assertive than the women who appeared in tales of courtly love, and who triumphed over adversity unlike the heroines of nineteenth-century novels. Mass circulation novels such as Mills and Boon romances, sold as Harlequin Enterprises in the USA and Canada, have made romantic fiction the biggest publishing sector in the world, providing women with hundreds of stolen hours of relaxation and pleasure. The brand publishes 100 titles per month and in 2008 sold 200 million copies worldwide, yet it is looked down upon and denigrated, perhaps because its audience is predominantly female. However, as Clare Somerville, then marketing director of Harlequin, pointed out in 2009:

> Our books appeal to average women ... [who] are exhausted looking after everybody. The hero is a nurturer who lets you be yourself, while someone off stage does all the crappy stuff. I get very cross when people say we denigrate women. I think we are one of the most feminist publishers in existence ... We don't trailblaze but we do talk to women about their emotions and their feelings and their dreams. We talk about relationships in the way that women really want them to be.

The gap between the romantic ideal of how women would like their relationships to be and their everyday lives is a perennial source of sadness and marital breakdown. In July 1981 romantic love seemed to be epitomised by the fairy-tale wedding of Lady Diana Spencer to the Prince of Wales. Eleven years later, Diana sat alone and desolate on a bench in the most romantic spot in the world, the Taj Mahal, attracting huge media attention. Prince Charles had already been photographed on the same spot prior to his marriage when he was quoted as saying that he hoped to return there with his wife. On this day, he had chosen to visit an Indian school of architecture to make a speech to industrialists. Speculation as to the state of their marriage followed, especially as Diana appeared so downcast and alone and told reporters that 'it would have been better if both of us had been here'. They parted ten months later. Their son Prince William said 'he hoped to forge new memories' when he sat on the bench twenty-four years later in 2016, following in his parents' footsteps but this time with his wife by his side. Barbara Cartland, a prolific writer of romantic novels with virginal brides and happily-ever-after endings, was Princess Diana's step-grandmother and she was quoted as saying, 'the only books Diana ever read were mine, and they weren't awfully good for her'.

16 | Hogarth's *Gin Lane*

Attitudes to Women Drinking

JANIS LOMAS

William Hogarth painted *Gin Lane* (1751) at a time when the average Londoner was drinking around a pint and a half of neat gin per week. Roughly 25 per cent of London households produced or sold gin.

The central figure in the painting is the grotesque half-naked prostitute, clearly drunk, her legs covered with syphilitic sores, taking snuff and totally oblivious to her child hurtling head first to its death. The remainder of the images are of a city in turmoil. The archway at the bottom left of the engraving is leading to a gin cellar. The cheapness of the gin is illustrated in the sign over the archway: 'Drunk for a penny, Dead drunk for two pence, Clean straw for nothing.' The straw is for somewhere to sleep off the effects of the alcohol. The drink was incredibly strong, around 57 per cent proof, and became an easy way to oblivion. Hogarth's painting conveyed an image of the dangers of drink for women, and especially of gin.

Hogarth produced *Gin Lane* and its companion painting *Beer Street* as part of a campaign to stem the epidemic of gin drinking that was sweeping the slums of London. He produced the engraving plates himself to keep the price affordable and ensured the engravings were widely distributed. *Beer Street* showed beer drinking as promoting a calm, ordered city, in contrast to the horrors of *Gin Lane*, where as well as the horrific central image, a carpenter and his wife are pawning their tools and pots and pans to buy gin, a man and a dog chew on the same bone, and a lunatic dances a jig with a spike on which a baby has been impaled while another hangs himself in despair. All in all, Hogarth's *Gin Alley* depicts the tumbled-down ruins and mob rule of a city in utter disarray and it is likely that the term 'Mother's Ruin' came to be applied to gin in the aftermath of Hogarth's engraving. A woman called Judith Dufour was said to be the inspiration for Hogarth's central figure. In 1734 this woman took her 2-year-old child out of the workhouse, strangled her and stripped her naked in order to sell her clothes to buy gin. She was later hanged for this crime. There was particular concern that women were compromising their ability to produce the children the nation needed to work in factories or fight in wars by drinking gin. Drinking large amounts of gin apparently made men impotent and women sterile, and it was perceived to have affected the birth rate in London, which had fallen significantly.

The roots of the gin craze lay in the years between 1700 and 1751, when people began to move from the countryside into cities like London, living in unprecedented

Does there continue to be more criticism directed at women for drinking than men?

In 1751, the average Londoner was drinking 1.5 pints of 57 per cent proof gin a week.

crowded, poverty-stricken conditions. Wages for the 'lower orders' were at starvation level and a desperate struggle for survival became the norm for many thousands of Londoners. Women's jobs paid much less than men's and were harder to find; for women unable to obtain work as servants or in sweatshops, prostitution was often the only avenue open to them and gin, once seen as medicine, became the affordable drink for those seeking oblivion from the miserable life they were enduring. Gin drinking staved off hunger pangs, blotted out the cold and was very cheap and sold on every street corner; by 1730 there were an estimated 7,000 gin shops in London in addition to the countless illegal drinking dens.

As a result of public disquiet and campaigns against the drinking of gin, in 1751 the Tippling Act was introduced, which increased the tax, and as economic conditions improved the consumption of gin lessened. It was to re-emerge in Victorian England in the proliferation of 'gin palaces' from the 1830s onwards. Designed to compete with beer shops, these were often large, imposing buildings and provided a welcome change from the slum dwellings which remained the lot of most Londoners. By the 1850s there were about 5,000 gin palaces in London, which social reformer George Sims claimed flourished in the slums as 'fortunes are made out of men and women who seldom know where tomorrow's meal is coming from'. For women, gin drinking and morally reprehensible behaviour were seen as intertwined; Eliza Cook in nineteenth-century London was apparently 'a woman of violent passions, given to swearing, thieving, drinking of gin and cat-skinning'.

Over time gin has retained a position in the marketplace and has also been associated with women in various ways. Women were informal small-scale sellers of gin, which was often identified as a woman's drink. Dram-shops, informal places where gin could be purchased in small quantities, were often run by women in their front rooms. The criticism of women drinkers continued and at the beginning of the twentieth century groups of Birmingham women took to drinking gin in teapots to hide their drinking from disapproving critics. In the 1940s and '50s 'Mother's Ruin' was considered to help procure a miscarriage. A hot bath accompanied by drinking a pint of gin was a combination tried by many a desperate girl trying to avoid the stigma of an unwanted pregnancy outside of marriage.

At the present time gin is having a resurgence, with 'designer' gins of various flavours being made by small producers. Cocktail bars and public houses specialising in different gins are fashionable, but the products they are selling bear little resemblance to the drink that caused so much misery in the eighteenth and nineteenth centuries. There are, however, resonances of the moral panic of the eighteenth-century gin craze in the anxiety and disapproval over contemporary young women's drinking, which remains open to so much more criticism than young men's drinking.

17 | Meissen Box with Portrait of Lady Caroline Fox

Family Fortunes and Their Role in Shaping Marriage

MAGGIE ANDREWS

The Meissen porcelain snuff box was given to the 2nd Duchess of Richmond as a present from her son-in-law, Henry Fox, in the middle of the eighteenth century. The picture underneath the lid was of the duchess's daughter Caroline, who four years earlier had thwarted her parents' authority and secretly married Fox.

The duke and duchess were well connected at the British court and intended their eldest daughter to marry someone of similar social standing, not a man nearly twice her age, surrounded by the whiff of scandal. Henry Fox was reputedly an atheist and gambler; he had one illegitimate child and another on the way. His brother had been openly homosexual before marrying the thirteen-year-old daughter of one of Henry Fox's mistresses. The duke refused to consent to a marriage between his daughter and this ambitious and cynical politician, who had neither title nor wealth. Caroline's elopement on 2 May 1744 caused a break with her parents. However, the duke's antagonism towards his son-in-law began to soften as Fox's political career blossomed; as Secretary at War, people talked about Fox as a future Prime Minister. Reconciliation followed, symbolised by the gift of the snuffbox.

The Duke and Duchess of Richmond subscribed to the view that affection was found within rather than prior to marriage, which was an institution where girls were a pawn to be used to build family alliances and wealth. Their own marriage was arranged between their fathers to settle a gambling debt, when the Earl of March, as the future duke was then known, was 18 years old and his bride only 13. After the ceremony the young lad proceeded to Italy with his tutor for three years. On his return, he prevaricated about visiting his wife only to be smitten by a young lady he saw at the theatre, who it was explained was 'the toast of the town, the beautiful Lady March'. Marriages arranged by parents usually entailed payments, a dowry paid by the bride's family or a bride-price paid by the groom for the woman's labour and reproductive capacity. Although the circumstances of the 2nd Duke's marriage were a little bizarre, they fitted with the principal of a dowry, a daughter's inheritance, being paid out when she left her family rather than when her parents died. For wealthy Europeans, marriages were usually preceded by contractual negotiations between parents; part of the dowry was invested to ensure the wife had spending money and would be provided for if widowed. Caroline's elopement lost her this

> In the twenty-first century, do money and family expectations play more of a role in modern marriages than we realise?

financial provision, but as both the marriage and Henry Fox's finances flourished this turned out to be immaterial.

Royal marriages served to seal international alliances and build empires. When the Duke of Richmond's grandfather, Charles II, married Catherine of Braganza, her dowry included territories in Bombay and Tangier; the marriage also recognised the new monarchy of Portugal. Negotiations for royal nuptials were often conducted at a distance; Marie Antoinette married the future Louis XVI of France by proxy when only a child. Subsequent introductions could be tricky; the 15-year-old Mary of Moderna reputedly burst into tears when she arrived in England and met her prospective husband, the future James II. The widowed brother of Charles II was twenty-five years her senior and Mary spent much of the following months weeping, although relations between the two improved in time. In 1795, the Prince of Wales greeted his fiancée, the 27-year-old German Princess Caroline of Brunswick, with a distinct lack of gallantry. Turning away, he requested of Lord Malmesbury, 'Harris, I am not well. Pray, get me a glass of brandy.' Unlike Caroline Fox, women in these situations were the pawns of their families' ambitions.

At the end of the nineteenth century, $25 billion came into Britain as American heiresses married British aristocrats.

The end of the nineteenth century saw a wave of American heiresses marry into the British aristocracy, injecting $25 billion into the British economy in return for titles. These young women's wealth was handed over to restore stately homes, pay gambling debts or merely cover their husbands' living expenses. Alice Thaw, daughter of a Pittsburgh railroad magnate, had to wait at the church on her wedding day when her future husband was arrested for debt, necessitating a renegotiation of the dowry terms between her father and her fiancé. In 1895 Consuelo Vanderbilt married Sunny, Charles Spencer-Churchill, the future 9th Duke of Marlborough and resident of Blenheim Palace. Consuelo's mother's ambitions for her to become duchess disregarded her daughter's attachment to a wealthy American. The bride recalled:

> Like an automaton I donned the lovely lingerie with its real lace and the white silk stockings and shoes ... I felt cold and numb as I went down to meet my father and the bridesmaids who were waiting for me.

Her husband was equally emotionally uncommitted to the marriage – but not to her wealth, which he spent restoring Blenheim before they separated ten years later.

In many contemporary cultures, women still face pressure to conform to their families' priorities or choices when marrying, and are tasked with avoiding bringing shame on their family. The Duke of Richmond's shame at his daughter Caroline's elopement led him to cancel a ball he was hosting and leave London, retiring to his country estate in West Sussex. Some individuals see shame in a much more sinister way; according to the Honour Based Violence Awareness Network, there are still 5,000 so-called 'honour' killings internationally per year. The practice continues, despite condemnation from leaders of major religions and legislation to outlaw honour killing in countries such as Pakistan. It is usually, but not always, carried out by men. In January 2017 Parveen Bibi confessed to killing her 18-year-old daughter Zeenat Rafiq for bringing shame on her family by marrying without her parents' consent.

18 | Newspaper Report of a Wife Sale

Dissolution of Marriage and Divorce

MAGGIE ANDREWS

The expectations and experiences of those who get married have varied over time and from one country to another; marriage may be understood as an intimate relationship, an economic necessity, even the basis of family and political alliances, or a legal institution which places financial obligations on the couple.

Dissolving a marriage was a complex process, and in eighteenth- and nineteenth-century Britain, at a time when wives had no legal status to own property and enter into contracts, the practice of a public wife sale developed. Sales were carried out in a public place, sometimes advertised in newspapers, on posters or by a town crier. One eighteenth-century newspaper announced:

> To be sold for Five Shillings, my Wife, Jane Hebbard. She is stoutly built, stands firm on her posterns, and is of sound wind and limb. She can sow and reap, hold a plough, and drive a team, and would answer any stout able man, that can hold a tight rein, for she is damned hard mouthed, headstrong ...

After the sale – which could be vetoed by the wife – was agreed, lawyers sometimes drew up a receipt recording the exchange, transfer of rights and obligations; hence they have come to be seen as a form of divorce for the poorer classes.

Ideas about marriage and sexuality, and consequently the legal framework in which couples come together and are torn asunder, are often shaped by religious beliefs. In 1215 Pope Innocent III elevated the ceremony of marriage to a sacrament, making divorce very problematic for Catholics. By contrast, in the north-eastern villages of eighteenth-century Japan, divorce was easy and common for the peasant class. Divorce did not carry a stigma and was commonly followed by remarriage. It required only a short writ to be handed from husband to wife – something husbands sometimes undertook under pressure from their wives. However at the end of the nineteenth century, with the introduction of new civil code intended to modernise Japan, divorce became more difficult to obtain.

Revolutionary France introduced divorce in 1792, but this was restricted under Napoleon and banned altogether in 1816. It was not re-introduced until 1884 and then required evidence of serious misconduct – adultery, ill treatment or desertion. In Britain up until the middle of the nineteenth century, it was necessary to petition parliament to get a divorce, which was expensive and usually restricted to the wealthy. Only eight women successfully divorced their husbands between 1700

SELLING A WIFE BY AUCTION

and 1857. Jane Campbell was the first, requiring a special committee of the House of Lords to hear evidence of her husband's adultery. Her petition only succeeded because the adultery had occurred with Jane's sister and so was considered incestuous. The salacious details of the comings and goings of the guilty pair, as recounted by servants, sometimes spying through bedroom doors, was printed in the House of Lords Journal.

When in 1857 divorce courts were established in Britain, they also undertook the restitution of conjugal rights (which compelled spouses to cohabit) and legal separations – an option many wives preferred due to the prejudices of the courts towards women in divorce cases. In 1889, Cecilia Eva Fowke successfully petitioned for a judicial separation from her husband, after eleven years of marriage and five children, on account of his violent and drunken behaviour, which included beating two of the children with a hunting whip. The new court made divorce cheaper; an undefended divorce case in the House of Lords might have cost between £700 and £800 but could be obtained now for as little as £40 or £50. Nevertheless, with agricultural labourers earning the equivalent of 75 pence a week, only those in

'Wife sales' were a form of divorce for the poorer classes in eighteenth- and nineteenth-century Britain.

SELLING A WIFE FOR 1s. 6d.

An extraordinary case of bigamy was heard at Stockport. The accused, Thomas Johnson, an elderly man, admitted having been married twice, and that both women were still alive. He had not, he said, lived with his first wife for thirty years before he married the second, and he thought the former had no claim upon him, especially as he had sold her for 1s. 6d. to a chimney sweep at New Mills, near Stockport. The prisoner was committed for trial.

desperate circumstances with ready cash resorted to the divorce courts. For many, divorce was not an option; sometimes husbands disappeared, couples cohabited, and court records indicate others took the risk of committing bigamy. In the 1880s Sarah Jane Stamp left her drunkard husband due to his cruelty. He went on to live with another woman and had two children while she, eight or nine years later, married William George Galliers. Unfortunately this union was also unsuccessful and she claimed it was impossible to live with him as he was 'in the habit of always throwing up my having committed adultery'. Sarah was convicted of bigamy in 1893 but only sentenced to one day's imprisonment.

In the 1960s and '70s it became easier to get a divorce in a number of countries. The 1969 Divorce Act in Britain enabled couples who had been separated for two years and were in agreement to divorce; this was also possible in France from 1975. Even at the end of the twentieth century, a number of countries continued to restrict divorce. Following a referendum, the constitutional prohibition on divorce was removed in Eire in 1996 while Malta only legalised divorce in 2011. The Philippines allows couples to annul their marriages but not to divorce or remarry. Divorce is still not permitted in Vatican City. The more liberal divorce laws introduced in the latter part of the twentieth century have led to concern about the consequences for both spouses and any children they may have. For many people, it is the death of one spouse rather than divorce that ends marriages. However, the division of property and income following a divorce frequently financially disadvantages women. A study in Australia suggests women typically experience a 73 per cent cut in their standard of living after a divorce, while a typical ex-husband enjoys a 42 per cent increase.

Many see easier access to divorce as liberating for women, but perhaps it has just resulted in more women living in poverty?

19 | Mrs Fawcett's Bag

Married Women and Property

JANIS LOMAS

When Millicent Garrett Fawcett was out shopping one day shortly after her marriage in 1867, a pickpocket stole her purse from her bag. She had known when she married that in legal terms she and her husband were not equal; nevertheless she was somewhat shocked that when the thief appeared in court the charge was that of 'stealing from the person of Millicent Fawcett a purse containing £1 18s 6d, the property of Henry Fawcett'.

She said it brought home to her that once a woman married all her possessions immediately became those of her husband, and she later recalled that she 'felt as if I had been charged with theft myself'. For Fawcett this incident was the impetus for many years of campaigning which culminated in her becoming the leader of the National Union of Women's Suffrage Societies, which by 1905 included 305 societies and nearly 50,000 members.

In the United Kingdom in the first half of the nineteenth century a married woman had almost no legal rights and was in many ways prevented from taking an active part in civil society. She was not allowed to vote, go to university, enter professions such as law or medicine, become a magistrate, become a town councillor or sit on any of the boards that ran schools, prisons or workhouses. Marriage was considered the goal for every woman; to be unmarried was to be second class and often an object of pity, even though unmarried women had more rights than their married counterparts. On marriage a woman lost all her rights because of the law of coverture. As the lawyer William Blackstone wrote in 1765: 'A husband and wife are one person under the law, and the husband is that person.'

> Why is it that the division of property remains one of the biggest battlegrounds when couples separate or divorce?

A married woman could not make a will, control wages, buy or sell property or make contracts. Although there was a variation in personal behaviour within individual marriages, under the law any belongings or money a wife brought into the marriage automatically became her husband's; he controlled her property, earnings and their children. The famous Victorian novelist Mrs Gaskell, whose books sold in their thousands, received no income from her writing and relied on her husband giving her a small allowance. In the USA, some states had already begun to allow women to have some legal status; Connecticut, for example, allowed women to write wills from 1809, while a series of laws passed between 1859 and 1884 gave married women in Canada some control over their property.

Before 1882 English law saw a husband and wife as one person, and that person was the husband.

In Britain, Barbara Leigh Smith, later Bodichon, although almost forgotten today, was another leading figure in the movement calling for married women to have legal rights. She was a driving force for change, forming a nationwide campaign group. Bodichon drew upon cases the group compiled of individual women's suffering when she wrote a pamphlet entitled *A Brief Summary, in Plain Language, of the Most Important Laws Concerning Wives Together with a Few Observations* in 1854. It cited hundreds of instances of women losing everything upon marrying a man who subsequently absconded and left them destitute. If such a woman was subsequently to earn or inherit any money, the errant husband could return, seize all she had and leave once more. It was widely read and influential; two years later she gave evidence to a House of Commons committee looking into the legal status of married women. The first step in giving married women more legal powers came when the Infant Custody Act was passed in 1839. This allowed mothers some rights over their children up to the age of 7 years, although only if the woman was seen as having an 'unblemished character', and many problems remained.

In March 1856, Bodichon drafted a petition presented to the House of Lords with 26,000 signatures, including those of the poet Elizabeth Barrett Browning and Mrs Gaskell, demanding that married women be given the same rights over property that men and single women enjoyed. Although the petition was rejected, just a year later in 1857 the Matrimonial Causes Act, commonly known as the Divorce Bill, was finally passed into law. Throughout the 1860s progress was slow but in 1870 the first Married Women's Property Act was passed. Parliament heard stories of heiresses whose husbands had spent all their money and absconded to America, leaving the woman to die in a workhouse, and men who had pawned the children's clothes to buy alcohol. The act, however, at last allowed women to keep any money that they earned and to inherit property. However, anomalies still remained and it took a further twelve years of campaigning before a more extensive Married Women's Property Act was finally passed in 1882, the culmination of many years of agitation by a number of resolute reformers. It gave married women rights that they had never had before, the right to their earnings, to own property, to make a will and enter into contracts. By 2014, 142 countries worldwide had legislation to protect women's property rights, but the operation of these acts suggests a complex story; women do not necessarily experience the control over their property within or at the end of a marriage they might wish to have. Nevertheless, for campaigning women, such as Millicent Fawcett and Barbara Bodichon, married women's property rights were a stepping stone towards women gaining full equality under the law and strengthened the case for women to be allowed the right to vote.

20 | *Mrs Beeton's Book of Household Management*

Cookery Books and Domestic Gurus

JANIS LOMAS

Beeton's Book of Household Management was first published in Great Britain in 1861; 2 million copies had been sold by 1868. It was more than a cookery book, transforming ideas about domestic life in a way few books have before or since, by laying down rules for the way things should be done in polite society. The book turned formal dining into a competitive pursuit, with etiquette and spectacle being as important as the food itself.

In later editions the tome became known as *Mrs Beeton's Book of Household Management*, suggesting the author was an experienced cook, the fount of all culinary knowledge. Yet Isabella Beeton was only 21 when she began compiling her volume on domesticity, shamelessly borrowing from other books, most notably those of Eliza Acton. After Isabella Beeton died at the age of 28 her kitchen bible was changed, expanded and continually re-published. It contained little of the original text yet she attained celebrity status. Some of her recipes, for example those for oyster soup, iced currants or parsnips boiled for one and a half hours, now seem dated, but the Beeton name remains a marketable brand; in 1995 Ginsters of Cornwall paid £1 million to use the Beeton name on their pasties and pies.

In the twentieth century the mediums of radio and television enabled a new wave of 'domestic goddesses' to gain celebrity status. As Britain threw off rationing and entered the consumer boom in the 1950s, Fanny Cradock's television appearances boosted sales of the more than 100 cookery books she wrote, which included guidance on how to add cream and green food colouring to gruyere cheese or to create a multi-coloured and layered jelly à la *zizi*. Fanny Craddock's image was the antithesis of Mrs Beeton; she appeared on the screen with her ex-army major 'husband' Johnnie in attendance to hand her utensils or remove food from the oven under her orders. The queen of the kitchen, she cooked in designer evening dresses, heavily made-up and decked out with sparkling jewellery, sometimes even a tiara. The apparently upper-middle-class perfect hostess, versed in French cooking, was portrayed as the lynchpin of a close and loving family life. The reality was very different from the image; she committed bigamy twice, abandoned both her children and was not actually married to Johnnie until the 1970s. Nevertheless, celebrity appearances in TV commercials sold soap, washing-up liquid and frozen foods.

> Do cookery books, rather than offering helpful advice, merely offer unattainable ideals that make women feel a failure?

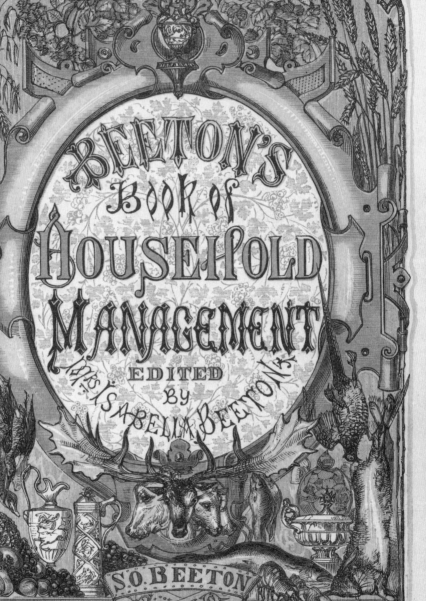

BEETON'S
BOOK OF
HOUSEHOLD
MANAGEMENT
EDITED BY
MRS ISABELLA BEETON

S. O. BEETON

248 STRAND   LONDON. W.C.

In 1995 Ginsters of Cornwall paid £1 million to use the
Beeton name on their pasties and pies.

In the USA, Julia Child is credited with introducing French cuisine to the American
public in a mammoth 700-page book *Mastering the Art of French Cooking*, published
in 1961. Two years later she successfully began demonstrating her recipes on
American TV and continued to broadcast until the 1990s. Her somewhat eccentric
presenting voice was underpinned by a thorough knowledge of French cooking and,
like Fanny Cradock, her various television series were accompanied by publications.
Julia Child remains a TV legend and her kitchen has been preserved so that it can be
visited at the Smithsonian Museum of American History in Washington DC.

The down-to-earth celebrity cook Delia Smith invited the TV cameras into her
home in the 1970s but it was Nigella Lawson, billed as the 'Domestic Goddess' in the
late 1990s, who combined idealised domesticity with sex appeal. She often appeared
in a red silk dressing gown, or was shown entertaining her friends and children with
the food she had cooked, then supposedly raiding her kitchen late at night, eating
leftover trifle from the fridge with her fingers. It emerged later that what appeared
to be her own kitchen was in fact a London warehouse designed to replicate her
home kitchen. Despite censorious coverage of her second marriage, which ended in
divorce, her books and merchandise continue to sell.

In the USA in the 1990s Martha Stewart also extended the idea of television cook
to lifestyle guru. Her cultivated image was as a beautiful country-house hostess
living an ideal domestic life with a close-knit family. Not only did she show how
to cook a perfect meal, she gave advice on every aspect of entertaining, crafting,
gardening, flower arranging and decorating, projecting a wholesome lifestyle
in which homemade was the key. She successfully launched magazines and an
extensive range of cookery and homeware goods on the strength of her name. When
in 2004 she went to prison for five months following an investigation over insider
trading, there were predictions that her brand image would be tarnished, but the
Martha Stewart range of products continues to expand.

Celebrity cooks from Mrs Beeton onwards have promoted idealised images of
domesticity, unattainable versions of women as perfect homemakers. Despite
evidence sometimes emerging that their own lives are less than ideal, their brands
of domesticity continue to sell merchandise, demonstrating the strength of the
domestic ideal which many women aspire to emulate. These women cooks have
been accused of promoting impossible standards and making working women feel
inadequate if they are not cooking in an immaculate kitchen or hosting a dinner
party after work. However, their books and television programmes remain a popular
fantasy, perhaps an escape from the harsh realities of everyday domestic life.

21 | The War Widows' Pension Form

When the Government Cares for Dependent Women

JANIS LOMAS

In Great Britain in the latter stages of the First World War, this record card confirmed a serviceman's widow's right to receive a regular pension from the state. If a war widow saw this document, it would have conjured up a variety of emotions. As the official stamp near the top right baldly stated, it confirmed that her husband had died, but the grief and worry of being left, as Clara Buckley was, with five children to bring up alone was probably also mixed with a feeling of relief. Finally, it proved she had not been left bereft of any means of support.

George Buckley served in the East Yorkshire Regiment and was killed in action on 17 July 1917. Clara was 32 when he died and they lived in Houghton-Le-Spring near Durham with their five children – four girls and a boy. When their father was killed, Florence, the eldest, was 13; Constance was 12, George was 10, Winifred 7 and Clara just 3 years old. On 21 August 1917 Clara received a £5 death grant for herself and an additional £1 for each child; she would then continue to receive separation allowance as if her husband were still alive for six months, until her claim for the war widows' pension was processed.

This system, introduced by the newly formed Ministry of Pensions in 1917, ended the delays and destitution of war widows which had marked the first years of the war, when widows had to rely on charity until their pension was sorted. It is therefore easy to see why this form was so vital: it meant a measure of security. Even though it was less than separation allowance, it confirmed that the government had accepted that the country owed her family a debt, that George had carried out his duty diligently and that she was therefore deserving of help. If George had been shell-shocked and had failed in his duty by desertion or committed another serious offence, as over 3,000 soldiers did during the First World War, his wife and children would not have received any financial assistance or a war pension. One of these cases was that of Gertrude Farr, whose husband Harry was one of the 306 British soldiers shot for desertion after a court martial lasting just twenty minutes, despite him clearly suffering from shell shock.

Thankfully, this was not the case for Clara Buckley; from 21 January 1918, Clara received 31s 3d a week. This amount would be reduced on 10 October 1919 by 5s as Florence would then be 16 years old; the pension would gradually lessen until the youngest child reached 16, at which time Clara would receive £1 a week for the rest of her life as long as she did not remarry or behave in any way that was considered inappropriate. As the Ministry of Pensions stated: 'Pensions to widows, children and dependants ... shall not be claimed as a right, but shall be given as a reward of service, and no pension shall be granted or continued to a widow who is unworthy.'

A war widow had to behave responsibly and be respectable; if not, her pension could be removed, and if she was not looking after her children properly they too could be removed from her care. Some war widows found themselves envied by others in their neighbourhood as they had a secure, if tiny, income. This envy could leave them open to any malicious charge from a jealous or malign informant. If they were seen out in the company of a man, or they went to the public house, a letter could be sent to the local War Pension Committee who would investigate any complaint against a war widow even if it was sent anonymously. In just seven months up to March 1918, the year that Clara received her pension, investigations against war widows numbered 805, and 177 war widows lost their pensions for unworthiness; the following year a further 939 were forfeited. While widows were under investigation, police reports and surveillance were used to decide on worthiness; in a close-knit community this could mean a widow's reputation was irretrievably lost even if no wrongdoing was ever proved. This form of 'policing' of war widows was to continue throughout the Second World War and for decades afterwards.

Disabled male war pensioners had none of the limitations applied to women and received their pensions free of income tax, unlike war widows. Despite these disadvantages, however, the war widows' pension represented the first gendered welfare provision in favour of women and was an initiative that almost certainly paved the way for the introduction of the widows' pension in 1925. This was because by that time government was beginning to see women who had married disabled ex-servicemen, who had since died as a result of their injuries, left destitute. If a husband lived seven years or more after the date of his injury wives could not claim the war widows' pension. This opened up the possibility of criticism of the government for its treatment of the families of dead heroes. James Hogge MP, speaking in the House of Commons in February 1919, quoted this letter written by a severely ill ex-soldier in 1919 to demonstrate how heartless this rule could be:

I am in a dilemma. It is now three years since I contracted this disease, and unless I die within four years my wife and children will be deprived of their pension. I know that by taking the greatest care of my life I might live a few years longer, but what a horrible feeling it is to me to think that by prolonging my life by care beyond that time limit by doing so I leave my wife and children destitute.

Should widows keep their pension if they remarry?

Although far from generous and hedged around by these and other restrictions, the war widows' pension and later the widows' pension did provide a safety net for women and set a precedent in enabling them to receive a benefit as a right. First World War widows also lost their pension if they remarried, a situation that was only changed in 2014, 100 years after the outbreak of the First World War, at a time when there was no longer an expectation that men would be breadwinners and wives financial dependants. The spouses of those in the armed forces, in the police or who are teachers all now receive an adult dependant's pension for life, whether they choose to remarry or not, and their personal life and 'respectability' are no longer a focus of public scrutiny.

22 | First World War Canadian Canning Machine

War, Food Shortages and Women's Institutes

MAGGIE ANDREWS

When on 4 August 1914 Britain declared war on Germany, Canada and the rest of the British Empire also became automatically involved in a world war. Some 619,000 Canadian troops took part in the conflict but twentieth-century warfare was not just fought on the battlefields but on the home front, in the factories and on the farms and in homes by housewives.

To countries in the grip of large-scale mechanised twentieth- and twenty-first-century conflicts, food became a weapon of war and it was housewives' role to source, conserve, preserve and use food wisely. Thus First World War British propaganda posters explained the 'Key to Victory' was in the kitchen, and Canadian home canning machines were sent to Britain to ensure that British housewives did not waste any of the precious fruit and vegetable crops.

During the First World War naval warfare made exporting and importing food treacherous. In April 1917 alone, 869,000 tons of Allied shipping was sunk. As the conflict destroyed and disrupted agriculture and displaced thousands of people, a food crisis developed. Prices increased, and shortages meant that housewives sometimes queued for hours for basic foodstuffs as European countries struggled to feed both their populations and their armies. Yet, for many, food was a symbol of home and of hope for the future. Women sent cakes and Christmas puddings to men in the forces, to remind them of home. Canada toiled not only to feed its own population but also to send supplies to Britain, which had greeted the outbreak of war with panic buying, price rises and anxiety over food supplies. Problems with the potato crop in 1916 meant that the city of Worcester was delighted to receive 800 sacks of potatoes, part of a gift from Canadians to Britain. According to the local newspaper:

> Each of the sacks contained 80 or 90lb of potatoes and these were distributed in the City Police Yard this afternoon to a large number of poor people. … There was a continuous procession of women, armed with bags and baskets and tickets which entitled them to have these filled. Each one received 15lbs of potatoes and went away with a radiant face and a well-filled basket.

These Canadian potatoes helped 200 housewives with the daily struggle to feed their families. By 1917 naval blockades exacerbated the food shortages and in Worcester 500 people waited six hours for margarine; some housewives kept their children off school to undertake the food queuing for them.

Despite the efforts of many housewives, 20 million people died of starvation in the Second World War.

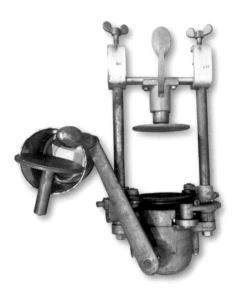

By this time rural housewives in Britain were already benefitting from another export from Canada – the Women's Institute (WI) Movement. This organisation had been founded in Stoney Creek, Ontario, as a branch of the Farmer's Institute, inspired by a talk from Adelaide Hoodless and supported by the Ontario government. The British Board of Agriculture employed a Canadian, Mrs Watt, to set up WIs in Britain to increase interest among village women in food production and food economy, and to improve the conditions of village life. Prior to the outbreak of the First World War Britain imported, from the USA, over two-thirds of the grain needed to make bread, the staple food of the working classes. As submarine warfare made this increasingly difficult, farmers were encouraged to produce wheat rather than meat and housewives urged to grow food in their gardens or allotments and adapt their diets to include more vegetables. The canning machines imported from Canada were often set up in village halls and the guidance of the WI enabled housewives to preserve the precious food they harvested in the summer. Women were bombarded with advice about food preparation and preservation as waste became abhorrent and in 1917 illegal. That year, as Sir Arthur Yapp pointed out, 'there was a world shortage of food … there was the most urgent need for economy in all foods'.

The Russian Revolution in 1917 was sparked by food riots, and both Austria and Germany also saw housewives rioting in response to the food crisis. The British government increasingly took over control of food supplies and distribution. National Kitchens offered simple, cheap communal meals and rationing was introduced in

WASTE NOT—WANT NOT

PREPARE FOR WINTER

Save
Perishable Foods
by
Preserving Now

January 1918. By this time, in Canada, drought, poor harvests and the long-term effects of the loss of skilled agricultural workers into the armed forces had taken their toll on food production. The government responded to the food crisis by setting up the Canadian Food Board, intended to persuade the population there to produce, preserve and prepare food more carefully. Canadian housewives were provided with a range of advice, disseminated via recipe booklets and posters like this one. During the conflict, Britain used its naval supremacy to subject Germany and its allies to a trade blockade; hunger became a weapon used against women and children. This blockade continued after the armistice in November 1918, until the signing of the Treaty of Versailles finally ended the war the following year. The British government's reticence in responding to protests demanding they 'Lift the Blockade' led to deprivation and malnutrition among German children. Two sisters, Dorothy Buxton and Eglantyne Jebb, set up the Save the Children Fund to ensure that this suffering should never be repeated. The organisation's aim was to 'attack the vast mass of child suffering which exists in the world today as a result of war and economic distress'.

> In modern warfare, when food is used as a weapon of war, women and children are arguably increasingly the innocent victims.

Within twenty years the onset of the Second World War created another food crisis and the WI set up canning centres in villages across Britain, using canning machines sometimes sent from Canada. One mother of five in West Sussex recalled how, after taking her eldest four children to school, she put her youngest in the pushchair and loaded on to it a packed lunch, colanders, wooden spoons and pans, and walked over 2 miles, twice a week, to help at a canning centre. There were several processes involved in canning: sterilisation, grading, packing, making syrup, sealing cans, labelling, and picking over. The group had to attend a course and pass, with a certificate being awarded to indicate that they had reached an adequate level of competence. The canning machine required a high level of skill and precision. She recalled:

You had to turn the handle and it had to be in neutral to start with and this is what caused so many problems. It had to be absolutely neutral to start with and it had to be turned exactly twenty times … I fell into it quite easily [but] the other four kept on having trouble with it.

The precision was important because faulty cans could explode rather dramatically. Despite housewives' efforts, starvation was the deadliest weapon of the Second World War, causing at least 20 million deaths, more than the 19.5 million military deaths. Using the starvation of civilians as a method of warfare is now a recognised war crime, but it still occurs. Some 2 million civilians died from starvation during the Biafra War, which took place between 1976 and 1980. In 1984 the Ethiopian famine was exacerbated by the ongoing civil war, killing nearly a million people. More recently the Syrian conflict has resulted in hundreds of thousands of women struggling to feed their families.

23 | Women's Aid Slogan
Domestic Violence

DICKIE JAMES

The slogan 'You Can't Beat a Woman' was created in 1976 by Women's Aid and used on T-shirts, mugs, leaflets, and in local and national campaigning posters for many years.

The image and slogan work together to portray a movement based on female solidarity in refuges for victims of domestic violence, which were often overcrowded and chaotic for the women and children who already lived in fear and had lost their homes. Yet the women who set up the refuges believed in the power of women-only spaces, and of women supporting women. They worked as collectives, with no management structure, against the injustice of women suffering violence in their homes, drawing inspiration from the idea that women pulling together, supporting one another, would not be beaten; hence 'You Can't Beat a Woman'.

Women's Aid came into being on the back of the Women's Liberation Movement, which had emerged as a force for change in the late 1960s and early 1970s. Uniting under the slogan 'The Personal is Political', a key focus of women's lib was combating women's oppression within the home and family. Women living with violence from their husbands and partners were often powerless, had nowhere to turn and were frequently blamed for their situations. The first 'women's shelter' had opened in Canada in 1965 and by the 1970s the idea spread to the USA; there are shelters and refuges now in forty-five countries in the world. Erin Pizzey opened the first refuge in Britain in Chiswick, London in 1972 and the refuge movement grew remarkably quickly; by 1974, nearly forty refuges had been set up across Britain.

The National Women's Aid Federation was established to bring members together as a campaigning voice, and to provide a network of support for women and children needing refuge across the UK; it still exists today. The early refuges were largely the result of local grassroots women's groups tenaciously lobbying their local authorities for houses to use as refuges, or squatting in empty properties. They had little in the way of funding and faced considerable hostility because they were challenging one of the most deeply rooted institutions of Western society – the family. The movement was founded on the belief that women and children had a right to the provision of safe accommodation if they needed to flee their homes because of domestic violence. Sandra, who escaped to a refuge in the Midlands in 1978, recalls how she and her two children shared a small bedroom with another woman and two children for months: 'It was really tough, but it was so much better than living in fear. You knew you were safe at last. Going into refuge changed my life forever.' Like many other women survivors

Living in Refuges

who became part of the movement, Sandra went on to become a volunteer and worked in a refuge for over twenty-five years.

The echo of 'You Can't Beat a Woman' has continued to sound through the history of the refuge movement in the UK. Women's Aid and its membership has relentlessly lobbied and campaigned for nearly five decades to achieve cultural and legislative change. In 1976 the first Domestic Violence Bill (the Domestic Violence and Matrimonial Proceedings Act) gave new rights through civil protection orders for those at risk of domestic violence; and in 1977 The Housing Act (Homeless Persons) acknowledged women and children fleeing domestic violence as homeless, gaining them the right to support from local authorities with temporary accommodation. More recently, the organisation has succeeded in demonstrating that domestic violence is a pattern of power and control rather than a series of isolated incidents, leading to the new criminal offence of Coercive Control in 2015. 'We wanted to change the world, to make it safer for women and children,' recalls Anna, who was a founder member of one of the early refuges in Staffordshire. 'We were a sisterhood. We wouldn't be silenced and we wouldn't be beaten.'

To a degree, this vision of a safer world for women and children has been achieved. Domestic violence is no longer invisible and has featured in soap operas, stimulating public debate. For example, in 1995, Channel 4's *Brookside* featured a storyline about Mandy Jordache, a woman who killed her abusive husband. The Women's Aid Federation today has a membership of around 500 domestic violence projects in England alone, and an expert knowledge base providing community outreach services as well as refuge. These specialist services argue for the continuation of women-only spaces and a therapeutic model that draws directly from a view of domestic violence as a gendered phenomenon. While it is acknowledged that there are male victims of domestic violence, the movement argues that female victims are at most risk, and that domestic violence is both the cause and consequence of gender inequality. The sector has largely fought to remain independent of statutory services, often having to balance its feminist political roots against the need for funding from institutions with a less gendered approach to domestic violence and its causes.

> In Britain, why is there an increasing emphasis on male victims of domestic violence when 81 per cent of victims are women and almost all of the most violent assaults are on women perpetrated by men?

Domestic violence continues to blight the lives of women and children in all societies across the world today. According to the United Nations, 35 per cent of women across the world have experienced either physical and/or sexual intimate partner violence or non-partner sexual violence. The British Crime Survey reports that on average two women are killed each week in England and Wales, and almost half of all women murdered are killed by a partner or former partner. The movement still struggles to change centuries of ingrained attitudes. Yet it remains a force for change, retaining the spirit of 'You Can't Beat a Woman' – a vision of women supporting women to become the agents of their own lives and futures, where women and children are safe in their homes, and a world where domestic violence is no longer tolerated.

24 | Porthleven Website Advert for a Food Bank

Food Poverty and Support for Women Struggling to Feed Their Families

JANIS LOMAS

The picturesque fishing village of Porthleven lies on the Cornish coastline; with a population of a little over 3,000, the village has large areas of social housing and its village website includes an advert for the local food bank with the strapline 'What's for tea, mum?'

Across the world women are more likely to be living in poverty than men; for hundreds of years many women have faced a daily struggle to feed their families and have had to turn to charities and governments for financial assistance, which has all too often been accompanied by disapproval and harsh judgements. In contemporary Britain the Trussell Trust runs a network of over 400 food banks, including the one in Helston, which the described poster encourages women to use. In 2016 the Trust gave 1,182,954 three-day emergency food supplies to people to whom the Citizens Advice Bureau, doctors, health visitors, the clergy, schools and social workers had given a food-bank voucher. In a determinedly non-judgemental way, food banks seek to support those who are in food crisis, despite living in one of the wealthiest countries in the world.

Providing for the poor of the community has always proved a challenge for governments. There has been a dichotomy between providing sustenance for those in genuine need and ensuring that the 'undeserving' did not benefit. From the seventeenth century onwards various schemes were tried in Britain. The poor have been divided into the deserving and the undeserving. The undeserving poor were those who could work but would not. The Poor Law decreed that these 'were to be whipped through the streets publicly, until they learnt the error of their ways'. The deserving poor were those who would work if they could but were unable; into this category came women without a husband but with young children, those with seasonal jobs who needed financial help to tide them over and those who were unable to work because of illness or mental or physical incapacity. In order to help the 'deserving poor' a poor relief rate was levied on property owners in every parish; overseers were appointed to collect this levy and oversee the schemes which were set up to give the poor work. Those too young, too old or not fit for work would be housed in almshouses or hospitals. Anyone who had moved away from their home parish to find work or to marry had to return to the parish of their birth to get assistance.

In 1834 the government introduced the Poor Law Amendment Act to reduce the cost of the Poor Law. This measure was designed to discipline an 'irresponsible'

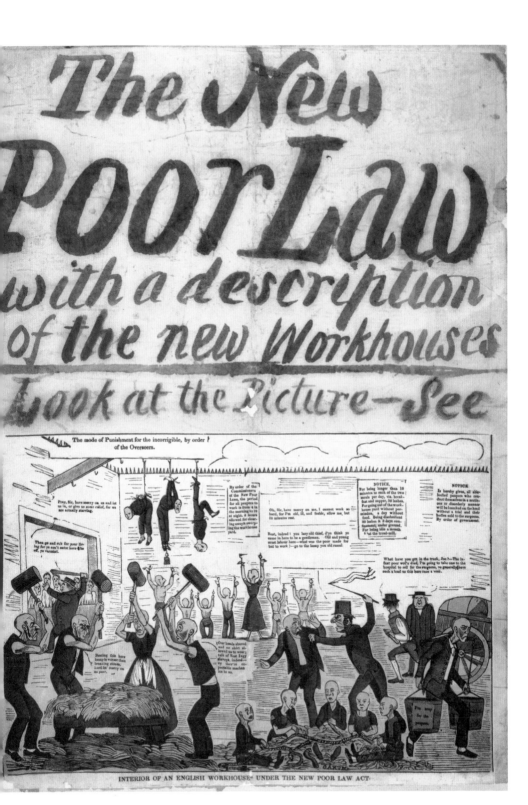

The New POOR LAW with a description of the new Workhouses Look at the the Picture—See

INTERIOR OF AN ENGLISH WORKHOUSE UNDER THE NEW POOR LAW ACT

Oxfam stated in 2016 that one in five people in Britain struggled to put food on the table and more than half a million relied on food banks.

growing population by severely restricting access to outdoor relief. Help was to be given largely through entry into a workhouse where conditions were to be 'less eligible' – that is, worse than outside the workhouse. Edwin Chadwick, the principal architect of the act, wrote that workhouses were to be 'uninviting places of wholesome restraint'. Under the workhouse system families were separated to prevent them having more children, and they were places which filled the poor with dread. The sentimental music-hall song 'My Old Dutch' was often sung against the painted backdrop of a workhouse entrance, to an audience who knew that elderly couples forced by poverty into the workhouse would be separated. The heart-rending chorus made their plight more poignant with the words:

> We've been together now for forty years,
> An' it don't seem a day too much,
> There ain't a lady livin' in the land
> As I'd swop for my dear old Dutch.

The early settlers to the United States largely followed the British system of help for the poor, with a mixture of outdoor relief and poor houses providing a patchy safety net for those deserving of support. The Great Depression created conditions that showed the failings of the system on both sides of the Atlantic, but particularly in America, which suffered the most. The Depression followed the stock market collapse on Wall Street in 1929, which led to an economic crisis in the United States. By 1933, when Franklin Roosevelt became President, 13 million Americans had lost their jobs. Roosevelt established programmes for economic recovery, providing work for the unemployed through public spending and federal aid for the most needy. The Food Stamps programme began in the USA in 1939 as part of his 'New Deal' and was designed to channel agricultural food surpluses to those in need. The programme operated by permitting people on relief to buy orange stamps equal to their normal food expenditure; for every $1-worth of orange stamps purchased, 50c-worth of blue stamps were received. Orange stamps could be used to buy any food; blue stamps could be used only to buy food determined by the Department of Agriculture to be surplus. The scheme ran for almost four years until 1943 when American involvement in the Second World War meant that unmarketable foodstuffs and widespread unemployment were no longer a problem.

Why, in some of the wealthiest countries in the world, are thousands of people struggling in a food crisis?

In 1961, John F. Kennedy made announcing a food stamp pilot scheme his first executive order, and President Lyndon Johnson made the scheme permanent in 1964. In the following decades the scheme has either expanded or been cut back, depending on various administrations. Eligibility rules have also been changed frequently to try to eliminate fraud and cut the costs of the programme. In 2008, the Food Stamps Program was renamed the Supplemental Nutrition Assistance Program (SNAP) and references to food stamps or coupons replaced by a debit card system known as Electronic Benefits Transfer (EBT). SNAP benefits increased temporarily in 2009 as a result of the recession but this ended in 2013. In 2016, 45.4 million Americans were receiving SNAP, of whom almost half were children. The majority of adult Americans claiming SNAP are women in single-parent families who face an uncertain future; President Trump has expressed his determination to reduce the scheme massively.

In many developing countries the only help for the poor comes from charities and religious organisations. Women and their children continue to be the most vulnerable members of society; across the world, food poverty remains the lived experience of millions of women, made more extreme as the gap between rich and poor widens. John Hendra of the United Nations, speaking in 2014, noted that:

Women are the face of poverty, in particular rural poverty, due to their lower access to productive resources and assets, capabilities and decent paid employment. What's more, persistent, multiple economic and social inequalities have exacerbated the feminisation of poverty in rural areas.

Dear BARCLAYCARD Centre,

I'm told that if I had a BARCLAYCARD I'd be able to sign the bill in thousands of shops all over the country—and pay you at the end of the month. What's more, they say the service wouldn't cost me anything, and I don't even have to bank with Barclays or the British Linen Bank. I find this hard to believe.

Please convince me.

Name

Address

C1/P

Post to: BARCLAYCARD, **OR** BARCLAYCARD,
20 Moorgate, 38 St. Andrew Sq.,
London, EC2 Edinburgh, 2

25 | The Barclaycard
The Importance of Credit for Women

MAGGIE ANDREWS

Barclays, a British high street bank, launched the Barclaycard on 29 June 1966. It sent out over a million of this new type of credit card, intended to be used by ordinary people. Much of the advertising and the card itself was often targeted towards women shoppers.

The young carefree woman was addressed in one advert, where she was portrayed tucking her Barclaycard into her swimming costume with the strapline 'Travelling Light'. The housewife was not forgotten; another advert explained that 'a wife needs to be able to buy things when they're wanted; clothes, items for the family and home, and gifts'. Barclaycard, it suggested, provided a new tool to help with one of women's perennial tasks – managing the household budget.

Women had, however, been involved as creditors and debtors in many countries prior to this, for example in nineteenth-century Peru and seventeenth-century Scotland. In industrial societies, domestic life has for many years relied upon women's ability to manage the family budget by whatever means they have at their disposal, including, crucially, access to credit. Yet women's spending and potential overspending has been a cause of anxiety for many years. Fears women will run up debts purchasing clothes or household items to obtain the home of their dreams accompanied the emergence of department stores in the nineteenth century and caused consternation in some quarters. In Britain, women's legal status as subordinate to their husbands meant that if a housewife bought items of credit, her husband was legally responsible for her debts. Women's shopping began to be seen as a risky business for their husbands, and also for some shopkeepers who found men resisted honouring debts their wives had incurred purchasing extravagances. Many shops found it easiest to insist that women purchased items with cash only.

Working-class housewives often relied on credit to prevent their families from going hungry or becoming homeless. Buying food on 'tick', to be paid at the end of the week when wages were paid, hiding from the rent collector and using a pawnbroker were part of many housewives' survival strategies in the inter-war years of the depression. George Peck remembered that Monday was pawnshop day:

Lots of people were in bad circumstances, five, six, eight or ten kids, you see … They used to go on Mondays, take a clean sheet off the bed and fill it full of stuff. Shoes and things like that would be put into the sheet and taken to the pawnshop, in a big bundle on their shoulder. They would pawn their husband's best suit, shoes or shirt, which was only used on Sundays.

In the 1970s single women often had to bring their father to sign to obtain credit or a mortgage.

When wages came in at the end of the week, housewives redeemed their goods. The interest they paid was one of the costs of living. In the inter-war years the pawnbroker had a central place in urban communities, often open six days a week, until 11 p.m. on a Saturday. Many pawnbrokers closed down when incomes improved in the post-war period but reappeared alongside poverty at the end of the twentieth century.

The introduction of credit cards in Britain was critiqued as an American influence, yet Barclaycard's innovation was in offering extended credit at an interest rate of 1.5 per cent a month to enable cardholders to budget the cost of expensive purchases over a number of monthly payments. In doing so they mimicked the credit that catalogues like Kays had been offering for many years. Catalogues enabled housewives to buy everything from children's school shoes to a new kitchen with regular weekly or monthly payments. Both catalogues and hire purchase providers coaxed housewives into the pleasures of shopping, reassuring them that by using credit they were able to buy better-quality, longer-lasting items which would banish their 'money worries'. Another way of managing large purchases was through saving clubs, when women put in a regular amount of money each week or month, and redeemed their savings with tokens to be spent at local stores or by purchasing items chosen from a Christmas catalogue. The Provident Saving Club had 1 million members by 1937.

How responsible is the gender pay gap for the phenomenon of women getting into debt?

In both the USA and the UK the ability to obtain credit, a mortgage, a credit card or an overdraft was an important feminist issue in the 1970s. Women seeking credit encountered an onslaught of detailed questions about their personal life, their marital status and their children. Many banks and building societies required single women to be accompanied by a man, often their father, when they applied for a credit card or mortgages. In 1974 the USA Senate passed the Equal Credit Opportunity Act making it illegal to discriminate on the basis of gender, race, religion or national origin in granting credit to people. The following year Judy H. Mello opened First Women's Bank which was 'the first bank in the United States to be operated by women and for women'.

For many women, credit cards are a symbol of freedom, power and independence. Little wonder, then, that in the twenty-first century many a postcard and poster carries the quote: 'A man asked a fairy to make him irresistible to all women. She turned him into a credit card.'

26 | Suffragette Teacups and Saucers

The Pleasures of Tea Drinking

JADE GILKS

Sharing a cup of tea has become very much a women's experience; in the 1930s US First Lady Eleanor Roosevelt likened women to tea, saying: 'A woman is like a tea bag; you never know how strong it is until it's in hot water.'

Evidence of tea as a communal activity among women can be seen in the writings of Jane Austen, at suffragette meetings, and is a prominent theme in the film *Tea with Mussolini* (1999). The commissioning of tea sets to aid the suffragettes' propaganda on both sides of the Atlantic can be seen as an acknowledgement of the significance of tea meetings and tea drinking to women. Tea drinking occurs around the world and has become integral to British identity; the term 'English breakfast tea' seems to have emerged in the USA to describe the consumption of this popular morning drink by the British in their colonies in the eighteenth century. However, a cup of tea has not always been a staple part of everyday life in Britain. Legend has it that Chinese emperor Shen Nung created the first ever cup of tea. Tea leaves are grown in countries such as China, Sri Lanka, Kenya and India where people were experiencing the refreshment of tea centuries before the Portuguese princess Catherine of Braganza married Charles II and brought tea drinking into the British royal family in the seventeenth century. Tea ceremonies, which continue to be part of Chinese and Japanese culture, originated in China; Zen monk Dai-o (1236–1308) brought the knowledge of the tea ceremony to Japan after he saw it practised in Chinese monasteries. Tea ceremonies continue to have a place at Chinese weddings where brides serve tea to their parents and prospective in-laws on the morning of their wedding, symbolising their gratitude for the love and support they provide.

Although now commonplace, enjoying the pleasure of a cup of tea was originally the preserve of those with the funds to buy tea or take tea in one of the London coffeehouses. Tea was so pricey that the wealthy purchased it and kept it locked away from their servants. Novelist Jane Austen, a passionate drinker of tea, kept the key to the tea cupboard in the house she shared with her mother and sisters in Chawton, Hampshire, and mentions it in many of her novels and even in letters to her sister, noting: 'We began our China Tea three days ago, & I find it very good – my companions know nothing of the matter.'

As tea was so expensive it was not shared freely and after it was used, servants had the task of drying out the tea so that it could be sold on and used by others. In the early nineteenth century tea was beginning to be consumed by the wider

population, to the dismay of some. William Cobbett, who did not share Jane Austen's enthusiasm for tea, complained:

> It is notorious that tea has no useful strength in it; that it contains nothing nutritious; that it, besides being good for nothing, has badness in it, because it is well known to produce want of sleep in many cases, and in all cases, to shake and weaken the nerves.

Notwithstanding Cobbett's criticisms, by the twentieth century tea had become embedded in ideas of Englishness and seen as a source of comfort and normality in times of crisis. As George Orwell noted of the British during the Second World War: 'All the culture that is mostly truly native centres around things which even if they are not communal are not official – the pub, the football match, the back garden, the fireside and "the nice cup of tea".'

Tea drinking as a communal activity was of particular importance during the Second World War; although tea was rationed in July 1940, women on the home front continued to enjoy the pleasure of a 'nice cup of tea'. The Women's Voluntary Service (WVS) handed out tea from mobile canteens on a regular basis to people working, at railway stations and to civilians bombed out during the Blitz. Patience 'Boo' Brand and Rachel Bingham recalled serving tea to people in shelters and to the Air Raid Precaution (ARP) wardens; all refreshments were sold at cost price, the WVS doing their job to help boost the morale of the country.

The tea bag was not introduced in Britain until the 1950s, when tea was finally freed from rationing; by 2007 tea bags made up 96 per cent of the British market, saving women a lot of time washing up and ending what had once been a popular women's pastime, foretelling the future by reading tea leaves. Tea has changed women's lives in other ways, with women now playing a vital role in tea production, supported by campaigns for fair trade and fair pay in the developing world. The tea industry provides security for women and empowerment for the high number of female smallholding farmers who grow tea, providing them with a route out of poverty. Tealeaf worker Rozina explains:

> Is the appeal of a cup of tea for women that, like chocolate and biscuits, they are a treat for oneself as opposed to caring for others?

> Today I'm now one of the elected members of our small tea growers' association. Now people look at me with respect. I want everyone in my village to be able to grow tea – so no one goes to sleep with an empty stomach like I used to.

Tea drinking has offered snatched moments of comforting pleasure in many women's working or everyday lives across the world. In recent years upmarket Georgian-style tea rooms, hotels and restaurants create spaces for women to indulge themselves a little by enjoying a luxurious afternoon tea. Since the introduction of tea there has been no looking back; the average tea drinker in Britain now enjoys at least four cups a day, indicating people remain as passionate about tea as Queen Catherine of Braganza was in the seventeenth century.

Part III
Science, Technology and Medicine

For thousands of years, science, technology and medicine have produced objects with a tremendous capacity to change women's everyday lives and reduce the domestic labour for which women are often responsible. A quick perusal of many homes will reveal an array of domestic technology which our great-grandmothers could not even have dreamed of: the electric kettle used to boil water is now commonplace and saves housewives from spending time heating water over a fire or indeed making that fire. Much modern technology has its origins in small technological developments many hundreds of years old – the washing dolly, for example, was a important stepping stone towards the washing machine which itself relies on the provision of electricity and water supplies.

It is hard to overestimate the huge amount of physical and often unpleasant work that women are saved from undertaking when their houses contain hot and cold water taps and flushing toilets – although versions of all of these can be found in ancient Roman cities such as Pompeii. The cleanliness of the public latrines in Roman cities may not have met modern standards but they saved women the laborious task of looking after the midden – a dump for domestic waste and human excrement that many properties in Britain had well into the twentieth century, which housewives were responsible for tending. An awareness of the Roman taps and sewage raises one of the most important questions in relation to women and technology – when, where and by whom are the priorities about spending on technology decided. For example at the beginning of the 1950s, Britain was spending money building atomic bombs yet half the rural homes in Britain had no inside water tap.

Finally, it is important to acknowledge the significant role women have taken in the production of scientific, technological and medical advancement, roles that have often been played down or gone unrecognised. Marie Curie was a rarity in that, even in her lifetime, her contribution to science was rewarded with a Nobel Prize; the desk at which she studied is therefore a key object in the history of women scientists. But as the diary of this famous scientist shows, she was a woman, not just a scientist; a wife and mother, making gooseberry jam as well as isolating polonium. Women scientists are still very much in the minority and it is perhaps interesting to ponder whether, if there were more of them, there might be more medical and scientific developments with the capacity to enhance women's lives. There have been some important medical advancements, such as forceps, which have helped to bring down maternal mortality rates, while for many women the invention of the Pill has enabled them to separate the pleasures of sex from the more dubious joys of procreation and multiple pregnancies. The advantages of these innovations are by no means available to all women yet, and there is much scope for further development and innovation.

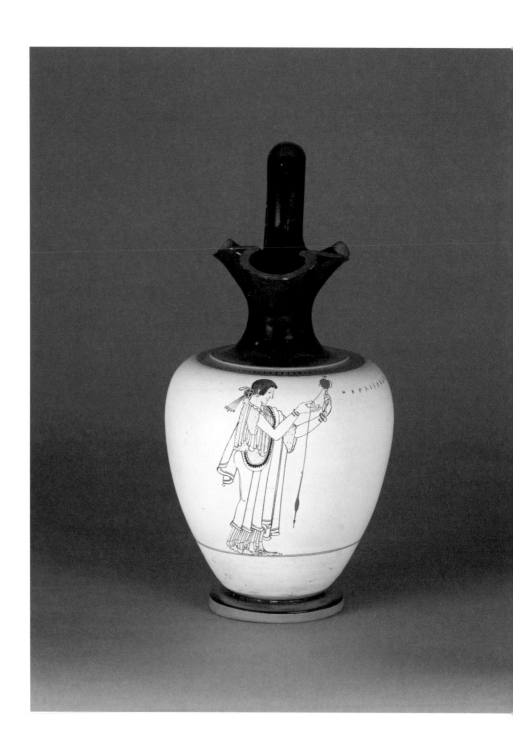

27 | Grecian Vase Showing Women Spinning

Making Cloth and Clothing

JANIS LOMAS

The Grecian vase in the British Museum, dating from *c.* 490 BCE, shows a woman using a spindle to twist fibres to make yarn. The earliest archaeological evidence of primitive spinning was from at least 20,000 years ago. Animal hair, plant fibres and then, from around 6,000 years ago, silk from silkworm cocoons were all used to produce yarns.

Woven textiles have been found in a Peruvian cave and dated to around 9,000–10,000 BCE, and cotton socks dating from around a thousand years ago were found in Egypt. These represent the earliest known examples of knitting, although it is thought that knitting was taking place much earlier but examples have not survived. Historically women were largely responsible for the entire process of textile production beginning with the cultivation of plants, their harvesting, cleaning, spinning, dyeing, and ending with the weaving of the yarns. Furthermore, women spinners and weavers did not simply produce utilitarian textiles; they often decorated them with colour, dyed them and embroidered them.

Spinning is the beginning of the process whereby fibre is converted into yarn, which can then be woven or knitted to produce fabric to make garments and household objects such as fishing nets, baskets for gathering and storing food, tents or shelter coverings. The earliest spinning was entirely by hand with the tufts of hair or fibre rolled down the thigh with the hand and additional tufts added by twisting the tufts together. Later a stone was used to aid the twisting process, followed by the development of the spindle and some time after that the whorl or weight at the bottom of the spindle. The whorl kept the spindle steady and helped it to rotate; this became the method used for centuries until the invention of the spinning wheel in the High Middle Ages (1000–1300 CE). The spinning wheel was probably first invented in India, although it is also known to have been in use in China, before spreading to Europe by around 1280 CE.

Spinning in the medieval period was considered such an important and all-consuming role that the term 'spinster' was synonymous with an unmarried woman. The spinster's skills would be needed when women married, and Gervase Markham, musing on the skills needed for a wife in 1651, noted that: 'After her knowledge of preserving and feeding her family, [she] must learn also how, out of her own endeavours, she ought to clothe them outwardly and inwardly.'

The spinning wheel was the first stage in the mechanisation of what had previously been a slow, laborious and largely domestic process. Often the girls and women in the family all worked at spinning in order to produce enough yarn to keep

The earliest archaelogical evidence of primitive spinning was from at least 20,000 years ago.

the weaver, who after industrialisation was usually male, fully occupied. It took five spinners to spin enough wool or cotton to keep one handloom weaver producing cloth. Women's role in spinning was changed by the Industrial Revolution, when textile production was often transferred from homes into factories. Crompton's spinning mule, invented in 1779, was operated by men – perhaps because it required more physical strength but also because men opposed women being employed. In Glasgow women who worked on the spinning mules were violently attacked by their male counterparts. Women instead took up work in weaving or in lower-paid roles assisting the male spinners. Hand spinning and weaving did not, however, disappear entirely. In the late nineteenth century generations of Scottish women were still all working preparing wool for spinning, and on the islands of Harris, Lewis, Uist and Barra in the Outer Hebrides of Scotland, Harris Tweed is still successfully produced and sold all over the world. Much of it is still woven in the crofters' own homes using wool dyed, spun and handloomed in the same way as it has been for centuries. Hand spinning and weaving is also still practised in many parts of the world. In some communities in Peru, weaving is the mainstay of the community alongside subsistence farming and has changed little over the centuries. Hats, scarves, bags, socks and sweaters are all woven using alpaca, vicuna and sheep fleeces. It has even been described as being a 'language' as each community or region has developed its own designs and dye colours, which distinguish them from each other and shape the communal identity of the people.

Why have what were once domestic chores for all women become leisure activities for some?

In Western countries in the twenty-first century, spinning, once a necessity for women – as it still is in many parts of the world – is now also a leisure pursuit. There are classes and tutorials on spinning and weaving all over the Western world. In the medieval period 'a wife's desirability was measured by the quality of her weaving'; as this is no longer the case, many women have embraced the satisfaction of producing craft items. As one hobbyist spinner wrote, 'people used to have to rely on knitting, weaving and spinning to clothe themselves and make household items on a daily basis. Now, the reason people do it is to enjoy the process.'

28 | Roman Tap from Pompeii
The Importance of Water and Drainage for Women

MAGGIE ANDREWS

The need to have a supply of clean water from wells and streams, or taps and pipes, has shaped, even dominated women's lives across the world for hundreds of years. Water is used for drinking, for cooking, for washing and if not readily available has to be fetched and carried, a task usually undertaken by women.

In many civilisations natural water supplies, from rivers and springs, have influenced where women make their homes; the need to harness natural water supplies has sometimes shaped the very structure of those homes. Roman houses often had roofs sloped so the rain would run off and collect in underground cisterns or pools, able to be stored for times of shortage. The Romans' appreciation of the importance of water was summed up by Vitruvius who wrote in 27 BCE that 'without water neither the animal frame nor any virtue of food can originate, be maintained or provided. Hence great diligence and industry must be used in seeking and choosing springs to serve the health of man.'

> Why is the provision of clean, fresh water to homes not a priority for every government?

The Romans were famous for their water and wastewater systems and their taps, and the pipes and viaducts they installed that brought water to homes, streets and public amenities including bath houses. Poorer women and servants visited fountain houses where they filled water carriers and transported them home.

Public spaces where women access water can also become places for companionship, gossip and chat, as tasks such as washing clothes are undertaken together. In many societies women have gone, and continue to go, to favoured spaces on riverbanks to undertake their washing. In seventeenth-century Rome women were still working together as laundresses at the same public fountains as their forebears had done centuries before. Women's access to water remains varied and haphazard, and drainage and sewage have been even more problematic in societies without the advantages of inside flushing toilets. Public health concerns, particularly in relation to typhus, led many cities to develop water supplies and waste systems from the middle of the nineteenth century. However, across the world, rural women have continued to suffer from a lack of convenient water supplies, needing to spend time each day fetching water for cooking or washing dishes and clothes. Bath houses and wash houses were organised in some areas; alternatively a family's weekly bath in front of the fire required the housewife to both fetch and heat water, and when bath time was over, carry the water out to be

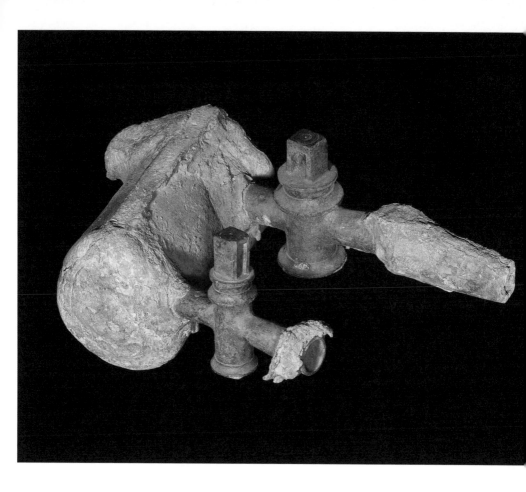

emptied into a ditch or drain. A Staffordshire housewife from Longdon explained how important water supplies were for her in 1936:

> I have lived in this cottage for over six years and for the first four and half years we had not a water supply on the premises and had to fetch it from a draw well 40 feet deep, from a cottage 70 yards away. We had to make three journeys a day, which would each take about half an hour ... My supply is now from a sink in the back kitchen ... You will understand what a blessing it is to us.

In 1950s Britain half the rural homes still had no internal water supply; in the early 1960s the Irish Countrywomen's Association organised a 'Turn on the Tap' exhibition at the Mansion House and a conference on rural water supply at An Grianan to launch their campaign for water supplies for all. For many rural women ensuring that their town, village or settlement had an adequate water supply was a key feminist campaign in the twentieth century, involving groups such as the Women's Institute movement in Britain and the Associated Country Women of

Globally women and children spend 200 million hours collecting water every day, time that could be spent doing so many other things.

the World. What was once a national or regional battle for water has become an international campaign to improve women's lives in the twenty-first century. The United Nations designated 1981–90 an International Drinking Water Supply and Sanitation Decade and in 2005–15 they again announced an International Decade for Action 'Water for Life' when they placed the involvement of women's groups and the importance of water for women high on their agenda. Nevertheless more than two-thirds of the population in sub-Saharan Africa have to leave their home to collect water and the responsibility for this falls predominantly on women. A lifetime of carrying water can have adverse effects on women's bodies, causing fatigue, musculoskeletal damage, degenerative bone and tissue damage, spinal pain and arthritis. The Food and Agriculture Organization of the United Nations (FAO) has pointed out that 'women are most often the collectors, users and managers of water in the household as well as farmers of crops. Women and children provide nearly all the water for the household in rural areas.'

Globally women and children spend 200 million hours collecting water every day, time that could be spent on so many other things. Mothers could work, and provide food for families; estimates suggest that in India women spend 150 million workdays every year fetching and carrying water, resulting in the loss of 10 billion rupees of national income. When young girls live without a ready supply of water, their education suffers; they arrive tired or late for school after fetching water. Little wonder that in the twenty-first century campaigning for water supplies remains a key issue for rural women's groups in many countries, where women's lives could be dramatically improved by taps like those in Roman cities 2,000 years ago.

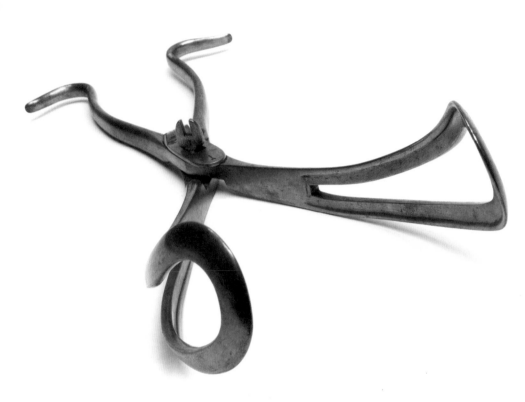

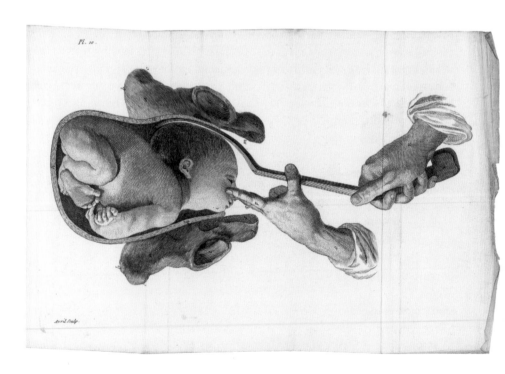

29 | Eighteenth-Century Obstetric Forceps
Medical Intervention in Childbirth

GILL THORN

Up to the sixteenth century childbirth was considered women's work. Men were not encouraged to attend and it was of little interest to doctors. Women in general were subservient to men, but taboos around childbirth were deeply rooted. If a birth was obstructed the midwife might fetch a spoon from the cooking pot to assist; only as a last resort would a barber surgeon (male, but of lower status than a doctor) be called, to dismember the child in an attempt to save the life of the mother.

Around 1588, barber surgeon Peter Chamberlen invented forceps, a game-changing device that saved the lives of both mother and baby. The forceps resembled two oversized, hollow spoons which could be placed around a baby's head and locked together to protect the skull. This innovation was so successful that he and his brother attended the ladies of the English court and travelled around Europe charging huge fees for their services. Driven by profit, they used drama to keep the secret of forceps through three generations, blindfolding the mother and banishing her attendants, banging sticks and ringing bells to disguise the sound of the metal instruments. About a hundred years later, when other barber surgeons were coming up with similar instruments, Hugh Chamberlen sold a single blade to a Dutchman.

The invention of forceps was a key factor in paving the way for doctors to take control of childbirth. In 1721 Jean Palfyne, a Belgian barber surgeon, presented his version of forceps to the Paris Academy of Science, noting that they might be improved with the addition of a curve to fit the birth canal. Others, including surgeons William Smellie in England and Andre Levet in France, refined the design. It became fashionable for wealthy families to engage a barber surgeon or physician, which made it acceptable for a man to attend childbirth. When forceps became widely available in Europe during the eighteenth century, only men could legally perform this 'surgery', as it was called. Surgery commanded high fees and doctors condemned midwives as dirty and incompetent. In the face of assumed male superiority it was difficult for women to retain their primary role in the birth chamber.

Some midwives fought back, complaining that forceps were used too readily in pursuit of profit. Elizabeth Nihell, in her *Treatise on the Art of Midwifery* (1760), accused William Smellie and his colleagues of forcing labour prematurely, to shorten normal deliveries for their own convenience or for experimental purposes. She suggested that few midwives defied the law and used forceps because they found their traditional skills of patience and a hands-on approach more efficacious, except in isolated cases. As doctors became increasingly involved in childbirth, this natural

Fewer than half of births in Britain now take place without some form of medical intervention such as caesarean section, ventouse or forceps.

function of the female body began to be seen as defective. Forceps were used more and more frequently. The blades became longer, allowing them to be used higher in the pelvis, ostensibly to shorten labour and spare the mother pain, although this increased the risk of brain injury to the baby and trauma to the mother.

English surgeon John Leake noted in his instructions on the use of forceps in 1773 that 'the safety of the patient more immediately depends on the operator's skill in this than in any other brand of physic or surgery'. He, and Julien Clement in France, established lithotomy, whereby women lie on their back with their feet up – often in stirrups – as the preferred position for labour. This position made it safer and easier for the doctor to use instruments, but a labouring woman lying on her back is rendered passive. A textbook written by forty-two men and one woman in 1966 claimed that the lithotomy position 'makes maintenance of asepsis easier and it contributes greatly to the convenience of the obstetrician. These advantages more than compensate for the somewhat unphysiologic posture and the discomfort of the position itself.'

Is there now too much emphasis on science and technology when women give birth?

During the Industrial Revolution widespread rickets caused more difficult births. In the United States at the beginning of twentieth century, however, forceps accounted for around half of all deliveries. Doctors advanced other reasons for their use. In 1920 Joseph DeLee promoted 'prophylactic forceps', which involved cutting a large episiotomy in the birth outlet and pulling the baby out, ostensibly to eradicate pain and trauma to the baby. By 1923 he had amassed a fortune, and was called the greatest American obstetrician of his time. His views popularised forceps for decades.

Doctors in the newly established National Health Service in Britain used forceps routinely. William Nixon and Eric Hickson, in their 'Guide to Obstetrics in General Practice' (1953), list the 'contents of the obstetric bag' for a home birth, advising that 'the type of forceps carried is an individual choice. A doctor will do the best work with the instrument to which he is accustomed.' Forceps became a quick delivery fix, rather than something to be used with great caution in the most difficult of situations. The female body is generally well designed to give birth, but the invention of forceps undoubtedly revolutionised childbirth, saving the lives of mothers and babies when a birth presented certain difficulties. It was also a catalyst for social change, ultimately allowing doctors (mainly male) to take over the management of birth from midwives (mainly female). Men and women have different perspectives. Science and technology have become more valued than intuition and patience. Strategies that were developed to treat the minority have increasingly been applied to the majority. Today obstetrics and midwifery continue to be quite separate disciplines.

30 | The Sewing Machine

Making Clothes at Home and in the Workplace

JANIS LOMAS

The first sewing machine was invented in England in 1790 by Thomas Saint; it was improved and refined over the next fifty years. First designed for commercial use, it revolutionised clothing manufacture leading to ready-to-wear clothing, and when in the 1850s machines for the home were introduced in both America and Western Europe, women's domestic needlework was also transformed.

Helen Blanchard, an American inventor, patented many improvements to the sewing machine in the 1870s and 1880s, including the first sewing machine to do a zigzag stitch and make buttonholes, and an over-seaming machine that could simultaneously sew and trim knitted fabrics. The first electric machines were introduced by the Singer company in 1889. As the domestic machine became more efficient, one British magazine proclaimed that 'in the history of the world the sewing machine has freed more women from the drudgery of manual labour than any invention to date!' A simple dress which had allegedly taken ten hours to make could now be produced in only an hour, and the time to make a man's shirt was reduced from fourteen hours to an hour and fifteen minutes.

Prices for sewing machines in Great Britain ranged from £6 to £15, making them initially only affordable to the better off; but monthly payment terms soon enabled them to become an essential item in many homes. In America from the 1860s, the Singer sewing machine company developed a network of salesmen to demonstrate and sign up customers to buy a machine on easy terms. This method of selling was extremely successful and quickly spread to other countries. Women, with their husband or father's agreement, could put a down payment on a machine and hope to recoup the weekly payments from making and selling the clothes they made. Owning a machine, and therefore the means of earning money and making better clothes for their family, made credit much more respectable.

Ownership of a sewing machine has often been the key to making a little go a long way. This was never more so than in Britain in the Second World War when clothes rationing meant an ever greater focus on 'make-do-and-mend' and dressmaking. Better value from the limited allowance of coupons was to be had by buying lengths of material and making up clothes yourself, or, for the better off, employing a dressmaker. Many women reckoned they learned to sew because of the war. One proud owner recalled that her sewing had previously consisted of buttons, shoulder straps and other mundane repairs. After her husband had found her a machine (sewing machine factories were given over to war production and second-hand machines were at a premium), she bought a book on make-do-and-mend and

it meant a complete revolution in her sewing skills: 'It was a real treasure – on it I made curtains, the children's coats, even topcoats and my own dresses.'

Sewing machines have also provided opportunities for women to work outside the home as clothing factories employed large numbers of women operatives, who were considered both cheaper and more nimble-fingered than men. The machines were used in sweatshops and by outworkers required to complete garments extremely quickly, often for poor pay. Some employers only paid for completed garments on a piecework basis and could reject garments that did not meet their standards. In Britain in 1906 Beatrice Skegg, a dressmaker who had worked in sweatshops, wrote to Ramsey Macdonald MP, as part of his investigation into conditions in the textile industries, pointing out:

When I was at business I never knew when I was going home, it was anything between 7 and 10 [in the evening] also 4 on Sat, it makes one's life a misery to be always at work and for such a few paltry shillings a week … The heads of the firms seem to have everything their own way. I know of one place in the town who make you go home for a quarter of the day if you are one min late but they don't mind how long they keep you at night that seems to count as nothing they don't get any overtime money or tea given to them.

Anita Dongre from Mumbai built up an international business from designing and making dresses on two sewing machines in her bedroom.

Protective legislation and the minimum wage has largely eradicated the worst aspects of exploitation in the Western world but sweatshops can still be found in many parts of the world including China, India, Sri Lanka, Bangladesh and Vietnam, where there is little legislation to prevent the exploitation of women machinists, who make garments for a pittance often to be resold in Europe and the USA for a huge profit. But, conversely, for a few women the sewing machine has also been a route, via sheer hard work and determination, to entrepreneurial success.

How is it that technology has empowered some women but destined others to work long hours for poor pay?

Anita Dongre from Mumbai began with two sewing machines, designing and making clothes in her bedroom. She now employs 2,500 people and sells to over 700 outlets, including exclusive shops in New York and Los Angeles; her profile was raised even further when the Duchess of Cambridge wore one of her dresses on her visit to India in 2016. Anita admits, however, that it has been difficult. She was one of thirty-two women who graduated in fashion design but is the only one who went on to make a career in design. As she said, ruefully: 'The others became homemakers. What lovely talent gone to waste.'

In recent years there has been a resurgence in dressmaking and homemaking skills and in women designing and making their own clothes and home furnishings as newer and more sophisticated sewing machines have allowed women's creative and artistic talents to flourish.

31 | Marie Curie's Desk

Women Scientists

JANIS LOMAS

Marie Curie was born in Warsaw, Poland, in 1867, the youngest of five children. There was no money for her to have a university education so Maria Sklodowska, as she was then, studied in her spare time while working as a governess, until her sister offered lodgings with her in Paris in 1891.

She was accepted at the Sorbonne where she studied mathematics and physics, met and married the scientist Pierre Curie, and began working with him in 1895. Toiling together in a damp storeroom at the bottom of the School of Physics in Paris, in 1898 they discovered two new scientific elements. Despite the poor conditions, they isolated both polonium (named after Marie's native Poland) and radium, the most stable, radioactive and useful of the two elements. In the same year that Marie recorded her scientific achievements while sitting at her desk, she also noted in her diary that she was making gooseberry jam, and her baby daughter's first words and steps.

Some members of the scientific community did not initially share the Curies' belief in the existence of radium until, in 1902, after four years of extremely hard work Marie and Pierre had prepared 0.1g of pure radium and determined its atomic weight as 225. Now no one could doubt that radium actually existed. Pierre experimentally burned his arm with radium and found that it could destroy tissue, which would then slowly regenerate; he realised that radium might be used against cancerous tumours. In 1903 they were joint recipients, along with Henri Becqueril who had first observed the radioactivity of uranium, of the Nobel Prize for Physics. In April 1906 Pierre was tragically killed crossing a road in Paris. Marie was devastated but was offered her husband's professorship – the first woman to be appointed to the post. She carried on working and figured out a way of measuring minute amounts of radium by the radiation it produced so the correct dose for cancer treatment could be calculated. For this work she was awarded the Nobel Prize for Chemistry. She was the first woman to win a Nobel Prize and remains the only woman to be awarded two Nobel Prizes for two scientific disciplines.

During the First World War, Marie developed and equipped mobile X-ray units that could be taken by car to where they were needed. She also equipped 200 X-ray rooms to be used to treat injured soldiers in field hospitals. In all, a million wounded men were treated with X-rays. She spent all the money she received from her Nobel Prizes on the French war effort. In 1934 she died, possibly as a result of radiation, the year before her son-in-law and her daughter Irene were jointly awarded the Nobel Prize for Chemistry; building on Marie's work, they had developed an artificial radioactive element. In 1939, their work in splitting uranium led directly to the development of nuclear power stations and unfortunately to the development of the nuclear bomb.

Women had been engaged in scientific research prior to Marie Curie; Laura Maria Caterina Bassi (1711–78), after becoming only the second woman to gain a doctorate, became the first woman to be appointed professor of physics at the University of Bologna in 1732. Yet nearly 300 years later less than a quarter of science professors in the USA and Europe are women and many outstanding women scientists do not receive recognition for their work and remain hidden from history. Rosalind Franklin undoubtedly contributed towards the discovery of the structure of DNA. While working at King's College, London she was treated as a lab assistant rather than a project head by her colleague Maurice Wilkins, who did not get along with her. He corresponded with James Watson and Francis Crick who were also working on DNA at Cambridge University and without Rosalind Franklin's knowledge he showed them her X-ray image of DNA, which gave them the breakthrough they needed. Unfortunately, Rosalind Franklin died at the age of 37 of ovarian cancer four years before Watson, Crick and Wilkins were awarded the Nobel Prize for their work, so she would not have been eligible to be awarded the Nobel Prize as they are not awarded posthumously. Nevertheless, Franklin's contribution was key to deciphering its structure and seems to have been forgotten or ignored until very recently.

Why are there still so few women professors of science?

Jocelyn Bell Burnell is a Northern Irish astrophysicist who was the first to observe and analyse radio pulsars while studying for a PhD with Antony Hewish. He shared the 1974 Nobel Prize for Physics with the astronomer Martin Ryle. She was excluded while Hewish was singled out for 'his decisive role' in the discovery of pulsars. Many prominent astronomers criticised her exclusion, including Sir Fred Hoyle. Speaking later on missing out on the Nobel Prize she said: 'I am not myself upset about it – after all, I am in good company, am I not!'

She has now received recognition for her work, which has been called one of the greatest astronomical discoveries of the twentieth century. She was made a dame in 2007 and in 2015 was honoured with the Prudential Woman of the Year Lifetime Achievement Award.

Unusually, Marie Curie became a professor of physics and received recognition for her work. Doctors began to use radioactive material to treat cancer tumours as early as the 1910s and now 100 years later many cancer patients avoid dangerous surgical interventions as their tumours are destroyed successfully by radiotherapy – thanks to the discoveries of Marie Curie.

32 | Mary Anning's Fossil of Plesiosaurus

An Early Woman Fossil Hunter

JANIS LOMAS

Plesiosaurus is just one of the several hundred fossils found by Mary Anning during her long career as a fossil hunter. Starting as a young girl under the guidance of her father Richard, she developed an eye for locating fossils in the cliffs around Lyme Regis, where she was born in 1799. She had little schooling but managed to teach herself geology, palaeontology and anatomy.

Well-known scientists corresponded with and visited Mary in her humble cottage in Lyme, bought fossils from her and wrote up her finds. While her father was alive the family scratched a living from fossil sales but after his unexpected death Mary, her mother and brother were penniless and reliant on parish relief to survive. Mary began fossil hunting in earnest; her brother, Joseph, also collected fossils and was credited with her first great discovery, an ichthyosaurus, in 1810; the 12-year-old Mary excavated it from the cliff face. Joseph took little part in fossil hunting afterwards and worked as an upholsterer – a much more secure living.

In the early nineteenth century a few academics, mainly French, began to study plant and animal fossils. In Great Britain, the study of fossils was the preserve of a small number of gentlemen, many of them Anglican clergymen. The related sciences of geology and palaeontology were also in their infancy and the idea that creatures became extinct was contentious, even blasphemous. An Anglican clergyman and author named George Bugg was one of many who were aghast at the idea that fossils were of creatures which were no longer on the earth, proclaiming: 'Was ever the word of God laid so deplorably prostrate at the feet of an infant and precocious science!'

Due to the family's poverty, Mary frequently sold the extraordinary collection of fossils of flying and marine reptiles she recovered from the cliffs around Lyme Regis. Her findings helped the careers of many in the scientific community who published papers and took the credit for finds that they had bought from Mary. However, she taught herself to read and understand scientific papers and in a career that lasted until her death at the age of 47 she went on to collect more ichthyosaurs, another plesiosaurus, a pterodactyl, a squaloraja and many others, all of which were fossils of species never seen in Britain before. Her findings were so astounding at the time that Georges Cuvier, the leading zoologist and anatomist, initially believed the plesiosaurus must be a fake. He later admitted his doubts were wrong and pronounced it a major find but only after seeing drawings done by Mary's fossil collector friend, William Conybeare, Dean of Llandaff. Many found it almost

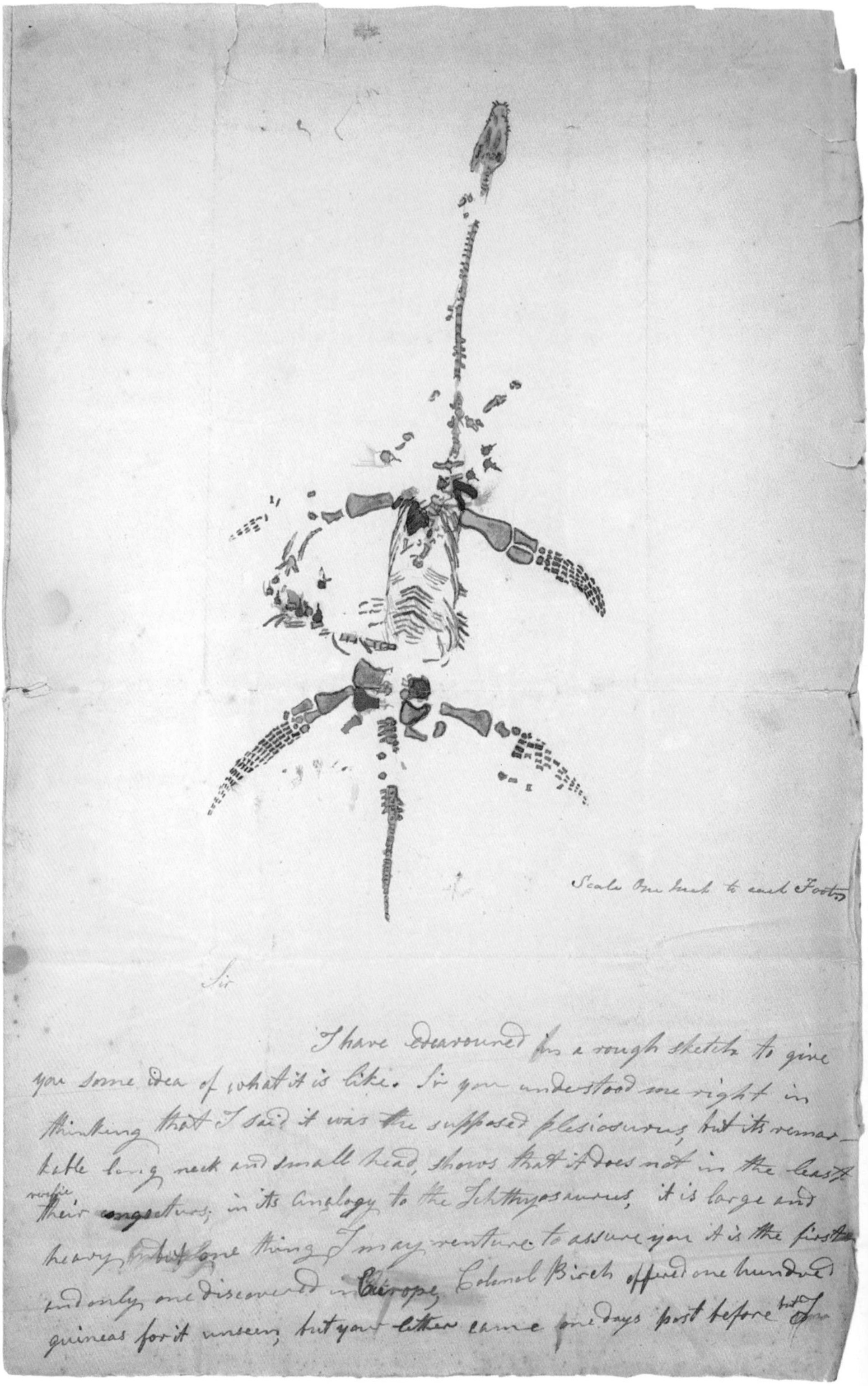

Mary Anning, one of the most influential fossil hunters, provided groundwork for Charles Darwin's *On the Origin of Species* (1859).

impossible to believe that an uneducated woman with no scientific training could have found, excavated, cleaned and mounted such unique fossil specimens, but after Cuvier's endorsement Mary's work was generally accepted. She also worked out that the fossilised stones (coprolites) she found inside the skeletons of the creatures were undigested food, which helped her to work out what the animals had eaten. When Lady Harriet Silvester visited Mary Anning in 1824, she recorded in her diary:

> The extraordinary thing in this young woman is that she had made herself so thoroughly acquainted with the science that the moment she finds any bones she knows to what tribe they belong ... by reading and application she has arrived to that greater degree of knowledge as to be in the habit of writing and talking with professors and other clever men on the subject, and they all acknowledge that she understands more of the science than anyone else in this kingdom.

Mary's fossil findings were crucial developments in the scientific reconstruction of the Earth's past, and provided groundwork for the theory of evolution propounded in Charles Darwin's *On the Origin of Species* in 1859. Mary was never wealthy and as she was female was never accepted as any sort of scientist. In the early twentieth century she was largely remembered for a tongue-twisting nursery rhyme written about her in 1908:

Why do women scientists so often fail to get the recognition they deserve?

> She sells seashells by the seashore,
> The shells she sells are seashells, I'm sure.
> So if she sells seashells on the seashore,
> Then I'm sure she sells seashore shells.

Mary was much more than a seller of shells, and in recent years her work has finally been getting the recognition it deserves; the Natural History Museum in London has made her finds the main attraction of their marine reptiles gallery while in Lyme Regis a museum dedicated to Mary Anning is now situated on the site of her cottage and fossil shop.

33 | The Washing Dolly

How Technology Helps Women Do the Washing

MAGGIE ANDREWS

Across the world and throughout history, housewives have been engaged in a constant battle to keep dirt at bay, to remove the grime and mess of everyday life from their domestic spaces by sweeping, hoovering and the laborious task of doing the family's weekly wash.

Laundry is perhaps the domestic task that has been changed most by technology. Women have undertaken the process of immersing items of clothing and bed linen in water, soaking, beating, scrubbing, and rinsing the dirt out of them by hand for millennia. The modern washing machine is the culmination of a number of technical developments, which have sought to make these laborious cleaning tasks a little easier for women; the washing dolly was one of its predecessors.

Without piped water, washing often takes place outside, in local streams and rivers or by clothes being placed in individual or communal containers of water to wash and rinse. The washing dolly was first used at the end of the eighteenth century, made of wood, about 1m high, with a handle at the top and legs spreading out at the bottom. By a mixture of both rotating and lifting the dolly up and down, women could agitate and therefore clean clothes in tubs of water. The dolly was more efficient and required less bending than scrubbing by hand. Mrs Aziz recalled how the early twentieth-century washing was done in Pakistani communities for the Reading Museum Washday Memories project in 2014. She explained how women used a laundry bat to beat clothes which were put in water boiled on open fires.

The sun's heat was used to dry the clothes in Pakistan, but for many women drying was one of the greatest challenges of washday. The introduction of the mangle in the middle of the nineteenth century assisted many women. This cumbersome machine was a popular item in many homes as it enabled women to feed clothes and sheets between two heavy rollers as they turned the handle to squeeze water out the fabric. Nevertheless, when interviewed for *Sussex Living* magazine in 2016, Mary White recalled, as a little girl of 8, helping her grandmother on washday:

> Always on a Monday unless it was Christmas Day ... When it came to the drying, hopefully it would dry outside but if it was a wet day, the washing was dried around the fires in the kitchen and living room. This could take several days and in the meantime the house smelled of wet washing.

Housewives sought assistance from children where possible, turning mangles, agitating the dolly and lighting fires to heat water outside or below a copper in the

corner of a scullery. In Britain in the early twentieth century it was not unusual for girls to be kept off school on washing day, either to assist their mothers or to look after their younger siblings while their mothers got on with the washing. Many urban homes did not have the space to do the weekly wash and communal open-air sinks were set up in some rural villages in the USA. Mrs McFarlen, also for the Reading Museum Washday Memories project, recalled washing in a communal washing house in a Glasgow tenement in Scotland in the 1930s:

We shared washing outside in a block that contained a big brick boiler with a cover ... we had two big sinks opposite the boiler and a big piece of wood. You put the sheet from one sink into the other to rinse it and then get it out again and back through the wringer. And we used to dry them on sunny days out on the grass ... a back green shared by everybody.

Those with the money to do so paid a washerwoman to help with the weekly wash, or in towns and cities sent larger items, particularly sheets, to laundries. There were 226 laundries in Chicago in 1909, employing more than 6,500 people. The majority were women, working long hours in an environment with accidents caused by hot irons and vats of boiling water. For housewives taking in neighbours' washing has also been a traditional way of earning extra money.

Why do women continue to devote more hours than men to domestic chores such as washing?

Although the patent for automatic washing machines was created in the nineteenth century, they were first manufactured in the USA in the 1930s. Initially available in launderettes, Bendix machines began to be sold for domestic use in 1937. By the twenty-first century they were widespread in Western countries; 97 per cent of homes in Britain had a washing machine in 2011, using it on average four times a week. According to the South Korean economist Ha-Joon Chang, the invention of the washing machine was more important than the internet, as it released women to undertake more productive tasks and join the workforce in greater numbers. He suggested in 2010 that 'without the washing machine, the scale of change in the role of women in society and in family dynamics would not have been nearly so dramatic'.

The washing machine is only one development which has reduced the time needed for the weekly wash; new synthetic fabrics, biological detergents and the electric iron have all played a part. However, there has been a corresponding rise in expectations of cleanliness and personal hygiene. Undergarments, shirts, skirts and trousers that would not have been changed more than once a week are now thrown into the washing basket or abandoned on the floor for the 'washing fairy' to clean. With women continuing to do more of the mundane and monotonous domestic tasks than men, washing still features strongly in their lives. In Australia, for example, women in full-time paid work continue to undertake an additional twenty-five hours of housework a week.

34 | Quarter-Plate Cameo Camera

Women Taking Photographs and Being Photographed

JANIS LOMAS

Women have been photographed since Louis Daguerre in France and Henry Fox Talbot in England created the first photographic images in 1826. Photographic images of women are gazed at in a multitude of spaces and places, in posters and pornography, their images examined, categorised and judged – often by men, although women have also been photographers.

Cameras enable people to produce images and then to manipulate, edit, airbrush and share these images. In the contemporary era of digital technology new opportunities have opened up to create and communicate meanings through photography, something many women have enthusiastically engaged with on social media sites such as Instagram. The first commercial camera was produced in France in 1839 but required a long exposure time, often several hours. The first photographic film using celluloid was developed in America by George Eastman in 1889 and the first Kodak camera came on to the American market in 1888. It came pre-loaded with 100 exposures which, once used, had to be returned to the factory for processing. Film cameras also developed around the turn of the century, making first the motion picture and later the television industry possible. The digital camera was developed in 1975 and is now the dominant method of capturing an image, with high-resolution smartphones enabling almost anyone in the Western world to take photographs wherever they are.

The portrayal of women in photographs is frequently somewhat different from how they appear in everyday life; they may be idealised, eroticised or have their images manipulated for propaganda or commercial purposes. The suffragette Evelyn Manesta was photographed after being arrested for damaging a painting in Manchester Art Gallery. It had been usual practice from the 1870s for all prisoners to be photographed on arrival in prison, but suffragette prisoners refused to allow their photograph to be taken. Women would struggle, bob out their tongues, or pull funny faces to thwart the efforts of police photographers, so instead surveillance cameras photographed the women in the prison exercise yards without their knowledge from 1913 onwards. The authorities wanted a clearer photograph of Evelyn Manesta to warn police officers of the danger she posed to public buildings and art objects. When she refused to oblige and struggled, a prison officer put her in a headlock and used the fingers of his other hand to grip her upper arm. However, in the published photo this manhandling was not visible, as it would have confirmed the suffragettes' complaints of police cruelty. The constraining fingers and arm were removed and replaced by a scarf.

In 1911 there were 11,899 male and 5,016 female photographers in Britain.

Photography has allowed many women to create, keep and leave their families with a record of their lives; family albums portraying domestic everyday expereinces of relations and relationships are treasured heirlooms. Women wealthy enough to gain access to cameras were also at the forefront of the development of photography as an art form in the nineteenth century. Julia Margaret Cameron, who began photographing family, friends and well-known people in 1863, is now recognised as one of the most important photographers of the era while Lee Miller's images taken in war-torn Europe in the early 1940s are widely celebrated.

Women and girls have not been averse to manipulating images themselves, and in 1920 an image produced by Francis Griffiths and Elsie Wright, two young cousins aged 9 and 16 years, was hailed as proof of the existence of fairies. The images, taken on a Quarter-Plate Cameo Camera, were produced by photographing cardboard figures of fairies cut out of a book and posed near the stream at the bottom of the garden. The five photographs produced caused a sensation and were reproduced in newspapers worldwide, fooling many including Sherlock Holmes's creator, Sir Arthur Conan Doyle, who considered them to be clear evidence of psychic phenomena. Sixty years later, in the 1980s, the cousins finally admitted they had faked the photographs for their own amusement, but once the images appeared in the newspapers they were too scared to admit it.

Why are women so often portrayed in photographs as idealised, fantasy or erotic figures?

Photographs are now manipulated digitally to enable photographs of women to conform to idealised images of what women should look like. This can lead girls and women to feel pressured to emulate such idealised versions of femininity through both extreme dieting and plastic surgery. In recent years, posting selfies on social media using smartphones has become ubiquitous but has also been linked to the perceived increasing obsession by women and girls with image and outward appearances, vanity and narcissism. A number of women celebrities and stars have criticised media manipulation of their photographs and the fantasy images that are consequently produced. Kate Winslet, who is famous for speaking out about the natural body being the most beautiful, objected to the size of her legs being reduced by about a third, saying: 'I'm completely physically comfortable with who I am.' Lady Gaga took advantage of the opportunity afforded her when receiving an award from *Glamour* magazine in 2013 to criticise a photoshopped imaged of her they had used on their front cover, saying: 'I felt my skin looked too perfect, I felt my hair looked too soft ... I do not look like this when I wake up in the morning.'

35 | The Electric Fridge

Women Inventors and the Benefits
of Domestic Technology

MAGGIE ANDREWS

Florence Parpart, a New Jersey housewife, is understood to have invented the modern electric refrigerator in 1914; she also invented a street-cleaning machine. There are a number of other examples of everyday items invented by women.

In 1846 Nancy Johnson had patented her ice-cream maker; repeated turning of the handle powered it to freeze the ice cream. Josephine Cochrane was responsible for the first dishwasher in 1886. Her machine used high water pressure, a wheel, a boiler, and a wire rack to produce the appliance, which she would never use – although it did make life easier for her servants. A gas-fired heating furnace, a key step on the way towards central heating being installed in many homes, was the brainchild of Alice Parker, one of relatively few African-American women to graduate from university in the early twentieth century.

Prior to Florence Parpart's invention a range of innovative methods were employed to preserve food: salting, drying, bottling, canning and ice were used; alternatively potatoes were stored in hay and carrots in moist sand in some cellars. Ancient Egyptians made ice by leaving earthenware pots of water outside on cold nights; in eighteenth-century English country houses, servants were expected to collect ice in the winter and store it underground in the specially constructed icehouses for use in the summer months. For many housewives and servants the refrigerator seemed a very welcome tool for preserving food. Fridges enabled milk and butter to be chilled, meat or even medicines to be stored more safely, and they relieved women of the necessity of shopping daily. A fridge offers the possibility of buying and cooking in bulk, keeping and re-using leftovers and thereby preventing waste. More recently the increasing use of fridges in Tanzania has been credited with improving health by cutting food contamination and enabling families to add high-protein foods to a diet that was previously dominated by grains and vegetables.

Florence Parpart was an astute marketer and promoter of her invention, helping to make fridges a desirable item for housewives with sufficient funds. The General Electric 'Monitor-Top' refrigerator sold for over $500 in 1927, so for most housewives a fridge was something they could only dream about and the appliances did not become commonplace until the 1950s. In Britain the uptake of this new domestic technology was even slower; only 2 per cent of homes had fridges in 1948. The Barrow-in-Furness housewife Nella Last acquired a fridge the following year, an event to which she devoted much time in her diary. She recalled that on 1 October:

In 1959 only 13 per cent of all British homes had a refrigerator, while 96 per cent of American housewives had one.

My husband came rushing in excitedly and said, 'How would you like a fridge for your birthday?' and said a shop had four in and the proprietor, an electrician who often works on big jobs for my husband, has promised him one.

She does not seem to have greeted the news with unparalleled enthusiasm, but reported she 'felt a bit dazed and indifferent' to the prospective arrival of what became a combined birthday and Christmas present. She did, however, note that 'if we have another summer it will be grand for we both like ice-cream, as well as the advantage of well-kept food, hard butter and marg, and crisp salads'.

After the fridge arrived neighbours came in to view it; getting a fridge was an exciting event for any family. The fridge's capacity to store ice cream was probably foregrounded when the item arrived in the home under the guise of being a child's birthday present. Nevertheless, even in 1959 only 13 per cent of all British homes had a refrigerator, in stark contrast to 96 per cent of American homes. Fridges required both the income to purchase them and a regular, reliable electricity supply – something not available in many rural areas across the globe. Hence in 2015 only three-quarters of the world's households had a fridge, with ownership as low as 24 per cent in India and 45 per cent in Peru. In India, however, fridges are high on family wish lists, coming after mobile phones and televisions.

> Does technology release women from domestic drudgery or further tie them to the kitchen and domesticity?

The electric fridge and other domestic technologies that have followed in its wake – including dishwashers, vacuum cleaners, microwaves, electric mixers and breadmakers – have been credited with transforming women's lives, saving labour and releasing women from domestic drudgery. Yet in recent years this has been questioned; women continue to spend significant amounts of time on domestic labour, and are struggling to meet the increasingly high expectations of cleanliness and food preparation that have accompanied the widespread introduction of domestic 'labour-saving' machines. In fiction and films fridges are sometimes seen to have a more sinister role; in the comic book *Green Lantern* (1994) the hero comes home to find that his girlfriend has been killed and stuffed in the fridge. This is a metaphor, perhaps, of the way in which domestic technology potentially stifles women and ties them to the kitchen when they could be focusing on other things. Such sentiments were expressed when in 2016 Indian External Affairs Minister Sushma Swaraj responded to a tweet from a disgruntled owner of a Samsung fridge with the comment which went viral and was widely praised: 'Brother I cannot help you in matters of a Refrigerator. I am very busy with human beings in distress.'

36 | The Ekco SH25 Wireless

Radio and Television Changing Women's
Domestic Lives

MAGGIE ANDREWS

The introduction of the wireless, as it was known, brought revolutionary changes to millions of women's domestic lives in the 1920s and 1930s. This technological innovation offered women music and camaraderie, education and politics, as they went about their everyday, often mundane, tasks in the home.

In Britain the *Radio Times* explained to women:

> You can sit by the fireside and hear great music, rousing songs, talks on every subject under the sun: plays constructed to appeal to the ear alone; your favourite comedians and dance bands ... The radio has brought to your fireside resources that can hardly be too highly prized. (15 November 1935)

Little wonder then that Mrs Mackay, who lived in the wilds of Colleden Moor, exclaimed only four years later: 'You cannot understand what the wireless means to us up here.' Likewise Margaret Bondfield, the very first female Cabinet minister, enthusiastically greeted the wireless, noting that 'the company of sound conveyed the world and its affairs into the tiny kitchens and living rooms which hitherto had isolated so many house-keepers'.

Newly enfranchised women listeners in the inter-war period were able to listen to politicians and opinion leaders, encountering the public world without leaving their firesides. Long before the internet, the wireless (and later the television) gave women access to the popular and political culture of the societies in which they lived.

The first experiments with wireless communication occurred towards the end of the nineteenth century when radios were used to convey messages between ships and ports. The HMS *Titanic*'s radio requested assistance when the ship hit an iceberg in 1912. It was not until the end of the First World War that wireless became a means of mass communication. Argentina, Canada and the USA all lay claim to regular wireless broadcasts in advance of those produced by Marconi in England in 1922. When the British Broadcasting Company (BBC) was formed later that year, its audience was, however, predominantly made up of technically confident men, engaged in solitary listening on homemade crystal sets with headphones. It was the mass production and distribution of factory-made radios, often made, like the Ekco SH25, out of Bakelite, in the 1930s, which put an end to the constant 'knob twiddling' of these early sets. An article in the *Radio Pictorial* welcomed 'tuning-in without

tears' and encouraged women listeners to 'see how easy it is?' Radio was quickly followed by television; the BBC's first regular television service began transmitting from Alexandra Palace, North London, on 2 November 1936. Early television sets were priced between £35 and £150, at a time when a new Model T Ford car cost £150. Consequently televisions could only be found in the living rooms of the wealthy few, and even then only those who lived close enough to a transmitter to get a signal.

In the 1920s it was suggested that wireless could help women lure their men away from the pub and the club, as it made their homes a more desirable place to spend time. Radio also apparently turned loneliness into leisure for single women, who at the touch of a button were provided with friends and a substitute family with whom to socialise. In the afternoons, when many mothers were preparing the evening meal, the BBC's Radio Aunties and Uncles occupied their little ones by providing a *Children's Hour*. When, in the 1950s, television became truly popular – the centre of almost every home – its schedule also included an afternoon for mothers with

Over 75 per cent of households in developing countries have access to a radio; they link women in their homes to wider communities.

dedicated children's programmes. During the day radio helped women combat the boredom of domestic life; entertainment and education accompanied cooking, cleaning and caring for children or elderly relatives. Then as now radio devoted a significant amount of airtime to music, and a plethora of friendly and flirtatious radio DJs have lifted women's spirits for more than eighty years. One woman listener explained in the *Radio Times* that 'light music is among the pleasures that weave themselves into our daily routine more and more often and more and more closely' (1937). An awareness that millions of other people are simultaneously tuning into a radio programme creates a shared listening experience, a community of radio listeners.

If for some the radio was soundscape to domestic tranquility, broadcasting also caused disharmony. Power over the choice of channel, and in latter years who operates the remote control, is also a weapon in subtle and not-so-subtle domestic tensions. Controversy has also surrounded women's limited involvement in the production of broadcast media. Many early radio stations considered women's voices unsuitable for broadcasting, although women took on roles as producers and organisers of talk programmes. In 2016 *Woman's Hour,* one of the most popular programmes on Britain's Radio 4, celebrated its seventieth birthday. Its success according to presenter Jane Garvey can be understood:

Why do women in twenty-first-century Britain still need the unique insight into women's lives that *Woman's Hour* offers?

> There simply isn't anything else like it … The running order is such an incredible cocktail of things that everybody will find something they are interested in, something they want to know more about, or something they want to tell their mother, daughter or friend – that's why it works.

The representation of women on radio and television has also come in for much criticism, as it often seems to be reinforcing stereotypes. For example Barn Dance radio in the USA in the 1930s used only the stock characters of the comedienne, the sentimental mother, and the cowgirl. Broadcast media's capacity to address millions of people many miles apart has led some to question its influence on women. In times of war and conflict, radio can be employed to speak directly to women in their homes. Hitler's fascist regime in Germany used radio to encourage housewives to support Nazi policies. More radically, community radio stations in Latin America and Africa have in recent years enabled marginalised women to gain a voice in a public sphere.

37 | The Contraceptive Pill

Birth Control Helping Women to Take Control
of Their Fertility

MAGGIE ANDREWS

Enovid, the very first oral contraception, was approved by the USA Food and Drug Administration in 1960 and available on the National Health Service in Britain the following year.

To those who had been struggling with mechanical means of birth control, condoms and caps, spermicides and safe periods, this seemed to be the greatest scientific invention of the twentieth century, so significant that it became know simply as the Pill. This new chemical contraceptive offered women control over their fertility and so enabled them to plan their careers, education and families. The novelist Margaret Drabble recalled:

> By the time the Pill was available I already had three children; I think I would have had a child a year if I hadn't started taking it. So, yes, it made a very considerable difference to one's life. You were able to make a choice, you were able to look after yourself, and I was pleased to do so.

Birth control was not a twentieth-century phenomenon; there is evidence of its use in antiquity, although not of its reliability. *Kahun gynaecological papyrus*, written in 1825 BCE, suggested packing crocodile dung into the vagina or alternatively applying a mixture made of honey. Withdrawal was the most common method of preventing contraception, mentioned in the Bible and still widely practised in mid-twentieth-century Britain. It did, however, rely upon male co-operation.

The initial Pill was a combination of hormones – progestogen and a small amount of oestrogen – which prevented women's monthly release of an egg cell from the ovary and therefore conception. At the time the chemist Carl Djerassi, who is often dubbed the father of the Pill, developed a process to synthesise hormones from Mexican yams during the 1950s, over thirty states in the USA still had laws preventing the promotion of birth control. Consequently and controversially the first large-scale clinical trials of the Pill were carried out in Puerto Rico and Haiti. The Pill proved very effective in preventing conception but a range of side effects including headaches, nausea, dizziness, bloating and even thrush were arguably played down; within five years 6.5 million American women were regular users of the Pill. In 1964 G.D. Searle and Co., Enovid's producers, earned $24 million in net profits from their innovative form of oral contraception. Debate over possible side effects continued; Barbara Seaman published *The Doctors' Case Against the Pill* in 1969 drawing attention to

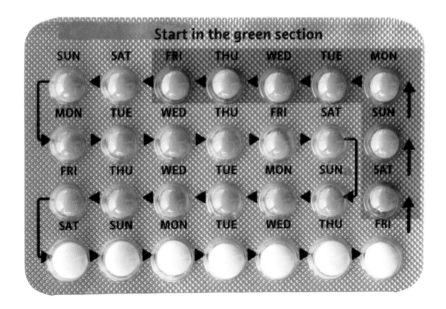

Start in the green section

the risk of blood clots, heart attack, stroke, depression, weight gain and loss of libido when on the drug. By the 1980s, progestogen-only pills had been developed, which although slightly less reliable as a form of birth control had fewer side effects. In the years that followed, the Pill has become the most common although problematic form of birth control in Western countries.

Controversy has surrounded the Pill's use; a number of religious groups questioned the morality of separating sexuality and procreation, and feared the Pill would lead to promiscuity. In 1968 Pope Paul VI published *Humanae Vitae*, a letter to the millions of Catholics across the world, which started from the assumption that:

> Why are so many women still discouraged or forbidden from using the Pill by religious groups?

> The transmission of human life is a most serious role in which married people collaborate freely and responsibly with God the Creator. It has always been a source of great joy to them, even though it sometimes entails many difficulties and hardships.

Humanae Vitae promoted chastity and self-discipline and concluded that Catholics should not use any artificial form of birth control, including the Pill, a controversial position that Pope Paul's successors have maintained for nearly fifty years amid much criticism. Melinda Gates, wife of billionaire and philanthropist Bill Gates, argues that the provision of birth control is an issue of social justice, vital to combat poverty in developing countries. She points out that 'about 358,000 women and 3 million newborns die each year worldwide due to pregnancy and childbirth, but

One of the methods of contraception suggested in 1825 BCE
was crocodile dung packed into the vagina.

other Catholics accuse Western Aid organisations of "Contraceptive Imperialism" in
providing the Pill to Africa and Asia'.

In Britain, it was married women who initially made up the vast majority of the
million women taking the Pill in 1969 and whose lives the new drug changed. Family
planning clinics were not allowed to prescribe the Pill to single women until 1974
and initially addressed all their patients as 'Mrs'. The Pill, for young women, as the
fashion designer Mary Quant recalled:

> Was hellishly difficult to get hold of at first. There was a lot of pretending one
> was married when one went to the doctor, and a minor disadvantage was that
> the early pills made one put on a couple of pounds. But that was nothing! Who
> cared? The other forms of contraception were so hellish.

Young, single women lent each other wedding rings or claimed they had menstrual
disorders to persuade doctors to prescribe them the Pill. The appropriate age for
women to take the Pill was by the 1980s also surrounded by controversy. Many
doctors, seeking to combat the rising rates of teenage pregnancy, began prescribing
the Pill to teenagers, a practice that was challenged by the Catholic campaigner
Victoria Gillick, herself a mother of ten children, who unsuccessfully sought to
prevent teenagers under 16 being prescribed the Pill without their parents' consent.

For many women, married or single, the Pill reduced the association between
sex and anxiety about pregnancy, something many found liberating. It has enabled
women to choose to engage in recreational sex on the same terms as men and
not necessarily within long-term relationships. However, some feminists, such as
Germaine Greer, have suggested that the Pill has not led to women having greater
choice and control over their sexuality but rather to an expectation and pressure that
all women will be sexually active and assumptions that they are sexually available,
liberating men more than women. Arguably the Pill places the responsibility for
birth control firmly on women rather than couples or men. Furthermore, more than
fifty years after the Pill was introduced, abortions continue to be needed. Many
women use the morning-after pill, which was introduced in 1999, and unplanned
and unwanted pregnancies continue to occur, while over 200,000 million women
across the world still do not have access to the Pill.

Would you be more careful if it was you that got pregnant?

Anyone married or single can get advice on contraception from the Family Planning Association
Margaret Pyke House, 27-35 Mortimer Street, London W1 N 8BQ. Tel. 01-636 9135.

The Health Education Council

Part IV
Fashions and Costumes

Fashion, clothes and costumes are perhaps an area that offers women hours of pleasure but also subjects them to many pressures. Clothes have a functional role to keep the wearer warm and to ensure they will not be scratched or hurt when doing certain tasks, and also serve to demark certain parts of the body as not available to be viewed by strangers or anyone outside the private spaces of home or bedroom. Fashions also shape the body, as a corset does; conceal and masquerade, as make-up can; or draw attention to particular parts of the body and sexualise the wearer, as high-heeled red shoes do. More recently the fashion for cosmetic surgery has seen women shaping their bodies more permanently.

Clothes are signifiers – they carry messages and meaning, suggest identity affiliations; even those who think they are ignoring fashion, by doing so are engaging with it. Women express their creativity and make a statement about themselves by wearing particular clothes or shoes, but they do so within a range of constraints. Financial resources limit what women wear, but more significantly social expectations define what women feel will be an acceptable costume for any occasion; expectations may be influenced by women's own social position or that of their husbands as some of the objects below such as Lady Curzon's peacock dress indicate.

What is deemed appropriate or respectable clothing for women is structured by age, marital status, class and ethnic identity at any particular historical moment. The jeans that so many women in Western cultures now wear would have shocked Victorian women.

Even in 1912 when the male impersonator and music hall star Vesta Tilley performed at the Royal Variety Show in London, the queen averted her gaze as she was appalled to be asked to view a woman's legs in trousers. Vesta Tilley's choice of costume enabled her to perform a role, and some of the objects that are explored in this section were similarly chosen for particular performances – such as Queen Victoria's wedding. Victoria's dress, like many clothes, was invested with political meaning. The choice of colour, the designer and the makers of the lace all conveyed messages about Victoria's role as Queen of the British Empire. Similarly the wearing of white veils and garments on White Wednesdays in Iran in 2017 or Mary Winter's lesbian liberation badge in the 1970s were overtly political, but for people with less power than a queen the consequences of these political protests can be severe.

A range of meanings are embedded in clothing and garments and, as the parents of many a teenage girl will be aware, what these meanings are may be contested. For women, clothes represent power, fun, autonomy and communication. It is perhaps summed up in the 2008 film about the Duchess of Devonshire's life, *The Duchess*. In an exchange with her husband on their wedding night, as he literally cuts her out of her garments, he says: 'For the life of me I can never understand why women's clothes must be so damned complicated', to which the duchess replies: 'It's just our way of expressing ourselves, I suppose. You have so many ways of expressing yourselves where we make do with our hats and our dresses.'

38 | Bronze Age Cosmetic Box
Women's Relationship with Make-Up and Cosmetics over the Centuries

SALLIE MCNAMARA

Evidence of women's use of cosmetics goes back thousands of years; cosmetic boxes from ancient Egypt are among the collections at the British Museum, while the hippo tusk make-up box in the Hecht Museum dates from the Bronze Age.

Traces of the ingredients, including kohl, ochre, wax, and perfumed oils dating from 1350 BCE, have been excavated from graves. Egyptians used red ochre for lipstick and cheek stain, burned almonds to paint brows black, henna to dye fingernails yellow and orange. Kohl was used around the eyes, predominantly by women in the Middle East, North Africa, the Horn of Africa and South Asia, and was said to deter flies, prevent infection and deflect the glare of the sun, as well as prevent cursing from the 'evil eye'. Face and body painting was universal, and included Aboriginal Australians and Aztecs; South African cave paintings dating back 100,000–125,000 years show use of red and yellow ochre, which for many was believed to be healing and magical. People blended their own cosmetics, some of which were poisonous: kohl includes lead, while vermillion, from powdered mineral cinnabar, was derived from red mercuric sulphide. Women's relationship with cosmetics goes back a very long way.

The use of cosmetics is entangled with differing cultural ideals of beauty and status. The practice of teeth-blackening, once popular in Japan, China and southeast Asia, and thought to signify female coming of age, has not been widely popular since. Pale skin, which the Chinese and Koreans believe to be the height of female beauty, has been revered across cultures, accompanied by rouge on the cheek and lips during the time of the Renaissance. Lead-based skin-whitening products were used by the wealthy in the eighteenth and nineteenth centuries; the poor, who prepared their own, blended less harmful ingredients such as chickpeas, almonds and milk. Skin lightening also has complex and contradictory political dimensions, particularly when used by African-Americans who are sometimes criticised as wanting to emulate or to pass as white. Nevertheless in the 1920s the popular entertainer Josephine Baker promoted skin-lightening products, while white women wanting to create a Bakeresque glow rubbed walnut oil into their face and limbs.

The nineteenth and twentieth centuries saw the development of mass-produced cosmetics and regulation of ingredients, and safer products, including French chalk and powder of magnesia for skin whitening, were introduced. Products promoted by magazines, photography, and later Hollywood film stars became more widely available to all classes via high street stores and local pharmacies. Beauty became a global business, and in the early twentieth century it was also a place for female

entrepreneurs including Madam C.J. Walker and Annie Turnbo Malone, who launched hair and cosmetic products sold by and to African-American women. Rivals Elizabeth Arden and Helena Rubenstein catered for wealthy white women, marketing cosmetics as both a luxury and necessity, and as a treatment. Adverts emphasised the scientific element of cosmetics' constituents. In the twentieth century make-up boxes became more portable, to cater for women's changing lives. The swivel metal lipstick case, powder compacts, block 'spit and brush' mascara and later the pen-shaped applicator were introduced, all able to be popped into a handbag rather more easily than the Bronze Age cosmetics box.

There have been criticisms of cosmetics throughout their history, sometimes with a moral dimension concerned about the element of concealment or deception in their use. Queen Victoria banned make-up use at court: the epithet 'slapper' derives from 'slapping on' theatrical make-up. The political aspects of twentieth-century identity politics led to the practice of 'conking' – that is, chemically straightening hair – being denounced by members of the Black Panthers in the USA during the 1960s and 1970s; they argued that Black African heritage was represented by curly hair, leading to the popularisation of the Afro hairstyle. Second wave feminism in the 1970s criticised stereotypes of female beauty, and the 'beauty myth' which led to the use of make-up which they saw as linked to patriarchal oppression and female subjugation. The angst and tensions around feminism and make-up continue. In a blog post Melissa Fabello, who argued that 'Makeup Isn't Inherently Anti-Feminist – But Your Body Policing Is', noted that:

When humanitarian Zainab Salbi entered the besieged Bosnian capital Sarajevo in the 1990s, women asked her to bring them lipstick.

While I'm empowered to decide that I want to wear makeup, I'm equally disempowered by a system that sells that to me as the 'right' choice to make. And the fact that I refuse to leave the house without makeup? That's definitely the result of internalized misogyny. And feminism taught me that.

The meanings and use of, and attitudes towards, cosmetics shift according to circumstances; 'red lippy' is used for morale-boosting purposes, but may be a symbol of defiance. On a suffrage demonstration attended by Elizabeth Arden in New York in 1912, women painted their mouths with bright red lipstick. Posters during the Second World War exhorted women to wear make-up with pride as 'Home Front Ammunition'. When humanitarian Zainab Salbi entered the besieged Bosnian capital Sarajevo in the 1990s, women asked her to bring them lipstick, saying 'I want that sniper, before he shoots me, to know he is killing a beautiful woman'. Celebrity-endorsed global brands now dominate the market, with more products for every part of the face and body, and varying skin tints. Different colours, which were first developed by Max Factor for use by Hollywood, conformed to dominant beauty ideals in the West, and thus were unsuitable for women of colour. However, model and businesswoman Iman launched her own brand of cosmetics in 1994, while other multinationals have seen the growing business potential and extended their ranges to include Asian women's skin tones. Ethical issues have been raised about cosmetics being tested on animals and the use of additives; an increasing emphasis is now placed on 'natural' products. In a return to the past, avocado oil once used by Aztecs, Mayans and Incas is today marketed in hair and skin products.

Beliefs that cosmetics have magical properties, are seductive, can change identity, create beauty or conceal age continue. While ancient Egyptians made anti-wrinkle cream with wax, olive oil, incense, milk, juniper leaves and crocodile dung, today marine-based serums suggest the same result. And cosmetic surgery is on the rise: Botox, a poison used to remove wrinkles and temporarily paralyse muscles, also attempts to deny the ageing process. Cosmetics remain one of women's most frequently reached-for beauty aids. The earliest known recipe for cold cream was an emollient of fats and water, formulated by second-century CE Greek physician Galen; it has now been surpassed by a range of unguents for all ages, skin types and colours, colonising every part of the body, and for many women their make-up case is one of their most essential possessions.

Can you wear make-up and be feminist?

39 | The White Veil in Iran
Religion, Islamophobia and the Politics of Dress

MAGGIE ANDREWS

The wearing of a veil or headscarf covering parts of the head or face has had multiple meanings at different historical moments. In 2017 women in Iran have begun to wear white headscarves and clothing on Wednesdays to protest against the strict dress codes and the hijab law brought in on 8 March 1979, which decreed that all women in Iran should cover their hair in public.

The inspiration for the movement came from Masih Alinejad, the originator of an online movement entitled My Stealthy Freedom, which campaigns against the mandatory dress code and publishes images of women whose heads are not covered. The social media hashtag #whitewednesdays gives women a safe public platform for protest. One woman walking down a street explained to a video maker: 'I'm so pumped up to be in this campaign … they imposed hijab on me since I was seven while I never felt committed to it and won't be.'

Across the world in the USA, since the election of President Donald Trump in 2016 many Muslim women, including Sameeha Ahmada, a psychology student at the University of Maryland, have chosen to start wearing the hijab, which has become a symbol of resistance to Islamophobia. She has explained: 'I do believe [the] hijab support[s] feminism … It's a step you are taking to further yourself within your own religion. No one forced me to dress this way.' Slma Shelbayah points out: 'I wear a headscarf to support diversity; since [the] presidential election, I don't feel safe to do so.'

In Britain the introduction of a poppy-themed headscarf to commemorate the Muslim soldiers who took part in two world wars has been criticised for its implication that apparently it is only Muslim women who have to prove, as Sofia Ahmed points out, that 'you're not a terrorist, a wannabe "jihadi bride", planning on running off to Syria to find your Isis prince in blood-stained camouflage'.

Some women wear the veil with pride, others with shame or fear – for in the post-9/11 contemporary world the veil has become imbued with multiple contradictory and complex meanings and wearing it or not has begun to be seen as a fiercely political statement. To many of today's youth it is as objectionable for people to be banned from wearing the hijab as it is to force them to wear it – yet history is littered with examples of women being subject to both of these restrictions.

The tradition of women wearing veils has had a place in the Jewish, Christian and Muslim religions for hundreds of years, but the origin of women wearing veils lies before these religions came into being. Women were reserving some areas of their lives and bodies – most particularly the hair, sometimes referred to as a woman's crowning glory, for the private world. Recent research suggests that in ancient Mesopotamia, Persia and Greece, the veil symbolised respectability and status. Women veiled routinely in ancient Greece to go into public spaces, where they were otherwise unprotected, and wished to avoid encountering unwelcome sexual attention. In medieval Europe many women wore veils covering their hair and also their chins, a practice that was replaced by wearing hoods in the Tudor period. Queen Isabeau of Bavaria was depicted wearing a veil as Queen of France in the later fourteenth century. Christian nuns also wore veils to suggest their modesty and piety, an illusion that was not always upheld. Brides in many wedding ceremonies have been veiled to symbolise their virginity and modesty.

Convents in the late medieval period generally focused on catering for the needs of the local community, a practice that has continued since; in the middle of the twentieth century, nuns still wore veils as they provided social care or educated girls. Karen Armstrong, who was for nine years a Catholic nun in North London in the 1960s, recalled in 2006:

> I spent seven years of my girlhood heavily veiled ... We wore voluminous black robes, large rosaries and crucifixes, and an elaborate headdress: you could see a small slice of my face from the front, but from the side I was entirely shielded from view. We must have looked very odd indeed, walking dourly through the colourful carnival of London during the swinging 60s, but nobody ever asked us to exchange our habits for more conventional attire ... I found my habit liberating: for seven years I never had to give a thought to my clothes, make-up and hair – all the rubbish that clutters the minds of the most liberated women.

The freedom offered by wearing a veil is echoed by Fatima Khan, a 20-year-old social sciences student in the USA, who argues: 'By covering my body, I am able to limit how much someone can objectify me and instead have the power to only be judged for my intellect, abilities and personality rather than simply my appearance.'

19-year-old Egyptian volleyball player Doaa Elghobashy wore ankle-length trousers and a long-sleeved T-shirt and hijab in a match against Germany; unusual garb, but why was it that all the media attention focused on her hijab?

Unlike Karen Armstrong, women in the twentieth and twenty-first centuries in many countries do face pressure to exchange their hijab for other attire. In Turkey wearing a hijab or headscarf was banned for those who worked in public service in 1978; this was extended to those in educational institutions in 1982 but reversed in 1984 and reintroduced in 1987, staying in place until 2013. Countries that insist on girls attending school bare-headed can lead to

girls being kept away from school and deprived of an education. In state-subsidised schools in Cameroon, adherence to the constitutional law has resulted in some girls taking off their hijab for school or attending private Islamic schools, often built with money from Saudi Arabian-based NGOs.

The obsessive preoccupation with women's headgear is unlikely to abate in the difficult climate of twenty-first-century political culture, when still it appears women are not allowed to make decisions about how they dress. Dalia Mogahed, director of research at the Institute for Social Policy, argues that a 'woman in a hijab is only covering her body and hair, not her voice or intellect ... To say that [a] hijab oppresses women is to say that the source of a woman's power, but not a man's, is her body, not her mind.'

The White Wednesday protest in Iran and the women adopting the hijab in response to President Trump in the USA suggest that women can use the preoccupation with the headdress in interesting political ways.

40 | Joanne Stoker Red Shoes
The Politics of Footwear

MAGGIE ANDREWS

These high-heeled red shoes epitomise the bold colours, stylistic designs and 'femininity' of the young British London-based shoe designer Joanne Stoker, who has explained: 'I love constructing shoes, watching all the components come together ... To create beautiful and conceptual shoes, stepping out to astound and delight.'

After an MA in footwear at the London College of Fashion and winning the First Into Fashion Award and the Footwear Friends Award, sponsored by the British Footwear Association, she was mentored at Jimmy Choo, the London-based fashion designer of high-end expensive shoes which often carry a price tag of around £1,000. Joanne Stoker established her own label in 2010 making hand-made shoes in London, now stocked in the upmarket London department store Selfridges.

Shoes are both functional and symbolic, portraying identity and status. Designer footwear like Stoker's red shoes merge art and consumerism, objects of female desire which articulate women's sexuality. Women's yearning to possess shoes has been condemned, as with the discovery that Imelda Marcos, wife of the president of the Philippines, owned over 1,000 pairs of shoes in the 1980s when many in the country lived in abject poverty. However, a decade later Carrie's obsession with designer shoes in the TV series *Sex and the City* (1998–2004) was hailed as an acknowledgement that feminism and femininity can be combined, and that women can have it all.

Historically fictional portrayals of women hankering after the pleasures of footwear have been less sympathetic. Hans Christian Andersen's story *The Red Shoes* (1848), like most fairy tales, punishes a girl for transgressing, desiring red shoes which made her want to dance and abandon responsibility, duty and religion. The story inspired other artistic products including Kate Bush's album *Red Shoes* (1992) where red shoes provided a subversive space where women artists could reclaim situations once controlled. Red shoes rarely have that radical potential. The magical powers of Dorothy's sparkling red shoes in the film *The Wizard of Oz* (1939) serve to transport her home. The film *Red Shoes* (1948) starred Moira Shearer as Vicky Page, a young ballerina torn by the choice she was forced to make between her art and romance. After giving up dancing to marry, she returns to the ballet, putting on her red shoes to dance again. Vicky's attempt to prioritise her creativity ends in tragedy when she is run over by a train, although there is ambivalence about whether her death is suicide or she was possessed by the red shoes.

Red dancing shoes can symbolise women's transgression, passion, movement and a rejection of domesticity, or feminine dependence and how women are restrained

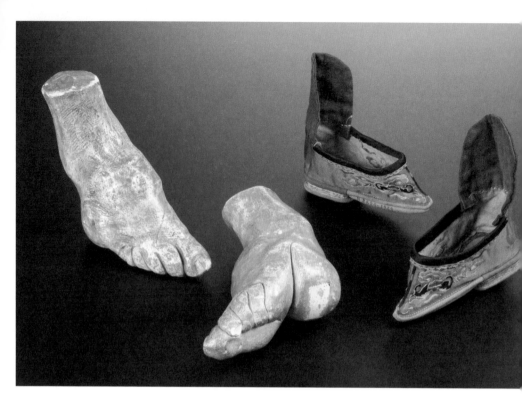

by being regarded as a sexual icon. A Chinese legend suggests that in the eleventh century the father of Empress Taki, who was born with deformed feet, announced that only small feet were truly feminine and desirable. The practice which developed, of applying tight binding to young girls' feet, caused intense pain and prevented foot growth and functionality. Women with bound feet were unable to work; they were playthings who were status symbols for their husbands or families. It has been estimated that in the nineteenth century, perhaps 40–50 per cent of Chinese women had bound feet, but the practice was forbidden for women in Manchu who instead wore platform shoes with tapering soles to mimic the appearance of bound feet.

Why are shoes such objects of female desire and articulations of women's sexuality?

Other countries also revered small feet; in the fairy tale *Cinderella* her ability to fit her small dainty feet into a glass slipper identifies her as a suitable wife for the prince. European travellers to Peru also noted the sensual appeal of small women's feet which were associated with virtue in the eighteenth century. Modern high heels, so revered as the height of femininity and fashion equivalent, can be seen in a similar light as they make walking or work difficult. Even shoe designer Joanne Stoker noted that as she is constantly on her feet all day, her 'feet have got used to flats!' Research indicates that wearing high heels can be linked to a range of medical conditions including bunions, osteoarthritis and tendon injuries; little wonder that some have

Imelda Marcos left behind more than 1,220 pairs of shoes when she and her husband, President Ferdinand Marcos, left the Philippines during the 1986 uprising.

described high heels as comparable to the restrictive corsets women wore in the nineteenth century. Yet many women, such as airline cabin crew or receptionists, are expected to wear high heels for work.

When Nicola Thorp arrived at a City of London accounting firm in 2015 to undertake a temporary receptionist role, wearing chic but sensible black flat shoes, her supervisor insisted she change them to ones with heels between 5cm and 10cm high. She refused, and pointed out that male colleagues were not required to conform to the same dress code; she was consequently sent home without pay. As she explained to BBC Radio London: 'I was expected to do a nine-hour shift on my feet escorting clients to meeting rooms. I said "I just won't be able to do that in heels".'

Dozens of professional women posted pictures of themselves wearing flat shoes to work to express their support and Nicola Thorp started a petition to make it illegal for a company to require women to wear high heels at work, which gained over 150,000 signatures, leading to a parliamentary debate. An inquiry overseen by two parliamentary committees received hundreds of complaints from women whose employers had required them to dye their hair blonde, wear revealing outfits, or constantly reapply make-up. All served to justify Nicola Thorp's observations that 'I was a bit scared about speaking up about it in case there was a negative backlash … But I realised I needed to put a voice to this as it is a much bigger issue.'

41 | The Corset
Clothing for Seduction or Subjugation

SALLIE MCNAMARA

The first recorded image of the corset was found in excavations at the Palace of Knossos, Crete, and dates from around 2000 BCE. While it is shown together with a crinoline as outerwear on the figure of the Cretan snake goddess, nothing is known of its actual function.

From these seemingly innocuous beginnings, in its long history the corset has garnered controversy: for some its links to tight lacing, either voluntary or enforced, symbolise female oppression, torture and fetishism, which causes ill health. For others it is a powerful representation of women's independence and ownership of their sexuality. Its development combines interlocking histories of changing ideas of femininity and the ideal female form, of class, advances in technologies, product development, and global trade.

The corset was not considered underwear until the fifteenth century. It was adopted by Catherine de Medici (1519–89), wife of Henry II of France, who apparently possessed an iron corset, although it may have been worn for orthopaedic purposes. For the Victorians and Edwardians the corset connoted respectability as it contained and enclosed the body. The very stiff corset indicated an inability to work, and was worn by both middle- and upper-class women, while working-class women wore the looser 'jumps' which allowed for freedom of movement, enabling them to work. The Victorians are synonymous with the fashion for tight lacing, a practice condemned by doctors for causing ill health, and satirised by writers and cartoonists. The Industrial Revolution played an interesting role here: the invention of the metal eyelet in 1823 meant corsets could be tightly laced without the material tearing, while in 1839 Frenchman Jean Werly patented the machine-made woven corset, after which they became more widely available.

Has the corset become a playful clothing item, worn by women taking control of and relishing their own sexuality?

The extreme tight-lacing corset was, and is, seen as an early example of fetish-wear; the smallest waists in the period measured just 16in. However, regardless of the fashion for tight lacing, few women went to that extreme. From the 1850s to the 1890s dress reformists, such as the Rational Dress Society in both the UK and USA, highlighted the perils of tight lacing, and campaigned for the reform of women's undergarments; from the 1870s, the Pre-Raphaelite art movement also favoured freer, unrestricted clothing. Nevertheless, the respectability conferred by wearing corsets was utilised and defended by Emmeline Pankhurst when fighting for female

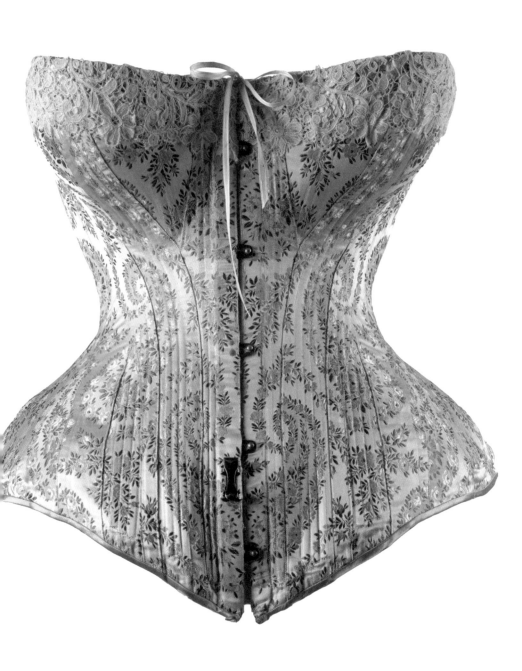

The first National Corset Week took place in 1952; garments for evening were glamorised with names such as Merry Widow, Pink Champagne and Charade.

emancipation, as the upright and contained figure gave propriety to militant suffragettes, and suggested their respectability to a conservatively minded public. Although representing an idealised Victorian and Edwardian femininity, the corset did not necessarily cross cultures. It was worn by women in the colonised British Empire, including India and Africa, but it was resisted by other non-European women, and caricatured elsewhere, notably in Japanese magazines in the 1880s. The popularity of the corset owes much to fashion and changing ideals of female body shapes, and also to politics and ideas of freedom. It had all but disappeared in the period between the French Revolution and the 1820s when looser, more fluid dress styles prevailed. The hourglass corset evolved around 1830, and remained dominant until 1900 when replaced by the 'straight-back' or S-curve. As women's lives changed in the early twentieth century, especially after the First World War, there was a decline in the corset's popularity. Attitudes towards the female body changed, with women's rising participation in sport and gymnastics. From around 1907, the fashionable figure wore a lighter, rubber girdle – lighter boning and steel had replaced whalebone in the nineteenth century – influenced by designer Paul Poiret's neo-classical designs. The androgynous female form dominated the 1920s.

Interest in corsets was revived after the Second World War when Christian Dior's New Look signalled a return to the hourglass figure, with a small waist and high bust, and subsequently the more voluptuous figure epitomised by Marilyn Monroe in the 1950s. The fashion was short lived, though; corsetry using lighter fabrics such as Lycra, elastic net, roll-ons and roll-on panties appealed to younger women. In the 1980s the lightweight plastic corset popularised by Vivienne Westwood again attracted a younger market, and was worn with ironic awareness of its different meanings and links to fetishism.

The corset is a paradoxical garment with as many uses and meanings as there are types – the corset, basque, bustier, waspie, corselette. It can be worn to support and control the figure, as part of or under a wedding dress, for erotic/sexual purposes, or as a fetish item. The pointed-breast corsets designed by Jean-Paul Gaultier and worn by Madonna on her Blonde Ambition tour (1990–91) redrew the garment as postmodern irony and a statement about female sexuality. In recent years the corset has been reworked by fashion designers and worn with a crinoline on the catwalk, and adopted as attire for hen parties. There is the tightly laced 'waist trainer', a slimming accessory said to have been utilised by reality television stars, while in contemporary fashion, the corset-style fabric belt is sometimes worn as outerwear. Debates will no doubt continue as to whether the latter shows women taking control of their sexuality or whether it is merely a fashionable moment within a patriarchal culture.

42 | Queen Victoria's White Wedding Dress

The Evolution of Expensive Weddings

MAGGIE ANDREWS

Queen Victoria wore a white wedding dress when she married Prince Albert in the Chapel Royal at St James's Palace on 10 February 1840. It was not the first white wedding dress; both before and after this date wedding dresses across the world have come in a range of styles and colours. The choices of fabric, style and colour for the clothes to be worn at the occasion of a woman's change from single to married status are both distinctive and shaped by tradition. They convey the bride's, or often her family's, sense of identity.

The clothes and adornments women wear for their nuptials indicate both the distinctiveness of communities and cultures that a bride is a part of, and her own personal choices. Across the world marriages are increasingly a romantic as well as a legal event and hence wedding traditions are constantly evolving and developing; but the white dress, of which Victoria's is the archetype, continues to be a popular choice. Victoria's wedding dress received considerable publicity in nineteenth-century Britain and across the Empire as she wore it in various guises for subsequent social occasions. She posed for photographs and portraits in the dress for many years after the ceremony, sometimes with Prince Albert. Although white has come to be seen as a symbol of the bride's purity in the wake of Victoria's dress, this was not the case when she married or before. Rather, white fabric had long symbolised wealth and social position, because without washing machines and biological detergents the work required to maintain clothing's whiteness relied upon the labour of servants. Victoria's cousin Princess Charlotte, who was expected to become queen, had also worn a white wedding dress, with metallic threads running through it, when she was married earlier in the century. Her marriage ended when she tragically died during childbirth in 1817.

> Why, with so many marriages ending in divorce, is so much money and effort invested in weddings?

Victoria's decision to use white silk, and to include the promise 'to obey' in the ceremony, suggested that although she was a queen she was also a romantically involved woman entering marriage just as her subjects did. Her identification with and leadership of the nation was also embodied by the choices made about the dress itself, which was made by a British woman, Mary Bettans, from silk spun at Spitalfields. William Dyce, the head of what was then known as the Government School of Design and subsequently became the Royal School of Art, designed the

dress which was covered in Honiton lace. Industrialisation was destroying the British lace industry and leading to poverty and unemployment so the commission to create the lace was welcomed by the village of Beer in Devon. By wearing Honiton lace Victoria was conveying her patriotic support for the British lace industry and providing them with some very useful product promotion. Many in the growing middle classes also chose to wear white wedding dresses, emulating Victoria's and Albert's public personas as the archetypal bourgeois family. Women of more modest means, however, had their white dress dyed a more practical colour after the wedding day to ensure it was sensible for everyday use. Even during the clothes rationing of the 1940s British women went to great lengths to be married in white, hiring and borrowing dresses, making them out of all sorts of fabric including parachute silk once the war was over.

There was no such enthusiasm in the USA for the white wedding dress of a British royal in the nineteenth century, but in time things changed and by the middle of the twentieth century white weddings were popular. Indeed, they gained some currency among communities of middle-class African-Americans in the years following the

Second World War. In the USA, weddings have a particular poignancy for African-Americans because the enslaved population were legally prohibited from marriage in pre-Civil War America. Weddings now represent a celebration of an individual's ability to exercise their own choices in their personal life including their right to marry, and also of communities affirming their citizenship and place in the nation. Furthermore, the conspicuous consumption involved in white weddings became a way of confirming the community's commitment to the American dream.

Queen Victoria described the events of her wedding day in her diary with little direct reference to her dress, although she recalled that:

> When I arrived at St James's I went into the dressing-room whereby 12 young Train-bearers were, dressed all in white with white roses, which had a beautiful effect. Here I waited a little till dearest Albert's Procession had moved into the chapel. I then went with my Train-bearers and ladies into the Throne room where the Procession formed.

Queen Victoria, like many brides, was attended and supported by other women on her wedding day; in her case the women were ladies and train-bearers. In traditional Moroccan weddings, the night before the ceremony the bride sits surrounded by a circle of women who offer protection and support, while one Athenian tradition involves the bride's female relatives making up the marital bed with hand-embroidered linens made specially for the occasion. In many countries, women help prepare, select or make wedding dresses. The role of the bridesmaids before the ceremony and the preparations of the bride's hair and make-up, painting her nails or hands with henna, are all part of women's support and care of the bride which takes place across many cultures.

In contemporary Western cultures, weddings are now often also highly commodified events. Indeed, it was in the wake of Victoria's wedding at the end of the nineteenth century that the introduction of special services by photographers, florists, caterers and dressmakers were offered, and the very first wedding fair was held in 1881. The money spent on weddings has grown ever since, and the cost of an average British wedding is now over £20,000; in the USA the figure is well over $30,000. Concerns about the cost of her dress would not have bothered Queen Victoria, but her dress is an example of the now dominant bridal fashion for dresses that are distinct from everyday wear, and the trend for the bride to have what is supposed to be a once-in-a-lifetime chance to be a star for a day. This tradition has expanded and developed as marriage itself has changed, so websites now advertise 'super cute lesbian wedding ideas', as it is pointed out that 'two brides are better than one'.

43 | Tsarina Alexandra Romanov's Emerald and Diamond Tiara

Jewellery as a Portable Nest Egg in Difficult Times

SCOTT EELES

The emerald and diamond tiara worn by the last Empress of Russia, Tsarina Alexandra Feodorovna (1872–1918), was made by two of the most skilled European jewellers of the time, Bolin and Fabergé, in 1900. Adorned with stones mined in South Africa, including a eye-catching 23-carat emerald, it was worn for formal occasions or parties.

Alexandra purchased the tiara herself, but most of her jewellery was accumulated through gifts, often from her husband, the last Emperor of Russia, Tsar Nicholas II Aleksandrovich (1868–1918). Her assistant, Madame Gheringer, noted that for Christmas of 1903 she received a star of white enamel with a heart in the middle of it, from the Duke of Hesse, and a Stern bracelet of nine sapphires with small diamonds from Empress Maria Fyodorovna. Alexandra amassed the largest personal jewel collection in the world (worth over $50 million in 1917 currency) which she kept in a private vault in her bedroom at the Alexander Palace.

Tsar Nicholas was an absolute monarch who could change Russian laws as he wished. Indeed in 1895 he described the desire of the representatives of other groups for a consultative role in government as 'senseless dreams'. He involved his wife in many meetings of diplomatic or military importance and she discussed ending the Russo-Japanese war with both First Minister Sergei Witte and her husband. However, during the 1905 revolution, the Tsarina was blamed for not convincing her husband to stay in the palace and listen to the demands of his critics. By the time the First World War broke out the liberal press, run by the emerging bourgeois classes in St Petersburg, had already mired the image of the Tsarina. The enigmatic and despised figure of Rasputin, a monk, had made his way into a position of dangerous influence in the Russian court after 'healing' the Tsarina's son Alexei, who suffered from haemophilia. Rasputin's position over the Tsar and the Tsarina was often described as 'witchcraft' corrupting the nation. The press and the Duma, the elected body of representatives for Russia, portrayed the Tsarina as an enemy of the people for allowing this to happen.

Women often wear jewellery to convey their own and their husband's status; jewellery can also be an investment or insurance, an asset to be sold or pawned if times are hard. When the political situation in Russia deteriorated and the privileged lives of the Tsar and Tsarina became increasingly precarious, Alexandra responded by ensuring much of her private wealth was kept as easily portable jewels. The 1917 Russian Revolution led to the abdication of the Tsar and finally to the infamous execution of the Tsar, Tsarina and their five children by the Bolsheviks in

1918. The emerald and diamond tiara was one of the items the Tsarina took with her when she was arrested, but it was seized by Bolshevik soldiers and lost among the tumultuous events that followed. Other aristocratic families were more successful in escaping Russia, with jewels stuffed in hems of skirts or dresses, a container of talcum powder, or beneath blankets in baby's prams. Jewels were intended to fund their new lives in exile. Olga Schilovsky, a Russian émigré, recalled her teddy bear being used to hide diamonds that her mother had been given by the Tsarina.

The social gulf between these wealthy women buying jewellery and ordinary women struggling to survive was immense. Rural peasant women worked with men, ploughing, growing vegetables, and making milk into butter and cheese alongside their domestic chores and childbearing. The situation for women in textile industries, working sometimes sixteen hours a day in sweatshops, was severe. Crude weaving machines cut and shredded hands, sometimes dismembering them so the workers lost their livelihoods. Women were reputedly smothering their children because there was not enough bread to feed them. On 8 March 1917 a demonstration of textile workers took place in the Russian capital Petrograd which spread across the city, involving tens of thousands of women, shouting for bread and down with the Tsar. Some carried banners demanding the Tsarist government 'feed the children of the defenders of the motherland'. Aleksandra Rodionova, a 22-year-old tram conductress, later recalled participating in the demonstration:

> Is jewellery often merely a status symbol for women and the men to whom they are married?

> The streets were full of people. The trams weren't running, cars lay across the tracks. I did not know then, I did not understand was happening. I yelled along with everyone ... I felt that all of life was falling apart, and I rejoiced in it.

These demonstrations of ordinary working women are often seen as the catalyst for the 1917 revolution and have been celebrated by socialists and communist countries since. In 1975, 8 March was adopted as International Women's Day by the United Nations.

44 | Lady Curzon's Peacock Dress
Clothes and Imperial Identity

JANIS LOMAS

At the end of 1902 and the beginning of 1903 the Delhi Durbar, or Court of Delhi, took place. It was a huge celebration to mark the coming to the throne of Edward VII, now crowned King of the United Kingdom and the British Dominions and Emperor of India.

One of the main events of the Durbar was the Coronation Ball held on New Year's Day 1903. As Viceroy of India, Lord Curzon was the emperor's deputy in India, ruling on the king's behalf. Lord Curzon's wife Mary was the vicereine representing Alexandra, Queen of Great Britain and Empress of India.

The entire Durbar was personally supervised by Lord Curzon with military precision and no expense was spared to ensure that it was on a scale never seen before. It was a brilliant spectacle and designed as an affirmation to the world of the permanency and legitimacy of British rule. From the arrival of the viceroy and vicereine on top of the largest elephant in the Indian sub-continent, the Durbar was a full programme of firework displays, garden parties, polo matches, tiger hunts, dances, military parades and band concerts with the Coronation Ball as its centrepiece. Some 4,000 guests were invited to the ball, which was held in the Red Fort. The Red Fort was the traditional home of Mughal rule and the dress that Lady Curzon wore to the event was more than mere clothing; it was designed to show India and the rest of the world that the British Raj was the legitimate successor to the Mughal throne. This demonstration of British power and grandeur recreated the pageantry of the ancient rulers of India but now sought to subordinate that older tradition to validate colonial power.

The dress that Lady Curzon wore was made in Paris by the House of Worth from cloth of gold with metal thread hand-woven in India by Indian craftsmen. The design was of overlapping peacock feathers of different sizes with copper, silver and gold coloured threads and in the centre of each of the feather designs was an iridescent emerald and blue scarab beetle wing that shone, and which many thought to be real emeralds. The bodice was lace with diamante strings threaded through and the hem was of glittery roses. Weighing over 10lb, the dress shimmered and sparkled in the electric light, newly installed for the occasion. Mary Curzon was very beautiful, almost 6ft tall with a spectacular figure, and it was reported that there was an audible gasp as she entered the room. A guest at the ball remarked: 'You cannot conceive what a dream she looked.' The dress created a sensation that was reported all over the world.

Mary's world was one in which she was always on show; she was there to be a symbol of power, pomp and display. Her dress was designed to accentuate this and signify Britain's greatness and that India was 'the jewel in the crown' of the British Empire. The Red Fort, where the ball was held, had originally housed the Peacock Throne made for Shah Jahan in the seventeenth century; in wearing the peacock dress the vicereine was symbolically referencing the replacement of the throne of the old rulers with the Raj and highlighting the importance the peacock held in both the Hindu and Islamic traditions. In using Indian craftsmen to weave the dress and a Parisian couturier to make the garment she attempted to marry together Eastern and Western traditions.

However, such a show of conspicuous wealth also highlighted the massive gulf between the world of the Raj and the vast majority of the population of India. The spiralling costs of the Durbar were considered inappropriate, especially as parts of the country were experiencing severe famine at the time. Rumours about the massive costs of the celebrations fuelled discontent, with estimates in some newspapers reaching as high as £5 million. The Coronation Durbar was dubbed the Curzonization Durbar as it was felt that it was more about the Curzons' own vanity and pomposity than the coronation of the emperor. Curzon later published accounts that showed that the actual net cost was only around £180,000, but even so, Curzon had to ask his rich American father-in-law to shoulder some of the cost. Curzon stated that the Durbar 'would proclaim to the world the greatness of the Empire of which India was an integral part'.

Has women's quiet but important role in sustaining colonial rule in countries such as India been overlooked?

For Lord and Lady Curzon the Delhi Durbar was the highlight of their time in India, as afterwards things began to go wrong for both the viceroy and his wife. Lord Curzon disagreed with Lord Kitchener, the military commander of India, over which of them had overall control of the ruling council, a fight Curzon lost. After this humiliation he resigned, returned to England and took little part in public life for the next ten years. Mary Curzon returned to England to await the birth of her third child, which was a third daughter, to the great disappointment of them both, as they desperately needed a male heir to the Kedleston estate. Soon afterwards Mary's health began to fail; she died three years after the Durbar, aged only 36. The permanency of British rule in India that the dress was meant to signify also proved illusionary. Within a few decades, on 15 August 1947, British India was no more and two new sovereign countries, India and Pakistan, finally achieved independence, amid chaos and bloodshed, bringing to an end almost 200 years of British colonial rule.

45 | Second World War Garden String Hat

Women's Ingenuity in the Face of Adversity

ELSPETH KING

This crocheted hat made of garden string epitomises the confluence of a 'beauty as duty' ethos and the desire for women to keep up appearances in an era of extreme shortages, thrift, creativity and make-do-and-mend in the Second World War in Britain.

The outbreak of hostilities had brought an almost immediate introduction of rationing, on 1 January 1940. Initially for food, it was extended to clothes the following year. Each item of clothing was given a points value and originally every person was allocated 66 coupons, which with careful use were considered sufficient to buy one complete outfit a year. This did not seem troublesome for most men. For women, trying to comply with the government's 'beauty as duty' ethos, which required them to keep up their appearance at all costs, to maintain the morale of servicemen, clothing rationing presented a minor crisis. In those worrying times hats were used as symbols of normality as well as respectability, despite the 1942 edict by the Archbishop of Canterbury that wearing them should no longer be thought of as compulsory for church. While some of the formality of dress did disappear, or was suspended for the duration of the conflict, for many the traditional trinity of hat, gloves and handbag did not. The challenges to maintaining this were significant, especially with the ever-fluctuating number of coupons, queues and shortages. New ways of maintaining appearances had to be found.

Imaginative new ways of fashioning and creating hats using materials hitherto untapped for clothing and fashion were approached with enthusiasm. Bottle tops, film spools and corks were used for jewellery while hats were imaginatively fashioned or 're-confectioned' (code for altered and decorated) from unusual materials including garden string, which in a 'grow your own' culture was readily available and importantly not rationed. Magazines were full of articles and plans on how to make clothes last longer or make new ones from existing clothes and readily available un-rationed items. One edition of *Good Housekeeping* magazine featured instructions on how to make six different crocheted hats, while department stores' dressmaking and alteration services offered to work 'miracles on wilting hats' to make them serviceable for longer. People became experts at 'primping' – adding artificial flowers and decorations to rejuvenate a hat. For those with no idea how to begin, classes were available and sewing machines could be accessed at sewing clubs. There are numerous references to hats in the diaries and accounts of the war. Molly Rich, a vicar's wife from London, recalled deciding to wear a turban (a popular replacement for traditional hats) when her hat 'died on [her] head during

a thunderstorm'. A 1941 edition of *Home Notes* magazine carried instructions on how to make a knitted turban. Military styles were all the rage, reflecting the hats being worn by the armed forces, and berets (often homemade) became particularly popular. One woman recalled making berets from an old coat and using a dinner and side plates as templates.

The make-do-and-mend culture was not unique to Britain. All countries involved in the war experienced shortages and rationing and many unique fashion statements emerged from this period of austerity and uncertainty. The United States did not experience clothes rationing in the same way as Britain. However, shoes for civilians were limited to three pairs a year; limitation orders placed an onus on

In 1942 the Archbishop of Canterbury issued an edict that wearing hats should no longer be thought of as compulsory for church.

manufacturers to reduce trimmings. No epaulets on coats, and no waistbands over three inches wide were allowed. As in Britain, millinery was not limited or rationed so many women used hats as a means of continuing to express their individuality, accessorising them with hatpins or decorations containing patriotic messages. In the USA, as in Britain, make-do-and-mend became the order of the day. Under Nazi occupation, France adopted a similar rationing system to Britain although most couture houses kept going as French women were reluctant to surrender their stylish reputation. There were limitations on fabric use and most people became adept at making do. 'La robe a mille morceaux' or the 'dress of a million pieces', pieced together from remnants, became popular. The ubiquitous turbans also made their appearance as popular headgear with the almost mandatory decorations of artificial flowers or even fruit. France even had a 'national suit' for men, bought by exchanging some coupons and also two old suits.

At the start of the war many German clothing companies were under Jewish ownership and were therefore shut down or taken into official ownership. Clothes rationing began in November 1939 and like Britain the points fluctuated according to the fortunes of war with a chronic shortage from 1943 onwards. Women were asked to 'aus alt mach neu' or 'from old make new' as make-do-and-mend became essential. There was copious restyling of old clothes and making clothes warmer against harsh German winters. One woman even reworked her dead husband's uniform jacket and made it into a winter coat complete with flowers covering the bullet holes. Models dressed in the Dirndl (the national dress) often featured on magazine covers.

Perhaps women's skills of 'making do' and ingenuity in the face of adversity are undervalued?

For the Japanese the war began in 1937 but it was not until 1942 that shortages really began to bite and official rationing of food and clothing began. Coupons were issued with 100 a year for city residents and eighty a year for country dwellers, but clothes also became almost impossible to find as nearly all textile production was given over to war needs. The government thought that Japanese women had many more clothes than American women and urged women to make do with what they had. Sufu, a poor-quality rayon, became the only material available for civilian use. Make-do-and-mend articles also appeared in Japanese magazines, including one on how to turn a kimono into trousers.

During the conflict, across the world, creativity and make-do-and-mend became an essential part of the war effort. For some it was a means of keeping spirits up and expressing individuality in the harshest of times, while for others it became a matter of survival – the garden string hat is a symbol of this determination and ingenuity.

46 | Mary Quant Cape

1960s Fashion, Freedom and Fun

LESLEY SPIERS

The cape, as an item of clothing, has a long history in fashion and has been worn by both women and men. They were common in medieval Europe, often decorated and highly stylised, or adapted and added to overcoats such as the Ulster coat worn by men in the Victorian period. However, this was an item also largely associated with women and was represented by various designs and lengths and accessorised according to the fashion of any given period.

The 'Alligator' cape, designed and made by Mary Quant, characterises Quant's design and style – often referred to as the 'London Look' – and her commitment to provide clothing that was more than just practical garments.

Mary Quant's cape incorporated a look based on a very simple shape allowing freedom of movement with panache and flair. This unpretentious coat embodied the key features of the new fashion that was championed and constructed by Mary Quant and other contemporary designers of this time. Bold colours, dramatic patterns and new blended fabrics not only symbolised a rebellious break from the older generations' sense of style and formality but provided young women with clothes that reflected the new social trends of the decade, ones which would allow women to fashion and display their bodies in their way. The miniskirt became an icon that was synonymous with freedom, and a new form of female sexuality and femininity.

The 1950s may have invented or introduced the concept of the 'teenager' in Western societies but the 1960s developed a new market designed with the teenager in mind, developing the key popular cultural influences of the time, including fashion. Against the backdrop of a decade that epitomised significant social, cultural and political upheaval new forms of expression, freedom and celebration were born. This new liberty for young women was captured most vividly in the fashion of the designer and icon, Mary Quant.

Born in London in 1934, the daughter of two teachers, Mary Quant was passionate about sewing and making clothes and later recalled: 'I think I always knew that what I wanted to do most of all was to make clothes ... clothes that would be fun to wear.' This early sentiment was reflected in the kinds of fashion and clothes that Quant designed and produced. Inspired by youth movements of the time, the clothes Mary Quant designed reflected a shift in fashion and social attitudes to sex, identity and outlook.

Following a brief time at Goldsmith's College of Art in London, Quant, together with her partner and future husband Alexander Plunket-Greene, and friend Archie

McNair, opened her first shop, Bazaar, on the King's Road, London, where she sold the highly fashionable ready-to-wear clothes she produced. Bazaar introduced not just a new style of clothing but a new style of shopping. The boutique experience Quant created took youth as a key source of inspiration. She later explained: 'I just knew that I wanted to concentrate on finding the right clothes for the young to wear and the right accessories to go with them.' The edgy décor of the shops and the loud pop music, including the Beatles and the Kinks, defined boutiques as places girls

Mary Quant became one of the key fashion gurus and icons of the 1960s and 1970s.

could hang out. Mary Quant's Bazaar was soon surrounded by other boutiques on the King's Road, Carnaby Street and Kensington High Street where Biba opened in 1964 selling soft retro clothing.

Fashion styles have, to some degree, always reflected the social, cultural and wider sensibilities of a particular era. Quant's clothing signified 1960s social change, a frenetic desire to move on from post-war austerity to a period of 'never having it so good' combined with the rising women's movement, articulating and demanding rights for women. In this atmosphere women were able to begin to break away from previous social traditions governing behaviour and embrace the optimistic fervour of the time. A growth in jobs, improvements in pay and better access to contraception afforded young women more independence and choice, which they exercised in the field of fashion. Increased disposable income encouraged women to cultivate their own style and break with the past. Designers of the time, including Mary Quant, responded to this in kind by constructing dramatic and experimental fashion that came to epitomise this period and the mood of the 1960s.

Is fashion one of the key ways in which young girls now express their identity?

While haute couture and Paris fashion continued to remain the province of those with money, new fabrics, designs and new mass production techniques helped to promote a particular style that was almost classless, and came to characterise the fashion and identity of youth and swinging London. Mary Quant became one of the key fashion gurus and icons of the 1960s and 1970s. She subsequently built on this reputation, enabling her to remain at the top of her game into the twenty-first century. For young women in the Western world, the fashion of Mary Quant and her contemporaries marked a turning point; from 1960 onwards young women and teenagers defined their own styles. Never again would youngsters wear purely – or sometimes even remotely – practical garments.

47 | Marilyn Monroe's Subway Dress

Hollywood Stardom

LINDA PIKE

The white dress worn by Marilyn Monroe in *The Seven Year Itch* (1954) has gained iconic status, and was sold for $4.6 million in 2011. In the film's most famous scene Monroe's white pleated halterneck dress, designed by William Travilla, blows up to expose her legs as she stands over a subway ventilation grating; it has been described as one of the most iconic images of the twentieth century.

It featured prominently on the film's publicity posters, with the black background and coloured titles emphasising its whiteness, dwarfing the image of her co-star Tom Ewell who, in the scene in the film, had looked on while whistling appreciatively. Monroe portrays a woman who is confident about her sexuality, yet also innocent and vulnerable, and most importantly a woman who is fun. She portrayed an unthreatening object of desire for men, an inspiration for women, the ultimate Hollywood sex symbol and film star who became the most famous woman of her generation. Her allure continues to fascinate fifty-five years after her death.

Born Norma Jean Mortensen in June 1926 in Hollywood, Los Angeles, Marilyn became a model and later signed to Twentieth Century Fox film studios, where she developed her screen persona and a new name. Marilyn was a tribute to actress Marilyn Miller and Monroe came from her grandfather. She dyed her brown hair blonde and was depicted in her early films such as *All About Eve* (1950) and *Monkey Business* (1952) as a starlet who wiggled. Her forte was undemanding comedy roles, then musical comedies such as *How to Marry a Millionaire* (1953) and – after becoming platinum blonde – *Gentlemen Prefer Blondes* (1953). She developed her unique walk that showed her sensuous physique in *Niagara* (1952), leading Fox studios to reinvent the term Blonde Bombshell. While she excelled in light entertainment, she was determined to develop as an actress, leading director Billy Wilder to cast her in *The Seven Year Itch* (1955).

The film centres around married Tom Ewell, left at home in a hot, New York summer while his wife and son are sent on vacation, and his infatuation with the upstairs tenant, played by Monroe. Her character, identified only as 'The Girl', thus defining age, gender and sexual appeal, is the object of Tom's lust as he feels restricted by his seven years of marriage – the 'itch' of the title. Her first visualisation is her unmistakable silhouette in a doorway and then in a white polka-dot dress, a pattern usually seen on children and associated with purity, thus depicting her innocence and naivety.

Monroe's white dress, which encapsulated the spirit of 1950s America, was sold for $4.6 million in 2011.

Marilyn Monroe was not afraid to flaunt her sex appeal, often wearing dresses two sizes too small that clung to her body, and not wearing undergarments as they would ruin the line of her clothes. Many film roles showcased her extraordinary figure, including the red tight-waisted gown in *Gentlemen Prefer Blondes* and the green corset in *Bus Stop* (1957). She is consequently remembered for the clothes she wore to heighten her sexuality as much as the roles she played. Yet the infamous white dress scene in *The Seven Year Itch* contributed to the unhappiness in Monroe's personal life. She was first married at 16, but at the time of the film had recently married her second husband, baseball star Joe di Maggio, who was eleven years her senior. He believed she would put her career on hold when they married and was jealous of her entertaining US troops in Korea; he considered her displays of her body an insult to him. The press, photographers and 5,000 spectators were invited to the filming of *The Seven Year Itch*, necessitating fourteen takes, with di Maggio furious because Monroe's pubic hair was reported to have been filmed. He was disgusted at how she was public property and they were divorced four weeks later.

Do women feel pressured to conform to the perfect body shapes on display in the media?

Monroe's appearance in the white dress encapsulated the spirit of 1950s America. She conformed to idealised images of sexual desirability, a curvaceous size 16, while the whiteness of her dress and her blondeness was the embodiment of the USA's perception of sexual and racial perfection. The dress epitomised Dior's New Look: a swing-skirted silhouette and tight waist symbolised innocence, with sexuality contained in the full-skirted outline and complemented by white earrings and shoes; she stiffens her body to emphasise her billowing skirt. As Monroe raised her skirt she created sexiness without nudity, indicative of the greater public acknowledgement of female sexuality that followed the publication by Alfred Kinsey of *Sexual Behavior in the Human Female* (1953) but preceded the greater permissiveness of the 1960s and 1970s. Monroe's 1950s film star phenomenon and embodiment of voluptuous sexuality was much copied by Jayne Mansfield, Kathy Kirby and Diana Dors, publicised as Britain's answer to Marilyn Monroe. Her sexualised image was the beginning of a trend which has increased significantly over the last fifty years; worldwide, young girls and women are now feeling pressure to conform to idealised – and often unobtainable – images of beauty and body shape, with which they are bombarded, now not only on film and TV but even more perniciously on social media.

48 | Lesbian Liberation Badge
Lesbian History and Campaigning

MAGGIE ANDREWS

In 1978 Mary Winter, a bus driver who worked for the Burnley Bus Company in Lancashire, wore her 'Lesbian Liberation' badge to work. Badge-wearing was a popular form of political protest at the time; furthermore she claimed it helped to stop unwanted sexual advances from men.

When the bus company ordered her to stop wearing it, she refused and was sacked. Her union did not support her, but with backing from women's groups she started a campaign. The famous actress Vanessa Redgrave, a member of the Workers' Revolutionary Party, called for Winter's reinstatement and held a demonstration outside the bus company offices in Burnley. There were no employment rights for lesbian, gay, bisexual and transsexual (LGBT) people in Britain at the time and the campaign was unsuccessful; Winter had lost her job for wearing to work a badge proudly expressing her sexuality.

The 1970s was the era of political lesbianism, when a number of women in the feminist movement in Britain and the USA argued that lesbianism was an important and correct choice for feminists struggling against sexism. A pamphlet entitled *The Debate Between Heterosexual Feminism and Political Lesbianism* explained: 'We do think, that all feminists can and should be lesbians. Our definition of a political lesbian is a woman-identified woman who does not fuck men. It does not mean compulsory sexual activity with women.'

While the ideas were adopted by only some feminists, pamphlets, badges and campaigns all brought lesbianism out into the open. Lesbianism was only actually illegal in some countries, including Malaysia and Botswana; in almost all countries it was, as in Britain, hidden, surrounded by disapproval and shame and firmly in the closet.

Lesbian history has played an important role in bringing women's same-sex relationships out of the closet and challenging prejudice, by recovering the narratives of lesbian women in the past such as Anne Lister, who lived in Shebden Hall in Yorkshire. Conservative in her outlook and politics, anxious to uphold the status her family name enjoyed in the locality and concerned about her reputation, she felt 'an oddity', lonely and isolated. She poured out her feelings in her diary, written between 1806 and her death in 1840, even writing that 'nature was in an odd freak when she made me'.

Anxious her sexuality would be discovered, she wrote the intimate parts of her diaries in a code of her own making, giving details of her love affairs with women she met. The

diaries were discovered in 1887 by her descendant, John Lister, who cracked the code with the help of his antiquarian friend, Arthur Burrell. The two men found them so shocking that Lister hid them behind a panel in Shebden Hall, where they remained until his death in 1933. In the early 1980s Helena Whitbread began the mammoth task of editing the 4 million tightly packed words of the diaries and in 1988 they were finally published.

Anne Lister and her descendants' concerns were about social disapproval only, for in Britain it has never been illegal for two adult women to have sexual relations with each other in private. In 1921 legislation was proposed to make 'acts of indecency between females' illegal, but it was rejected on the grounds that it was best not to mention lesbianism, as it might give women ideas. In the House of Lords, the Earl of Desart opposed the legislation, saying:

> How many people does one suppose really are so vile, so unbalanced, so neurotic, so decadent as to do this? You may say there are a number of them, but it would be, at most, an extremely small minority, and you are going to tell the whole world that there is such an offence, to bring it to the notice of women who have never heard of it, never thought of it, never dreamed of it.

The bigoted parliamentarian's efforts were to no avail; the trial in late 1928 of Radclyffe Hall's autobiographical novel *The Well of Loneliness* attracted huge publicity. It was prosecuted under the Obscene Publication Act principally because it portrayed lesbian relationships without suggesting they were 'in any way blameworthy'. The trial brought lesbianism much more visibility and numerous supporting letters were sent to Radclyffe Hall.

The LGBT movements that blossomed at the end of the twentieth century challenged and sought to undermine assumptions of heterosexuality. In a number of countries Gay Pride marches, magazines such as *Diva*, music by openly lesbian singers such as KD Lang and films such as *Basic Instinct* (1992) are indications that lesbianism is now at least sometimes portrayed in mainstream popular culture. However, the inclusion of lesbian couples in children's fiction remains rare. The Lesbian Avengers were formed in 1992 in New York City as a direct action group of women, fed up with lesbian invisibility. They have fought homophobic initiatives, such as the banning of the book *Heather Has Two Mummies* by some education authorities, and organised Dyke Marches in Washington and San Francisco.

Would lesbian women suffer discrimination in the workplace if they wore a lesbian liberation badge now?

In the twenty-first century, in almost a quarter of the countries in the world, lesbianism continues to be classified as a criminal act. In Sudan, Iran, Saudi Arabia, Yemen, Mauritania, Afghanistan, Pakistan, Qatar, UAE, parts of Nigeria, parts of Somalia, parts of Syria and parts of Iraq being gay is punishable by death. In some other countries lesbians remain vulnerable to 'rape conversion', have endured sexual violence, are forced into heterosexual marriage or find that the state sanctions violence against them by family or community. In India 78 per cent of lesbians surveyed said they had felt suicidal or had experienced violence in some form. A woman in Cameroon, not allowed to see her children because she had come out, explained:

> My brothers told my children's fathers that I was a lesbian. Immediately a family meeting was convened, and it was decided that I should not bring the children up. I had no say, because I am a lesbian. I still try and contact my children to visit them, but the fathers deny me visits.

Nevertheless, in twenty-first-century Britain there is now more recognition of the rights of same-sex couples. The Civil Partnership Act gave legal recognition to lesbian and gay couples in 2005 and since March 2014 lesbian couples have had the option of entering into a civil marriage. Despite this, lesbian women still face discrimination, although they now have legal redress when this occurs. In 2007, two nurses working in a Cornwall care home were sacked, allegedly for mistreating patients. When their case went to court they received £350,000 compensation as the charge was totally unfounded and their dismissal was deemed solely because of their sexual orientation.

49 | The Silicone Breast Implant
Cosmetic Surgery

MAGGIE ANDREWS

In spring 1962 Timmie Jean Lindsey, a mother of six, became the first woman to undergo breast augmentation surgery, in Houston, Texas. The procedure inserted silicone gel-filled implants into her breasts, taking her from a B to a C cup.

Her operation was only a few years after the launch of both *Playboy* magazine and Barbie dolls, and when film stars Marilyn Monroe and Jane Russell were famous for their hourglass figures. Even many years later, at the age of eighty, Lindsey recalled: 'I thought they came out just perfect ... They felt soft and just like real breasts ... I don't think I got the full results of them until I went out in public and men on the street would whistle at me.'

Women have attempted to increase the size of their breasts, by inserting materials including ivory, glass balls, ground rubber, ox cartilage, and other synthetic substances, since the 1880s. In the 1940s breasts were injected with liquids made of substances which included paraffin and petroleum jellies, silicone fluid and medical-grade silicones. Such procedures, although sometimes satisfactory in the short term, carried side effects, including respiratory distress and pulmonary embolism, and even coma and death. Nevertheless thousands of women underwent breast injections in Las Vegas before it was outlawed in Nevada in 1976. By that point silicone breast implants were becoming more common. In 2014, 1.7 million breast operations were performed across the world; it is the most popular form of cosmetic surgery, particularly in Britain.

While women's body shapes may be influenced by ethnicity, genetics, exercise and metabolism, cultural representations construct ideal body shapes, ones that many women never attain naturally. Prostitutes in Japan at the end of the Second World War had industrial-grade liquid silicone injected into their breasts to increase their size, believing American servicemen preferred women with breasts larger than those of Asian women. Since 1959 the Mattel company's Barbie doll, less than 28cm tall, with adult features, has provided little girls with an unrealistic ideal. Barbie is white with masses of blonde hair, a tiny waist and ample breasts. Despite criticism, several hundred million Barbie dolls have spread this particularly iconic image of idealised American femininity around the world. This is only one version of idealised femininity; the popularity of the model Twiggy in women's magazines of the 1960s and 1970s suggested a more androgynous, slender, prepubescent femininity. Indeed in many countries – such as the USA – breast reductions are more common than breast augmentation. In soft-porn magazines such as *Playboy*, Barbie-style ample breasts remained in mode and silicone implants offered women the possibility of

combining the prepubescent look with ample breasts. More than 20 million cosmetic procedures now take place across the world each year, 90 per cent of which are performed on women, something many find problematic, objecting to the pressure on women in image-conscious industries such as the media to conform to idealised youthful femininity. Botox, which reduces the effects of ageing by injecting a small amount of a potentially lethal toxin into the face to paralyse facial muscles, has also become popular. The actress Julie Christie admitted she had a face-lift to try to keep working in the Hollywood film industry, while the talk show host Joan Rivers joked: 'I had so much plastic surgery, when I die they will donate my body to Tupperware.'

Some feminists draw attention to the aggressive advertising campaigns of the cosmetic surgery industry, the complications that sometimes occur after procedures and the lack of regulation of practitioners who carry out procedures. For others feminism is about self-determination; writing in *The Guardian* newspaper in 2016, Sara Pascoe explained:

> I used to be so outraged with friends and relatives who had enlargement surgery. I believed that when a woman felt her figure was insufficient or incorrect she should be furious with the culture that generated those feelings,

Prostitutes in Japan at the end of the Second World War had industrial-grade liquid silicone injected into their breasts to increase their size.

not change her body ... I've had to learn that women telling other women what to do is not feminism.

Many women assert their right to shape and present their body as they choose, arguing that cosmetic surgery and dentistry and procedures such as botox build self-confidence; however, research indicates that women with breast implants are three to four times more liable to commit suicide than those who have not had such procedures.

There are indications that the uptake of cosmetic surgery may have peaked in Britain; there was a significant downturn in the industry in 2016. This may be a consequence of a shortage of money in austerity Britain, a response to some of the recent health scares over implants, or an indication women feel more comfortable about their bodies, as writer and former model Natasha Devon suggests. The co-founder of Self-Esteem Team, which gives classes to youngsters on mental health and body image, has argued:

Why were 90 per cent of the 20 million cosmetic procedures that took place across the world in 2014 performed on women?

When I was modelling more than 15 years ago, the casting director had a very definite idea of what they wanted ... and invariably that meant conforming to a very narrow beauty ideal ... Now, the models who get booked are the ones with the largest Instagram following. Increasingly, these are people who represent a broader range of shapes, sizes, ages and races. In turn, this representation of diversity has, I believe, contributed to people feeling more comfortable in their own skin.

Part V
Communication, Transportation and Travel

Over the last 200 years women's worlds have expanded immeasurably thanks to new modes of transport, travel and communications systems, as the objects in this section demonstrate. Where historically many women may have been domestically orientated, they have been able to embrace trains, bicycles, cars and planes to shift out of their homes locally, nationally and internationally. Some had a spirit of adventure; the objects examined here give an insight into some pioneering women, explorers, travellers and aviators, such as the pilot Amelia Earhart who flew across oceans, broke records and attempted to circumnavigate the world in the 1930s. Other women have had travel forced upon them; nineteenth-century convict women were sent to Australia by the edict of the law courts. Other women have become refugees due to natural disasters, conflict or, like some homesteaders travelling west, have travelled as a result of a decision made by their spouse.

For many women, travel and communication are a means of escape; reading a magazine or letters from a loved one, or talking to someone on the phone, can feed the imagination and enable women to engage with ideas and people beyond their own horizons. Phones, letters and now the internet reduce isolation and maintain relationships. Those with the resources to do so have used travel and communications to escape the social expectations of their era, choosing to dress or behave in ways unimaginable in the hometowns in which they were born. Perhaps this is why there has been a degree of anxiety and concern over women's new-found freedoms, whether they be cycling, driving or even, as will be discussed below, motorcycling.

The American social reformer, women's rights activist and anti-slavery campaigner Susan Browell Anthony, writing at the end of the nineteenth century, perceived cycling as a hugely emancipatory experience for women, giving them mobility to go to work, to see friends and to engage in politics. It was a train which Emily Wilding Davison famously used to travel from London to Epsom on 4 June 1913 to promote the cause of women's suffrage in Britain, and the Mini which in the 1960s gave many women the chance to buy their first car.

50 | *Woman* Magazine

Articulating Discontent and Maintaining
Feminine Charms

MAGGIE ANDREWS

The magazine *Woman* was first sold in Britain in 1937, quickly becoming popular by modernising women's traditional domestic roles as wives and mothers. Its weekly circulation reached 750,000 in 1939 and 2.5 million in the 1950s and 1960s, when it was the magazine of choice for women from teens upwards.

Like many magazines, its fashion, fiction and features, editorials and advertising addressed women as guardians of home and relationships, as shoppers, and as managers of personal and domestic budgets. Women's magazines date back to *The Ladies Mercury*, published in London in 1693, and *The Lady's Magazine*, published in the USA in 1792. However, it was the inter-war era, with the enfranchisement of women and the increasing professionalisation of housewifery, which produced an explosion of new titles including *Good Housekeeping* (1922), *Women's Own* (1932) and *Women's Journal* (1927). *Woman* was one of over fifty publications on sale in Britain, each providing regular doses of practical advice, reassurance and self-indulgent relaxation but also interrogating what it meant to be a 'woman', inviting readers to navigate the tortuous path between feminism and femininity and exert power in private as wives and mothers or in public through their purse and their vote. *Good Housekeeping* carried articles on 'Catering for the home', and 'Budgeting the income' but magazines also held out fantasies of personal and political change; *Woman's Magazine* explained that 'the responsibility resting upon women as citizens seems to grow week by week, as the possibilities opening up before them are more fully revealed'.

Does the success of women's magazines lie in their ability to acknowledge change and articulate discontent or irritation?

Magazines have directly promoted feminism; *The English Woman's Journal*, first published in March 1858, was located at 19 Langham Place with the Society for Promoting the Employment of Women (SPEW). The group, mostly upper-middle-class women of independent means, who ran the magazine, became known as the Langham Place Group. They aimed to change society to ensure all women were educated and able to earn their own living, reform laws on married woman's status and to secure the vote for women. *The English Women's Journal* printed articles by women struggling to improve the status of women, and the suffrage movement in Britain likewise produced publications such as *Votes for Women* (1907–12), *The Suffragette* (1912–15) and *The Women's Dreadnought* (1914–24) to promote their cause. *The Woman's*

TWOPENCE

Woman
THE NATIONAL HOME WEEKLY

Beginning . . .
LAUGHTER Makes LIFE
Three-part Romance by Kathleen Hewitt

N°1
JUNE 5, 1937

Journal became a semi-official organ of the two major suffrage movements from 1870 to 1931 in the USA.

The majority of mass-circulation women's magazines, while giving some space to women's political issues, focused principally on femininity and domesticity. In the USA, *The Ladies' Home Journal* (1883) gained 1 million subscribers by 1903 when its December issue contained features such as 'The Christmas dining room: how the room and table should look' and 'Making the invalid happy on Christmas Day'. During the Second World War, magazines on both sides of the Atlantic encouraged

The circulation of *Woman* magazine reached 2.5 million in the 1950s and 1960s.

women to maintain their femininity despite shifting roles. *Good Housekeeping* announced in 1939 that it was 'Christmas as usual' in a feature, while a cosmetics advert pointed out: 'Uniform, yes, but not uniformity. The girl in the services kit preserves her own personality, her own charm.' Magazines acknowledged change, and allowed women to articulate discontent or irritation but promoted attention to 'beauty details' and the maintaining of feminine charms.

Glossy post-war publications relying on advertising revenue, and consequently promoting consumerism, became a target of criticism from many women's groups. On 18 March 1970 a group of feminists staged a sit-in at the *Ladies' Home Journal* office in New York to complain about how a magazine staffed predominantly by men defined women's interests. The protestors sought to improve working conditions for the magazine's female employees and broaden *The Ladies' Home Journal*'s content beyond its focus on happy homemakers. Their suggestions for alternative features included 'How to get a divorce', 'How to have an orgasm' and 'How detergents harm our rivers and streams'.

The protest ended with some limited success. In the years that followed, feminists again set up their own magazines; *Ms* magazine was launched by Gloria Steinem in the USA; *Spare Rib* was founded the same year in Britain. Its organising collective explained its aims in the manifesto as 'achieving collective, realistic solutions to women's problems, to involve women in discussing how we can contribute originally and effectively to society and consciously avoid being elitist and alienating'.

The magazine's monthly struggle to challenge, debate and interrogate the exploitation of women lasted twenty-one years before the financial pressures of running an independent feminist magazine finally defeated them in January 1993. By then many mainstream women's magazines were also exploring feminist issues such as rape, single parenthood, abortion and divorce reform. *Cosmopolitan,* under the editorship of Helen Gurley Brown in the late 1960s, targeted single career woman and encouraged them to embrace their sexuality, a proposal which boosted sales so that it is now distributed in over 110 countries in 35 languages.

Marie Claire, when launched in Britain in 1988, sought to colonise the vacant ground offered by *Spare Rib*'s demise. Features on Monica Lewinsky, foot binding in China, and life for a single mum in urban tower blocks, contributed to its self-styled image as 'the only glossy with brains'. In the twenty-first century it has thirty-five different editions so it can be sold in countries as diverse as Japan, India and Poland, offering readers both the pleasures of consumer femininity and a flirtation with fantasies of political engagement and feminism, commensurate with the new visibility of women in positions of power.

51 | Ladies' Carriages in Trains

Keeping Women Safe from Sexual Harassment
at Men's Request

MAGGIE ANDREWS

While many young boys have grown up with the dream of becoming a train driver, women have always had an ambivalent relationship with trains. Early critics of the first locomotives were concerned 'that women's bodies were not designed to go at 50 miles an hour … uteruses would fly out of [their] bodies as they were accelerated to that speed'.

Trains offered women mobility, the chance to travel, visit relatives and find employment further afield, but initially the majority of rail travellers – and until the Second World War, workers – were men. The railway station and the trains were masculine spaces; the Harvey Houses, restaurant-inns dotting the western landscape near the Transcontinental Railroad to California, provided travellers with dinner served by Harvey Girls in the late nineteenth century. These young ladies, who had to be between the ages of 18 and 30 and unmarried, wore long black dresses and white aprons and had the security of a year's contract of employment. They apparently provided a civilising influence on the Wild West.

Train travel involves women and men being in close proximity to one another, in carriages and at stations, which caused some anxiety. A woman living outside Manchester in the nineteenth century noted that 'ladies always avoided the business trains if they possibly could. It was highly embarrassing, a sort of indelicacy, to stand on the platform surrounded by a crowd of males who had to be polite but were obviously not in the mood for feminine society.'

Are women-only spaces in trains a safe, relaxed space or a way of avoiding the problems of sexual harassment?

For some women, such as Irish domestic workers travelling to Britain, stations were both sites of transition, as they embarked on a new life in a foreign country, and places of temptation and immorality known to be frequented by prostitutes. Alternatively, women like Ada Nield Chew climbed aboard numerous trains travelling across the country to campaign for women's suffrage in Britain at the beginning of the twentieth century. Her small daughter frequently accompanied her. By this time, concern over the dangers women travellers might face from male sexual predators had led to the introduction of women-only carriages on many trains, a practice that continues today in some countries.

Ladies' carriages were introduced in Britain in the 1840s, and the rule that a 'carriage is always reserved for ladies if required' operated on all trains on the

South Eastern Railways ten years later. The scandalous story of Colonel Valentine Baker in 1875 fuelled demands for women-only carriages. Baker was an army officer and friend of the Prince of Wales who indecently assaulted a 22-year-old woman, Rebecca Dickinson, in a first-class carriage. Although after 1868 emergency cords were a legal requirement on trains, Dickinson was unable to call for help. Justifiably frightened, she attempted to climb out of the train window. For nearly 5 miles, until the train stopped at the next station, she hung halfway in and halfway out of the carriage window of a moving train. Baker was subsequently arrested and faced a humiliating trial.

The demand for ladies-only carriages, however, came from men. Ladies' carriages began to be associated with elderly spinster ladies and most women preferred to travel in standard accommodation with other people about. Only 248 of 1,060 seats were occupied in the ladies-only carriages on the Great Western in one period in 1888, while 5,141 women travelled in smoking compartments. Some railway companies took the decision to abolish ladies-only carriages, offering instead to provide a ladies-only compartment if requested. In 1977, British Rail gave up the practice of ladies-only carriages or compartments and recent suggestions that they should be re-introduced have been controversial and criticised by women. Laura Bates, founder of the Everyday Sexism Project, pointed out that they convey a 'message that harassment and sexual abuse is inevitable and somehow innate, which is not only hugely insulting to the majority of men but also gives a free pass to perpetrators. It very much plays into victim-blaming, which is already a huge problem.'

Women in countries with a far higher reliance on public transport who find themselves subject to sexual harassment, however, often see things in a different light from white British feminists. Many women cannot wait for men to behave in ways that they ought; they have to deal with the ways men behave now. The overcrowding on stretched public transport, particularly during rush hour, brings men and women who are strangers into close physical proximity with one another – something otherwise reserved for intimate relationships. Trains and buses, so vital for women's independence and participation in the public sphere, also unfortunately facilitate sexual harassment. In 2012, the attention of the world fell on the case of Ms Pandey, a psychotherapy student, violently raped by six men on a bus driving around Delhi for over an hour. She died two weeks later in a Singapore hospital and the lurid details of her ordeal that emerged during the trial emphasised the tenuous security women have on public transport. Little wonder then that women-only passenger carriages and women-only pink buses are once again making an appearance in Japan, Egypt, India, Taiwan, Brazil, Indonesia, Belarus, Philippines, Dubai, Korea and Mexico. For women the shift from the private domestic sphere into the public sphere is dependent on safe, reliable transport and these women-only spaces in public transport provide a welcome sense of relief and safety, which has proved vital in Bangladesh to enable women to continue to work in some of the garment factories, or in South Africa for women to access healthcare for HIV.

52 | The Mask of Warka

Early Women Travellers Finding Escapism
and Adventure

JANIS LOMAS

The Mask of Warka, also called the Lady of Uruk, is around 5,000 years old, carved of marble and thought to be the earliest accurate representation of the human face. It probably depicts Inanna, the best-known goddess of ancient Mesopotamia (now known as Iraq).

Discovered in 1939, it is one of the most important artefacts in the National Museum of Iraq, which largely owes its existence to Gertrude Bell. This British woman was determined that the antiquities found by the archaeological expeditions excavating various sites in Iraq after the First World War should remain in Iraq. When the Iraqi government established the Baghdad Antiquities Museum in 1926 it incorporated the objects she had been collecting since 1922. Bell became the museum's first director, but unfortunately, suffering from illness and depression, she died of an overdose of sleeping tablets later that year.

She was a remarkable woman. Born in County Durham in 1868, she was one of the first women to graduate from Oxford University with a first-class honours degree in modern history, after just two years of study. As women were not admitted to become full members of Oxford University until 1920, she could not graduate in the traditional way. Before the First World War she had travelled round the world twice, and in 1913–14 she undertook an arduous three-month camel journey across the desert from Damascus to Baghdad and back, during which she took 700 photographs and made detailed notes, which it was said 'made her the most serious woman traveller of all time'. She also published a number of academic books, was a skilled mountaineer and linguist. After the First World War Bell played a major role in the founding of Iraq, bringing together the three provinces of the Ottoman Empire: Mosul, Baghdad and Basra. She was also instrumental in the crowning of her preferred choice of king when Prince Faisal came to the throne in 1921.

Bell was one of a number of women travellers; pilgrims were the first to leave a record of their journeys but in the seventeenth and eighteenth centuries women with money travelled to fashionable areas of Europe doing the Grand Tour, as upper-class gentlemen did but in smaller numbers. Suitably chaperoned, this was just about permissible but women who went further and travelled to more out-of-the-way places and to other continents risked their reputation.

Some women did not care about this and it was precisely to escape that they travelled. Lady Hester Stanhope, who was born in 1776, had been hostess for her unmarried uncle William Pitt the Younger when he was Prime Minister. After his

death in 1806, she was rewarded with a generous pension of £1,200 a year by the government and, when her brother also died in 1810, she was freed from domestic responsibilities and soon left England and first sailed to Athens. After a storm, when her ship was shipwrecked en route to Cairo, she borrowed Turkish men's clothes and travelled across the Middle East astride an Arab stallion. She was the first European woman to cross the Syrian desert and her expedition to Ashkelon was the first archaeological excavation in the Holy Land. She eventually settled near Sidon, Lebanon, in a remote former monastery. Perhaps as a result of a fever which might have damaged her brain, she began to believe she was a mystic woman

of destiny, writing that 'all Syria is in astonishment at my courage and success'. She
fed any beggar or refugee who came to her door, behaved rather as a medieval ruler
and as a result became heavily in debt and ever more reclusive until her death in
1839. Despite her sad and lonely end, she herself felt that 'I have no reproaches to
make of myself but that I went rather too far'.

Isabelle Eberhardt was born in Switzerland in 1877; her mother was a Russian
émigrée but, unusually for a middle-class family at the time, not
married to her father. In three years from 1897, she lost all her
family to suicide, illness and sudden death. She had frequently
dressed as a boy in her youth and now set out wearing Arabic
male clothing and travelled through Algeria and the Sahara,
as she wrote, 'alone, with a whole world of dashed hopes,
disappointment and disillusion behind me, and of memories
that grow daily more distant, almost losing all reality'.

Do women find
travelling appealing
because they can
escape the social
constraints of their
lives at home?

Eberhardt seems to have travelled to escape the losses in
her life, which she desperately tried to forget. Despite marriage
to a young Algerian soldier, she had a series of sexual encounters,
took drugs and finally died in a flash flood in the desert, aged only 27.

All these three women travellers' lives ended sadly but they were incredibly brave,
choosing lives of travel and adventure rather than settling for the restricted life of
a spinster available at home. They undertook journeys on horse – and camel – back,
which even today would be daunting; they learned local languages and shared a
love of the Middle East and the people they encountered. They may have had to pay
a price for their freedom but they lived the lives they chose without regard to the
conventions of the ones they left behind.

53 | The Covered Wagon
Making a Home on the Move

JANIS LOMAS

In the period 1840–70 the overland trails to Oregon and California were opened up. Fuelled by the farming depression from 1837 onwards, the promise of free land – and after 1848 by the prospect of gold and silver mining – approximately 350,000 men, women and children made the extremely perilous 2,400-mile journey from small towns situated along the banks of the Missouri river, such as Independence, St Joseph's and Council Bluffs. Most of those making the long westward crossing were migrants who had already made long journeys to reach Missouri.

The Prairie Schooner and the Conestoga Wagon were the two most popular wagons to make the long journey to the west when pioneer families were opening up the trails. The Prairie Schooner, so called because it looked, with its long sturdy frame and high white canopy, like a ship when it was 'sailing' through a sea of grass on the prairie, was lighter than the Conestoga Wagon and was generally considered better able to withstand the journey over rough terrain, across rivers and mountain ranges. Drawn by a team of oxen or horses, the covered wagon could travel 10–20 miles a day. Usually the young children rode in the wagon, sometimes with their mother, and older children walked alongside while the men rode with them or went ahead with the livestock. At night some slept in the wagons while others camped in a tent on the ground. Wagon trains could be 5 miles long when they set off but usually broke into smaller, more manageable units as the journey went on.

It was a different experience for men than it was for women. For young men, it was often seen as an adventure, a chance to prove their bravery with the prospect of untold riches and a new life carved out of the wilderness, but women almost always went reluctantly. Husbands decided to go and young wives had little choice but to follow. Many migrant wagon trains were composed of extended kinship networks but women's diaries and letters often contain heart-wrenching accounts of the pain of leaving behind the women friends and family that they had always relied upon, to set out on a journey into the unknown with every likelihood that they would never see their home again. The age of the average homesteader was between 16 and 35 years, meaning that men were at the peak of their strength, but for women the position was often very different. They were at the height of their childbearing years and often already had several small children. It has been estimated that one in five were pregnant, gave birth or became pregnant on the journey. The prospect of giving birth on the trail must have been a very daunting one but pregnancy and approaching birth could not be allowed to slow down the trek. Wagon trains typically set off in April or early May and hoped to accomplish the journey in four

to five months, but it often took much longer and it was imperative to reach their destination before winter really set in, provisions ran out and livestock died.

Women had to undertake all the tending to babies and small children, and their safety was a constant anxiety. They also had all the cooking and washing to do, as well as setting up tents every night and helping their husbands with the livestock, repairing wagons and unloading and loading goods before and after treacherous river crossings. They also had to walk alongside the wagon to collect 'buffalo chips' (dung) or, if there was none, to collect weeds to make fires to cook the evening meal. Approximately 9 per cent of all those who set out died along the way. On such uncharted territory it was easy to have an accident; children fell out of wagons, there were occasional Native American attacks, men died trying to find new routes, while starvation, drowning, fever and dysentery were common; most disastrously of all, the cholera epidemic took thousands of lives. If left widowed, women were expected to carry on alone and still stake their claim.

The most enduring myth of the pioneers, and one that survives to the present day, is the frontier thesis. Although published in 1893, echoes of it can be heard in speeches by politicians and legislators to the present day. Frederick Jackson Turner's

It has been estimated that one in five women homesteaders were pregnant, gave birth or became pregnant on the journey.

thesis advanced the argument that the frontier was the defining concept that forged the American nation. Turner saw the western frontier as a place of heroism, triumph, and above all progress, dominated by the feats of brave white men whose suffering, heroism and resilience in enduring the most overwhelming difficulties gave Americans a democratic, materialistic individualism.

Historians have in the second half of the twentieth century largely debunked Turner's ideas and pointed out that it leaves out the experiences of women and the Native American inhabitants who had lived in the west long before the settlers brought 'civilisation' and largely destroyed their way of life within a generation. Many pioneer women who travelled west did so reluctantly, enduring dangers and discomfort in a situation where men and women were mutually dependent and deserving of recognition for the contribution they made. Other women set off on their own: the 1862 Homesteading Act guaranteed free farmland to heads of households if they stayed on the land for five years and made improvements to their plot, and women who were single, widowed or divorced were eligible to apply.

Many headed west into Dakota Territory, including Eliza Jane Wilder who, despite health problems, lasted the necessary five years. Elinore Pruitt left Denver in 1909 and set out for Wyoming with her 2-year-old daughter after her husband died in a railway accident. She went to be housekeeper of a cattleman, whom she eventually married, and to stake a claim to a plot of land. For many women like Eliza Wilder, arrival at their destination did not mean the end of their difficulties, but their presence on the frontier was essential. For the majority the west was no promised land but they triumphed over hardship and endured, bringing up families in incredibly difficult circumstances. The homesteaders were pioneering travellers and some like Elinore Pruitt loved the landscape and the freedom of a more outdoor life; she wrote to her friend Mrs Coney of her joy in looking at the scenery from her cabin one morning: 'Fancy yourself in a big jewel-box of dark-green velvet lined with silver chiffon, the snow peak lying like an immense opal in its centre and over all the amber light of the new day. That is what it most looked like.'

Does making a home on the move, whether it be a homesteader wagon, caravan, or barge offer particular challenges or freedoms to women?

54 | The Rajah Quilt

How Women Faced Being Forced to Start a New Life in a New Country

MAGGIE ANDREWS

Travel, for some women, offers the chance of adventure and freedom; but many others are forced to leave their homes, families and all that is familiar fleeing from political, religious or ethnic persecution.

Civil wars and conflicts, economic deprivation and displacement have forced women to travel; in the 1970s the Vietnam War uprooted women from Vietnam and Cambodia, some of whom went to the USA. More recently conflict in Sudan and Syria has ousted many women from their homes. The Rajah Quilt of 1841 was made by the 180 women who travelled on board the *Rajah* from Woolwich, England, to Van Diemen's Land (later renamed Tasmania). They had no choice about their journey; as convicted felons their punishment was transportation to Australia.

The first Transportation Act of 1718 enabled courts to sentence felons to seven years' transportation to America, where women were usually expected to work as servants or in the fields. Transportation came to a stop in 1776 with the American War of Independence, but began again the following year, this time to Australia. In the years between 1787 and 1852 approximately 25,000 women convicted of crimes, which varied from poaching hares to murder, were punished this way. Some women were hardened London criminals, often perceived to be at least part-time prostitutes; others were first-time offenders or the victims of a miscarriage of justice. The majority were first offenders, young, literate, skilled or semi-skilled and guilty of petty theft.

Elizabeth Carpenter was convicted for stealing clothes when waiting in the queue at a pawnbrokers, while Jane Humphries was caught stealing a copper and a kettle. Both were sentenced to seven years' transportation in 1830. The experience of transportation for women was varied and uncertain, and could involve a wait of many months before they had completed the journey from regional gaols to London and thence in irons to the ship that could, in turn, be shipwrecked. The voyage was long and cramped; a space of 2m x 2m was considered sufficient for four convicts, and disease and consequently death were not uncommon. On arrival in Australia the women undertook indentured labour, sometimes as domestic servants. They were often also expected to provide sexual services. Little wonder that social reformers, such as Elizabeth Fry, attempted to alleviate the plight of the convicted women before, during and after their voyage.

Elizabeth Gurney was born into a wealthy Quaker Norwich family in 1780; after marrying Joseph Fry in 1800 she gave birth to six children in nine years. From 1813,

after a friend told her of the appalling conditions in Newgate Prison, she combined family life with her work in prison visiting and reform. She set up the Association for the Improvement of the Female Prisoners in Newgate, and with her colleagues promoted religious education among the inmates to encourage habits of order, sobriety and industry. Elizabeth Fry also visited women on convict ships waiting to leave London, and with her followers held religious services and provided the women with a knife and fork for daily meals, a Bible, and knitting and sewing materials; the latter were used to make the Rajah Quilt.

The embroidered and appliquéd patchwork coverlet is 325cm x 337cm in size, and provides an example of the skilled and artistic co-operative work that women can achieve even in horrendous conditions. The following inscription is stitched into its border:

The Rajah Quilt was made by 180 convict women travelling to a new life in Australia in 1841.

To the ladies of the convict ship committee, this quilt worked by the convicts of the ship Rajah during their voyage to van Dieman's Land is presented as a testimony of the gratitude with which they remember their exertions for their welfare while in England and during their passage and also as a proof that they have not neglected the ladies kind admonitions of being industrious. June 1841.

Many of the women on the convict ships were mothers, and, then as now, the sentences of the courts were imposed on children's lives as much as they were on their mothers. In Britain each year, approximately 20,000 children suffer the pain of separation when their mothers are in jail. Regulations regarding transportation in the early nineteenth century stated that 'Children whose ages do not exceed, if boys 6 years and girls 10 years, will be allowed to accompany their mothers but if either such convicts should have a child at the breast she must not be removed on board said ship'. Their mothers had to make tortuous decisions about whether to take their children with them or to be separated from them, probably forever. Consequently on one journey in 1834 the *George Hibbet* sailed with 150 convict women and 41 children on board.

When mothers are found guilty of crimes, are sentences imposed by courts as much on children's lives as their mothers'?

Women continue to undertake dangerous and uncertain journeys with their children in tow; Rima, a Syrian refugee and widow with two small children, who joined a stream of refugees from Turkey to Western Europe, recalled:

Walking through the night was terrifying ... I had a bag on my back and I put my daughter in it. She was ill; she had a temperature of 41°C. The most frightening point was when a man on a motorbike wanted to carry my little boy – he said he'd take only the boy, not the girl. I thought he might snatch him ... Now, there are no bombs, but we are freezing and still afraid.

55 | Emily Wilding Davison's Purse and Return Ticket

A Feminist Martyr

JANIS LOMAS

The Epsom Derby is the biggest race of the British flat racing calendar; in 1913 it was of particular interest as King George V had a fancied horse running in the race and was due to attend the race meeting.

Held on 4 June on Epsom Downs, the race attracted huge crowds. Suffragette militancy was at its height and, as the race came to its climax, Emily Wilding Davison ducked under the rail and walked into the path of the galloping horses. She reached up to grasp the reins of the king's horse, Anmer. The horses were at full gallop, travelling at over 35mph, and the force of the impact dragged her under the hooves of the horse, causing the jockey to fall. The horse stumbled but recovered and the jockey sustained slight concussion but no broken bones; Davison never regained consciousness and died four days later. Ever since there has been a debate about whether she intended to throw herself under the hooves of the king's horse deliberately, and by her suicide become a martyr to the cause of women's suffrage, or whether her actions that day were simply foolhardy – or, as Queen Alexandra described it, 'the abominable conduct of a brutal lunatic woman'.

Davison was clutching her purse when she ran into the path of the galloping horses, and contained within it was a return ticket to London. She also had an engagement that evening and plans to go on holiday with her sister in the very near future. So it would appear that she had every intention of returning home from the races that day. We will never know for sure her intentions but perhaps some of the answers can be found in a review of her involvement in the Women's Social and Political Union (WSPU), more usually known as the suffragettes.

She was an educated woman who had studied at Royal Holloway College and Oxford University. She worked as a schoolteacher before giving up her career to devote all her time to the suffrage cause in 1906. She was always a maverick figure who never asked permission before carrying out radical actions, and was never regarded as one of the inner circle by the suffrage leadership. She was imprisoned nine times and, as time went on and the promises to grant time for a bill to debate women's suffrage were constantly blocked by Herbert Asquith's government, she became increasingly frustrated and her actions became more extreme.

Davison had been arrested at different times for stone throwing, setting fire to pillar-boxes and even planting a bomb. She went on hunger strike and was force-fed more than forty-five times. On one occasion she resisted force-feeding by barricading herself in her cell. A prison warder responded to this by running a

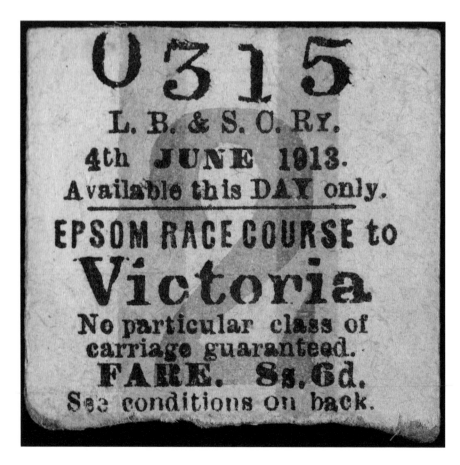

0315
L. B. & S. C. Ry.
4th JUNE 1913.
Available this DAY only.

EPSOM RACE COURSE to
Victoria
No particular class of
carriage guaranteed.
FARE. 8s. 6d.
See conditions on back.

hosepipe of freezing cold water into her cell, which rapidly filled with water; she almost drowned as a result. Davison later wrote: 'The thought in my mind was that the moment for the sacrifice, which we have all agreed will probably be demanded, was at hand ... I had no fear.' Upon her release, she successfully sued the prison authorities for this action and secured damages against them. On another occasion, after having endured starvation and force-feeding, in a desperate act she attempted to throw herself over the prison balcony on to the floor below. After her death the press seized on these words and actions to show that her death was suicide; however the inquest into her death returned a verdict of misadventure, enabling her to have a Christian burial and memorial service.

The latest examination and digital enhancement of the footage of the race seems to point to Davison's intention being to plant a flag on the king's horse, so he would end the race wearing the suffragette colours. She was probably somewhat naïve and lacking in knowledge as to the speed of galloping horses and the danger her actions would place her in. Davison's death, or martyrdom as the suffragettes saw it, had both an immediate and a long-term effect. As the event had been filmed, it was shown in cinema newsreels, and her funeral was a huge spectacle watched by 50,000 people with 6,000 suffragette supporters marching in procession, many dressed in the suffragette colours of purple, green and white. An empty carriage for the re-arrested Mrs Pankhurst and young suffragettes dressed in white carrying lilies, followed by older suffragettes dressed in black, made an arresting spectacle for the black and white film cameras that were filming the funeral procession. Her funeral was a show of strength and support for the WSPU and afterwards her body was taken by train to her childhood home, Morpeth in Northumberland. She was 40 years old when she died and to this day supporters place flowers on her grave every year on the anniversary of her death.

Do women martyrs help their political cause?

Even though there is no evidence that her death furthered the cause she so passionately believed in, the filming of her actions on Derby day and of her funeral procession made Davison a celebrity and the WSPU's use of spectacle to get publicity for their cause ensured it would be an unprecedented event. Although at the time many dismissed her as a crank, the spectacle of public mourning undoubtedly produced a range of media images which adorned the pages of the world's press and have been viewed in perpetuity, on newsreels in cinemas, in television documentaries and now via YouTube, arguably creating the blueprint for political funerals in the mass media age.

56 | The Phone Box
Telephone and Telecommunications

MAGGIE ANDREWS

Significant developments in communications systems stretch back to the nineteenth century; Morse code was introduced in 1836 and Alexander Graham Bell exhibited a working telephone at an exhibition in Philadelphia in 1876.

Women soon became strongly associated with this new technology, which offered a range of working opportunities and enabled housewives to bridge the gap between their private world and the public sphere, to talk to friends and relations far away, make social arrangements and organise their lives.

Talking on the earliest telephones required focused attention and was not easily combined with housework. In the 1920s one American farmer's wife took to peeling potatoes with the telephone receiver placed in the bottom of a large aluminum pan to amplify the conversations she was having. According to the *McClure's Magazine* in 1914 other farmers' wives were whiling away tedious afternoons listening to their neighbours' conversations via the shared or party lines many homes had, an early example of criticism directed at women for wasting time on the phone. Most women had few opportunities for such diversions. The home phone was a luxury item and trekking to public phone kiosks, first introduced in Berlin in 1881, was time consuming. Forty-two per cent of American households had a phone in 1929 but only 32 per cent had a phone in 1940, after the financial hardship of economic depression and wartime. Similarly in 1940s Britain only better-off families would have been 'on the phone', which was likely to be located in one fixed position in the hall, allowing little privacy for women to 'idle away the time' in conversation.

The early telephone systems required users in their homes, businesses, or public spaces to be manually connected to one another via the telephone exchange, where switchboard operators sat in front of huge plug boards. The first such operators were young men, but they were soon replaced by young women who were less abrupt, more polite and were paid much lower wages.

Emma Nutt became the world's first female telephone operator on 1 September 1878; her sister became the second a few hours later. The women's height, weight, and arm length were tested to ensure they could work in the tight spaces required, as switchboard operators were expected to sit for long hours with perfect posture on straight-backed chairs, not talking to one another. They were required to respond to customers quickly, efficiently and politely, and reportedly said 'number please' approximately 120 times an hour for eight hours a day. The soft tones of a helpful and reassuring female voice were seen to be ideal for this role, and many of the working opportunities for women in telecommunications continue to reinforce

gender stereotypes. Almost since the invention of the telephone, women have been required to act as receptionists, answering phones and being endlessly polite as they respond to the needs of others in offices and industries. Little wonder that when the speaking clock was introduced in Britain in 1936, Jane Cain was chosen as its first voice.

During the Second World War the British government recruited women to the Special Operations Executive (SOE) to act as radio operators. These young women undertook the dangerous task of using Morse code and the MKIII Suitcase Radio to send messages to the intelligence services in Britain about the German troop numbers and positions in occupied France between 1940 and 1944. As an SOE agent, Violette Szabó drew upon her experience as a switchboard operator for the Royal

The first public phone kiosks were introduced in Berlin in 1881.

Mail delivery service until she was captured and executed by the SS at Ravensbrück concentration camp, one of fifty-five SOE female agents who died in the line of duty. In the years that followed the Second World War, telephones became an increasingly common form of communication and were understood to reduce housewives' isolation and boredom. Prank, threatening or obscene phone calls could, however, make women feel vulnerable in their homes. Some women were reluctant to be listed in the telephone directory in any way that suggested they were a woman living alone, fearing it would encourage such calls.

Do telephones reduce women's and girls' sense of isolation?

The introduction of mobile phones offered women new levels of power and control. The Motorola's DynaTAC, first on sale in 1983, took ten hours to charge and only provided thirty minutes of talk-time, and was therefore the prerogative of wealthy business people only. Mobile phones have become smaller and cheaper, and private communication via telephone is now readily available to women. Women can now be in contact with their dependants, their employers and emergency services wherever they are. Although this may have its disadvantages, nine out of ten women feel safer with their mobile phone. However, as Cherie Blair pointed out in 2015, access to mobile technology is limited by the quality of networks and disposable income; 300 million women 'do not yet benefit from access to a mobile phone', which has the potential to make a significant impact 'on improving the social and economic status of women, families and entire communities'. Few modern teenage girls in Western societies could imagine life without their phone on which they talk and text, take photographs and access social media. They are both a mode of communication and a fashion accessory. But in India, where there are three men on Facebook to every woman, one rural woman pointed out that 'men have the latest touchscreen phone whereas women only have basic mobile phones'.

57 | A First World War Love Letter
Using Letters to Maintain Relationships

HAYLEY CARTER

Alice Amelia Brown Constable (Mela) devotedly wrote nearly 400 letters to her fiancé Cyril Sladden during his time on active service between 1914 and 1919. The couple became engaged in May 1913 and married after the war. Cyril was never far from Mela's thoughts. When carrying out her wartime role as a nurse, her intentions and experiences were shaped by her feelings for Cyril.

In September 1914 she wrote to him, explaining:

> The nursing will be the very thing for me, dear. I shall nurse the patients tenderly, oh so very tenderly because I shall be thinking of you and praying that if you are ever ill, while away from me, that some other nurse will do the same for you.

Like many couples in wartime they faced uncertainty and physical separation; letters provided their only reliable form of communication, creating a shared private space for them to live in their imagination. They mostly wrote of private thoughts, shared memories of times spent together and also hopes and desires for a happier future together to come. Unusually, the majority of both Mela and Cyril's letters survived to provide an intriguing insight into their personal relationship and their experiences of everyday life during the First World War. During the conflict, loved ones could receive a letter within twenty-four hours of it being written. The receipt of a letter, postcard or note provided physical evidence to sustain women's hope that their husbands, fiancés or sweethearts were still alive. Letters were a symbol of love, a connection vital to building and maintaining any type of relationship during war when the physical or intimate contact couples desired could only be attained during brief periods of leave. At night-time separation proved most difficult; Mela wrote in September 1916: 'I must go to bed now, sweetheart – to dream of you, I hope. Oh when will the time come when my dreams shall be realities? Some day – and it will be a glorious some day – won't it, dear?'

All over the world couples like Mela and Cyril used letters to maintain and build relationships and to engage in ever-continuing conversations, which now provide a captivating testimony of their experiences, passions and the challenges they faced conducting courtships in extraordinary circumstances. For women who lost their loved ones in war, the letters they had received gained even greater emotional significance. The unseen collections that have remained hidden, bundles tied with string, forgotten in dusty attic boxes or stashed in drawers, remain the only

It is weary waiting for your return Sweetheart but just now & again I can imagine you write me. In the words of Somerset's song you "come to me in the silence of the night", you "come in the speaking silence of a dream - "Speak low, breathe low" - so long ago my Love, how long ago". There have been exquisite moments which I can never forget & which live again in my imagination. But oh. dear heart - these are nothing in comparison to the Reality. God grant we may live through them all again together, & grant me strength to submit if it be His will that we shall never do so. But I feel He will be merciful. In the mean time we must watch & pray — until that joyful day of re-union.

God bless you, dear Love - All my heart's love -

From

Yr. ever devoted

Mela.

Since I've worked in the officers' wards I've realized your worth even more than I did before - Men are weak things in many ways & one sees their failings so much in hospital - Some of them are "fine" men of course -

BIRMINGHAM E
10.30 AM
19 SEP 16

ONE PENNY

Capt: Cyril. E. Sladden.

9th Worcesters.

13th Division.

Mesopotamian Exped. Force.

"D".

tangible evidence some wartime relationships occurred. Fred Marriott and May Darke were brought together and separated by war; after only having met twice, they married on 25 September 1915. They both wanted to have children and May received comfort from Fred. When she wrote and told him of her disappointment at not conceiving, he replied:

> I hope that there will be better results the next time and you will not have to do any cycling for a while if you think it was that that stopped it last time. For it would have been near time now. But what is to be will be. Yes I would be one of the happiest men if we had a little boy or girl but everything comes to them that wait so it might be our luck for it to come to us.

Despite many false hopes of further leave, their short and fervent relationship was mostly conducted through letters before it ended in heartbreak when Fred died during the Battle of the Somme, twenty-one days shy of their first wedding anniversary.

In Britain, the First World War is known as the first literate war, thanks to the introduction of compulsory education in the 1870s. This conflict gave many an opportunity to use their education to communicate with loved ones; previously letter writing was often reserved for women of wealth and privilege who built and maintained friendships and relationships through letters.

Women's obligation to establish lives in their husband's home, wherever his work took him, could mean relocating to another county in the hope of a better life. In the mid-nineteenth century, Jane Carlyle wrote to her friend Mrs Janie Aiken, telling her of the challenges of creating a tranquil home for her author husband, recording 'the immensity of needlework I had accomplished in his absence, in the shape of chair-covers, sofa-covers, window curtains &c., and &c, and all other manifest improvements which I had put my whole genius and industry, and so little money'.

Women sustained family ties and lifelong friendships, and constructed conversational relationships between absent friends through letters, which spanned a range of topics, spread news and gave advice, as Queen Victoria did to her granddaughter Princess Alice:

Have new communication systems usurped or replaced women's letter writing?

> I must emphasise that give and take ... So many girls think to marry is to be independent and amuse oneself, whereas it is the reverse of independence:

two wills have to be made to act together. It is only by mutual agreement and mutual yielding to one another that a happy marriage can be arrived at.

Before electronic communication the bonds between women, however great the physical distance that separated them, were maintained through letters. Far from being gossipy memos, women's letters reveal an affectionate and supportive connection based on shared interests through which women sometimes sought to exert influence beyond the domestic sphere in which they were writing.

Correspondence was also a safe and non-judgemental arena for political discussions. Thus the American feminist Lucy Stone wrote to explain her support of black male suffrage on 4 August 1869: 'I believe that just so far as we withhold or deny a human right to any human being, we establish a basis for the denial and withholding of our own rights.'

In today's world of mass media, instant communications, and the continuing evolution of modern technology, the postman's morning visit rarely brings anticipation or excitement; few people put pen to paper. The art of letter writing has been superseded by emails and instant messaging; the only address required often includes an @, perhaps making it difficult to appreciate the care and time that went into sustaining friendships and relationships like that of Alice Constable and Cyril Sladden, relying on the written word.

58 | Frances Willard's Bicycle
Transportation, Exercise and Freedom on Two Wheels

MAGGIE ANDREWS

Frances Elizabeth Caroline Willard was an American educator, suffragist and temperance reformer who called for the 'total prohibition of alcohol, opium and other addictives' and became president of the Women's Christian Unions in 1879.

A graduate of Northwestern Female College in Evanston, She was the president in 1871 and later dean after its merger with Northwestern University. Her slogan 'Do everything' was intended to encourage women to lobby, petition, preach, educate and improve the world, and it applied to her own tenacious determination to learn to ride a bicycle at the age of 53 in the 1890s. She described her bicycle, known as Gladys, as the 'most remarkable, ingenious, and inspiring motor ever yet devised upon this planet', remarking that 'she who succeeds in gaining the mastering of such an animal as Gladys, will gain the mastery of life and by exactly the same methods and characteristics'.

Willard was at the forefront of a cycling revolution, which in the 1870s was restricted to men with the funds to purchase a penny-farthing machine. With solid iron tyres, no brakes and one wheel very much larger than the other, bumps and bruises often accompanied learning to ride a penny-farthing. Women were restricted to riding tricycles or tandems. It was the invention of what was known as the 'safety bicycle' with equal-sized wheels and pneumatic tyres that changed things in the 1880s.

The bicycle became popular first in France and then in the USA, where Susan Browell Anthony, social reformer, women's rights activist and anti-slavery campaigner, suggested in 1896 that cycling had 'done more to emancipate women than anything else in the world', remarking: 'I stand and rejoice every time I see a woman ride by.'

The new hobby necessitated the abandonment of some of the more cumbersome Victorian women's clothing and gave a great boost to the Rational Dress Society. To avoid long skirts getting caught round pedals women began to wear divided skirts or, more controversially, knickerbockers. For many young middle- and upper-class young women the appeal of cycling lay in escaping chaperonage, despite the formation of a Chaperone Cyclist Association in London whose chaperones came complete with excellent references and their own cycles. Other women enjoyed bicycling with groups of friends, relishing the physically exhilarating healthy outdoor pastime. All cyclists were subject to taunts from young boys shouting 'monkey on wires', but it was female cyclists who faced the greatest condemnation. *The Women's Realm* in 1896 considered them without the 'faintest remnant of the spirit of allurement which conscious or unconscious, is women's supreme attraction'.

It was women's posture 'astride' a bicycle that evoked some of the concern; some considered it likely to lead women into prostitution. Doctors were concerned that the saddle would cause pelvic inflammation, inflamed fallopian tubes or infertility, or that women cyclists would develop masculine muscles or even an unattractive 'bicycle face'.

By the 1890s the craze for cycling stretched across the world and in Australia women took part in long-distance endurance riding. Mrs Maddock rode approximately 600 miles from Sydney to Melbourne in ten days in the company of her husband, a solicitor's clerk, going on to take part in 100-mile time-trial races, in which contestants completed the course in twelve to fourteen hours. Mrs Ellen Schwaebsch became the first woman to cycle over the Australian Alps in 1897. Female cyclists became a symbol of modernity; pictures of them appeared in magazines and newspapers, and can be found in many families' private archives. To some these were unsettling images, indications of the presence of the 'new' or emancipated woman.

There is nothing that symbolises modernity and freedom for women so much as a bicycle.

The bicycle moved from luxury to necessity in the twentieth century. A special Elswick bicycle for ladies was produced with enamelling in the colours of Mrs Pankhurst's Women's Social and Political Union – purple, white and green – for supporters of women's suffrage. By this time a new mode of transport was available to those with sufficient funds: the motorcycle. Women motorcyclists met with what proved to be a more tenacious form of ridicule and scepticism. An irate reader of the *Motorcycling* magazine put pen to paper to exclaim in 1903:

> To my mind woman was never made for an engine driver, and has not that cool nerve required so often in motoring. I saw a lady motorist riding a Singer lady's machine for the first time somewhere in Cambridge, and without being ungallant, I don't want to see another. Her nervousness was pathetically obvious, and her facial expression was an index to the sustained nervous tension under which she was labouring. I am sure the natural constitution of the gentler sex is not such that they can abstract any pleasure or physical good from such a pastime as motoring, which requires strong nerves, and a cool and ready hand and head.

Is the motto 'Do everything' one that women should still adhere to?

Whatever this man's views, across the world, in the years that followed, bicycling, motorbikes and motorcars offered women both transportation and emancipation.

59 | Amelia Earhart's Little Red Bus

Danger, Skill and Piloting Planes

JANIS LOMAS

Amelia Earhart acquired her 5B Vega, which she called 'Little Red Bus', in 1930. The Vega plane, made by the Lockheed Aircraft Company, was considered sturdy and streamlined; it was fast and popular with those pursuing speed and distance records.

It was not what some might consider a feminine machine, but Amelia Earhart, who became one of the best-known and most successful early aviators having gained her pilot's licence in 1922, held many incredible records including being the first woman to fly solo across the Atlantic Ocean. Her ultimate goal was to circumnavigate the world at its widest point and it was during this attempt in 1937, with only 7,000 miles to go, that her plane disappeared without trace. In her last letter to her husband Earhart wrote: 'Please know I am quite aware of the hazards. I want to do it because I want to do it. Women must try to do things as men have tried. When they fail their failure must be but a challenge to others.'

Amelia Earhart was by no means the first or the only woman aviator; from the earliest years of manned flight in 1903, women were part of the story of aviation, overcoming huge obstacles to take to the air. Early flights were extremely hazardous and fatalities occurred frequently as intrepid women risked their lives to fly. Raymonde de Laroche gained her pilot's licence after seeing Wilbur Wright demonstrate flying in 1908 in her birthplace, Paris. She is generally credited with being the first woman to hold a pilot's licence, in 1910. In the next few years she held the women's distance and altitude records but she was not allowed to fly during the First World War and was killed testing an experimental aircraft when she was trying to become the first woman test pilot in 1919.

> Must women, as Earhart suggested, 'try to do things as men have tried'?

For some women, planes were only one of a number of machines of transportation they mastered. Belgian-born Hélène Dutrieu was the world women's cycling champion in both 1897 and 1898. She then became a motorcycling stunt rider, performing tricks such as the 'jump of death', and soon afterwards took to flying. There was a minor scandal early in her aviation career when it was revealed to the press that she did not wear a corset while flying. She had her flying suit designed in Paris and during an aviation demonstration week in Burton-upon-Trent, England, in 1910, she took passengers for a flight. The First World War cut short her flying career so she drove an ambulance instead and later ran a military hospital. After the war she became a journalist.

Early women aviators were in many ways an unconventional group. On the day before her wedding Amelia Earhart wrote her soon-to-be husband a letter, telling him that she was reluctant to marry, and 'on our life together I want you to understand I shall not hold you to any midaevil [sic] code of faithfulness to me nor shall I consider myself bound to you similarly', ending with 'I must exact a cruel promise and that is you will let me go in a year if we find no happiness together'.

Harriet Quimby, the first American woman to hold a pilot's licence in August 1911, wrote screenplays for early silent movies, drove her own car, lived alone, smoked cigarettes, and was an accomplished journalist. She gave flying exhibitions and in April 1912, after borrowing a plane from Louis Bleriot, became the first woman to fly solo across the English Channel, relying solely on her compass to navigate for much of the way. The sinking of the *Titanic* overshadowed news of her accomplishment and a few months later she too was killed in a plane crash.

Bessie Coleman was the first African-American female pilot, having learned to fly in 1920. Born into a poor, cotton-sharecropping family, and one of thirteen children, she worked two jobs and travelled to France to get her pilot's licence as American flight schools did not allow African-Americans of either gender or any women to learn to fly in the United States. As she wrote: 'The air is the only place free from prejudices.' She worked as a barnstorming pilot, performing tricks like loop the loop and figures of eight to large crowds all over America for the next five years to buy her own aeroplane. She wanted to run her own flying school to teach women like herself

In 1937, as she attempted to circumnavigate the world, Ameila Earhart's plane disappeared without trace.

to fly so they didn't have to face the same difficulties that she had. She refused to perform at venues that did not allow black people to attend. She died in 1926 as a passenger in her new plane.

The other celebrated female aviator of the inter-war years, Amy Johnson, was born in Hull, England, and became the first British woman to qualify as an aeroplane mechanic and to fly from Britain to Australia. She was at the height of her fame when the Second World War broke out. She then joined the newly formed Air Transport Auxiliary, which was responsible for transporting all new planes from the factories to airfields, thereby freeing up pilots for combat duty. In 1941, while carrying out one of these flights in bad weather, her aircraft developed engine trouble and she bailed out over the English Channel. Her body was never found.

These women, whose lives often ended tragically, helped to make aviation safer and more accessible for those who followed their lead. Helen Richey became the first female airline pilot, for Central Airlines; she was, however, a co-pilot. It was not until 1973 that Emily Howell Warner became the first woman captain of a scheduled US airline. The women pioneers of aviation proved that women could break down the barriers and perform the same role as male pilots, but they had to overcome a great deal of prejudice in the process. As Cornelia Fort, an American aviator in the Second World War, wrote: 'Any girl who has flown at all grows used to the prejudice of most men pilots who will trot out any number of reasons why women can't possibly be good pilots ... The only way to show the disbelievers, the snickering hangar pilots, is to show them.'

60 | The Mini Car
1960s Mobile Freedom for Women

MAGGIE ANDREWS

The very first British Motor Company (BMC) Mini rolled off the production line in Oxford, England, on 8 May 1959. The little cars, just over 3m long, were designed by Alec Issigonis to be fuel efficient, in the wake of the 1957 Suez Crisis. Four adults could comfortably squeeze into the car, which came with an ashtray as the designer was a chain smoker, but no seat belts or radio.

Women really benefited from this economically priced, handy runaround. For housewives in the Western world the Mini sparked a revolution, enabling them to undertake the weekly shopping or the school run without relying on the sometimes dubious dependability of public transport to transport them, their shopping bags and children home. The Mini, and other cars, gave women new freedom to escape the domestic sphere. By December 1962, 500,000 Minis had been built; the millionth Mini was completed on 3 February 1965. Its success spurred other manufacturers to produce smaller, cheaper cars targeted at women and the young, who still make up a significant share of the mass market for automobiles. Little wonder that the Mini was voted the most significant car of the twentieth century by 100 experts for *Autocar* magazine in 1990. For youngsters the Mini has become as emblematic of the swinging sixties as the miniskirt.

The car itself, however, is often seen as an icon of masculinity, and women's aptitude and competency at the wheel has been questioned for over 100 years. Yet there have been female drivers since the first cars began to appear at the end of the nineteenth century. Indeed it was Mary Anderson who invented the first windscreen wiper in 1902, and only two years later a society-columnist for *Motor* Magazine noted that 'judging from the number of motors that one sees driven by women on a fine afternoon, one would imagine that nearly every belle in Washington owned a machine'.

Should larger, women-only parking spaces be abolished?

Early cars were both prohibitively expensive and unreliable, and thus motoring pioneers, such as the Duchess of Uzes and Camille du Gast, the first woman to drive racing cars, were very wealthy. Nevertheless a number of motoring publications such as *Motor* and *Country Life in America* included images of women driving and maintaining their vehicles. In the First World War female drivers came into their own, undertaking tasks such as driving ambulances behind the lines in France; the Girl Scouts in the USA introduced an Automobiling Badge requiring girls to demonstrate skills in driving, auto mechanics and first aid.

In Scotland in the aftermath of the conflict, Dorothée Pullinger, as manager of the Galloway Motors factory in Tongland, celebrated women's enfranchisement by producing a car in the purple, white and green colours of Mrs Pankhurst's suffragettes. The vehicle was described as 'a car built by ladies, for those of their own sex'. Sales were small but a car became an increasingly desirable item for women, particularly if they lived in rural areas. In the 1920s, an American farmwoman explained to an inspector from the United States Department of Agriculture, who questioned her decision to prioritise purchasing a car before indoor plumbing, that 'you can't go to town in a bathtub'.

It was during the second half of the twentieth century that there was a significant increase in the number of female drivers in Western countries. Dodge manufactured a pink two-door coupé called La Femme aimed at women, and sold it with matching accessories such as a comb, cigarette lighter and lipstick case. It was, however, its price that made the Mini so significant; sold for £378 10s in Britain and around $800 in the USA, it was affordable to women on average incomes. By 1972 44 per cent of driving licences issued in the USA were to women, while in Britain over 40 per cent of cars were owned by women in 2013. More expensive and luxurious cars continued to be marketed towards men; the numerous adverts, car magazines

By December 1962, 500,000 Minis had been built; the millionth Mini was completed on 3 February 1965.

and car shows which utilised semi-clad women to garner men's interest became a target for criticism from 1970s feminists.

Despite a number of successful saloon racing drivers such as Liane Engeman from the Netherlands who drove Minis in the BSRC (the forerunner to the British Touring Car Championship) from 1966, criticisms and jokes about women's driving continue. Far fewer women are Heavy Goods Vehicle drivers or bus drivers than men. Furthermore, there is an assumption that women lack the spatial awareness to park their vehicles competently. Despite scientific studies that contradict this, a number of countries, including Germany, Austria, Switzerland and China, provide special larger parking spaces for women, to make it easier for them to manoeuvre their cars. Women do continue to drive smaller cars than men – the Mini remains a popular car for women – but this is because on average women earn less money than men. The purchase price and fuel economy mean that the Mini and Mini-like cars are the choice of many women who seek the freedom and independence of a car. This is a freedom not available to many women on low incomes, or until recently in Saudi Arabia, where the law prohibiting women driving has been successfully challenged by a campaign entitled Women2Drive, which involved women portrayed images and videos of themselves driving on social media.

Part VI
Women's Work and Employment

Women have always worked, but their labour has not necessarily been recognised, rewarded or paid as they have often undertaken work within the home, farm, business or trade of their husbands, fathers, brothers or owners. Indeed, much of the paid work that women have done and continue to do is an extension of the caring and nurturing roles that women undertake in domestic environments. Many women have been employed as domestic servants, dairymaids, teachers and nurses. Some such roles have now become less appealing for women; few young girls choose to go into domestic service, while others such as nursing were increasingly professionalised during the twentieth century. The achievement of State Registration for Nurses was for example a prestigious achievement.

In many of the working roles women have undertaken over the years, including slavery, domestic service and secretarial work, sexual harassment seems to have been almost expected. In others, a little flirtation seems to be assumed to be part of the job. With the poor wages and limited employment options that some women have faced in the past, it is not surprising that many women have chosen or felt they had no option but to turn to prostitution. This is illuminated by Harris's List of London prostitutes, produced in the eighteenth century.

Many women workers continue to struggle with the double burden of undertaking paid work only to come home to engage in unpaid housework. Some of the objects tell the story of women who entered traditionally male professions, such as medicine, by dressing up and pretending to be men. The Royal Shakespeare Theatre is an object designed by a woman, Elisabeth Scott, who had broken through the glass ceiling and achieved success in the 1930s. However, in the contemporary working world some women in high-flying professions have felt unable to combine motherhood and a career.

What remains a consistent issue across all historical periods and the countries of the world is that women earn less than men, and the struggle for both equal pay for equal work and to close the gender pay gap continues in employment and pensions. Notwithstanding such difficulties, women have relished the new opportunities that the workplace offers, and many have found in work fulfilment, affirmation and a new sense of identity. Even more importantly, the financial independence that wages provide have been fundamental in women's struggle for equality.

61 | The Bayeux Tapestry
Embroidery, a Domestic and Feminine Craft

JANIS LOMAS

The Bayeux tapestry, which is believed to have been created in circa 1086, is one of the earliest surviving embroideries of the Middle Ages, depicting the Norman Conquest of England in 1066. It is approximately 70m long and made up of nine panels. It was embroidered with ten shades of woollen yarn; its vivid colours come from vegetable dyes.

The origins of the tapestry and who carried out the work remain the subject of debate. Some say it was commissioned by William the Conqueror himself; others suggest it was his half-brother Bishop Odo, Edith of Wessex, Eustace, Count of Boulogne, or even William's wife, Mathilda. The actual stitching has been attributed at times to both French and English needleworkers; in the nineteenth century it was even suggested Queen Mathilda stitched the entire work herself.

Given the size of the tapestry it is unimaginable that one person stitched the entire embroidery, but the claim helped to cement the link between embroidery, royalty and the feminine ideals of womanhood, reaffirming needlework and embroidery as genteel work for women. Embroidery was, however, practised by both men and women in the Middle Ages, an expertise developed within guilds, in workshops attached to grand houses and in monasteries and convents where it was considered an art form. By the seventeenth century embroidery was used to inculcate femininity in young girls; considered an innately female occupation, needlework began to be practised almost entirely by women. Its royal and aristocratic associations were established in the eighteenth century when it was used to demonstrate that a husband could keep his wife and unmarried daughters at home, undertaking the feminine pursuit of needlework rather than rough domestic work which would coarsen women's hands. As embroidery became associated with femininity it began to be seen as a craft, while painting, more frequently the preserve of men, was considered fine art.

Do traditional women's crafts offer wonderful scope for women's camaraderie and political discussions?

Over the centuries women's apparently natural affinity with embroidery has been the subject of comment and controversy. Jean Jacques Rousseau thought that a love of embroidery was natural to women 'but at no cost would I want them to learn landscape [painting], even less the human figure'; while Sigmund Freud diagnosed constant needlework as the occupation that 'rendered women particularly prone to hysteria'. However, a careful examination of some of the subject matter women chose to stitch

suggests they sometimes used their needlework to subvert ideas of docile, obedient femininity. Rozsika Parker writes that the frequent use of popular subjects such as Susanna and the Elders or Judith slaying Holofernes shows that both girl and women embroiderers 'celebrated "masculine" behaviour in women through the very medium intended to inculcate femininity'.

In the USA embroidery was practised by early Dutch and British settlers who used the stitching of samplers by young girls to teach them the alphabet, numbers and the needle skills to make clothes and furnishings for their families. Once again, women and girls having the time to engage in embroidery could indicate a family's prosperity. Stitching quilts was initially undertaken to create items to keep warm but the intricacies of design and the skills needed to produce them meant that they became family heirlooms. As one woman explained: 'After all, a woman didn't leave much behind in the world to show she had been there. Even the children she bore and raised got their father's name. But her quilts, now that was something she could pass on.'

Quilts, tapestries and embroideries are also part of the legacy of many women's political groups who turned the associations between needlework and domestic and demure femininity on their head. Suffragette protestors of the early twentieth century produced all manner of embroidered works, including parasols and large

By the seventeenth century embroidery was used to inculcate femininity in young girls.

banners displaying their motivations and aims, praising their leadership and allying themselves with women like Joan of Arc, Marie Curie and Boudicca. Their messages were direct: 'Votes for women', or 'Alliance and defiance', 'Dare to be free' and 'Courage, consistency, success'. When imprisoned or on hunger strike, they embroidered handkerchiefs with signatures of the suffrage prisoners. They used embroidered works to replace traditional ideas about women and femininity with women portrayed as strong agents of change.

During the Russian Revolution, from November1917, women employed embroidery to show an appreciation of Russian traditional crafts rather than foreign ideas; in the second half of the twentieth century women's liberation or peace movements used embroidery as a way of subverting the idea of passivity and docile femininity. One woman living in a hippy commune explained: 'In my hippy phase … we all embroidered … it functioned to establish you as a member of a tribe.' In the 1970s Kate Walker used the traditional form of the sampler and subverted it by stitching it with sayings such as 'This is a present to me' and 'Wife is a four letter word'.

Traditional needlework skills – quilting, tapestry, embroidery, knitting – are also collective occupations providing an excuse for women to get together .The shared occupation helps them to overcome loneliness and develop skills and friendships. Co-operative quilt making often involves twenty or thirty women working and enjoying a leisurely gossip and camaraderie, a tradition the current fad for 'stitch and bitch' clubs continues. As a member of a quilting club in the 1930s recalled:

We always used to meet about two o' clock and hope to work till four and then stop and have a cup of tea. And we used to make scones, and a sandwich cake or something and we would share it out. We used to enjoy it. All the tales that we told over the quilting frame. Well you could imagine. Everything was discussed, it was really entertainment making quilts.

62 | Bill of Sale for a Slave Girl

Slavery, Race and Exploitation of Women

MAGGIE ANDREWS

In 1835 a judge recorded the transfer of ownership of a young black girl between two members of the slave-owner class in Arkansas, USA. The judge assured anyone who read the document he would defend the sale 'at all cost'. The 'Bill of Sale' referred to 16-year-old Polly, sold for $600.

Selling Polly treated her as less than human, made her an object, a chattel; it articulated slave owners' belief in their own innate superiority over other races. Such beliefs led to Mrs Margaret Douglas being sentenced to a month's imprisonment for teaching black children to read and write in Norfolk, Virginia, in 1853 and could also result in black women being subjected to physical and sexual abuse.

The bill of sale hides the objectification and subjection of slave auctions. Mary Prince's narrative of life as a slave in Bermuda, Turks Island and Antigua, recalled the humiliation of being sold at the age of 12:

> He took me by the hand and led me out into the middle of the street, and, turning me slowly round exposed me to the view of those who attended the vendue. I was soon surrounded by strange men who examined and handled me in the same manner that a butcher would a calf or a lamb he was about to purchase and who talked about my shape and size in like words – as if I could no more understand their meaning than the dumb beasts. I was then put up for sale. The bidding commenced at a few pounds, and gradually rose to fifty-seven when I was knocked down to the highest bidder.

> Slavery corrupts societies and leaves legacies in attitudes to black women and other groups now involved in modern slavery. Why, then, is it so hard to abolish?

Women slaves worked in cotton and tobacco fields in the USA and toiled on sugar plantations in the Caribbean. They also became house slaves, undertaking any of a wide range of laborious domestic tasks to support their owner's lifestyle in an era without modern technology. The precise nature of their work depended upon the wealth and size of the household. Mary Prince describes how her mistress:

> Taught me to do all sorts of household work; to wash and bake, pick cotton and wool, wash floors and cook ... she caused me to know the exact difference between the smart of the rope, the cart whip and cow skin when applied to my naked body by her own cruel hand.

Know all Men by these presents
that I Martin Bridgeman of Jackson County
in the Territory of Arkansas for and in
consideration of the sum of Six Hundred dollars
lawful money of the United States of America
to me in hand paid the receipt whereof is hereby
acknowledged, have this day granted bargained
and sold, and by these presents doth grant
bargain and sell unto W^m H Wood of Jackson
County in said Territory. his heirs and assigns
One Negro Girl named Polly aged about
Sixteen years, Yellow complection and
black Eyes, so have & to hold the said Negro
Girl unto the s^d H Wood his heirs and assigns
for ever, And further that I warrant and
shall defend the Right and titles to said
Negro against all costs Suits or Suits at
law, or in Equity that may have been, or
may hereafter be commenced by any person
or persons whatsoever — In witness whereof
I have hereunto set my hand and seal
this Twenty Third day of December One
Thousand Eight Hundred and Thirty five

Witness   his
                          Martin Bridgeman   (Seal)
Thomas R Peel   mark
John Nall

The State of Texas
County of Montgomery Before me H. B
Boston clerk, of the county court, in & for said County

When one of the other slaves died Mary also had the milking of eleven cows each morning and caring for cattle added to her chores. House slaves, as Mary Prince discovered, were vulnerable to sexual abuse. Children from such liaisons, or from sexual relationships between slaves, were the property of their masters.

For some women the pain of seeing their children enter a life of slavery was unbearable. In 1856 Mary Garner escaped from slavery in Kentucky with her four children, her husband and his parents. They made their way to Ohio, a free state, before the slave catchers ambushed them. Before she was recaptured Mary slit her baby daughter's throat, later explaining she would have cut her other children's throats to prevent them returning to slavery. Toni Morrison used Mary Garner's story as the basis for her award-winning novel *Beloved* (1987), made into a film in 1998.

The transatlantic slave trade created wealth for a number of British cities, banks and stately homes; when Britain abolished slavery in 1833, compensation was paid to slave owners. These included many seemingly 'respectable' British women, such as Rose Milles, a widow who lived in Pishiobury, Hertfordshire. In 1865, the Thirteenth Amendment was passed in the USA, ruling that: 'Neither slavery nor involuntary servitude, except as a punishment for crime whereof the party shall have been duly convicted, shall exist within the United States, or any place subject to their jurisdiction.'

However, the cultural and social attitudes that sustained slavery were not so easily abolished, and black women still live with the bitter legacy of slavery and racism. Stereotypical portrayals of black women as matriarchs, mammies and jezebels continue to permeate popular culture. Furthermore, despite legislation, the practice of slavery still occurs in clandestine forms in the twenty-first century.

Modern slavery is a multi-billion-dollar industry and estimates suggest it generates over $35 billion annually. The United Nations asserts there are 27 to 30 million people caught in the slave trade industry, two-thirds of whom are women. In a globalised world, with regional variation in poverty and refugees created by conflict, many women wish to migrate to other countries. Traffickers prey on the vulnerable, confiscating their passports and enslaving them into domestic work or the sex industry. However, as Anne Gallagher argued in *The Guardian* newspaper (2016), the victims of modern slavery are varied and hidden:

A Yazidi girl forced into sexual slavery by Islamic State has little in common with a Rohingya asylum seeker sold into forced labour on a Thai fishing boat. Both are worlds apart from a Hungarian woman forced into commercial sex work in the UK to pay off her recruitment debt. Each of these situations is the result of complex interplay between social, economic and political circumstances.

63 | Harris's List

Prostitution: One of Women's Oldest Professions

JANIS LOMAS

Harris's List of Covent Garden Ladies was published yearly from 1757 to 1795. Each edition listed 120–150 prostitutes working in this area of London, giving their ages, addresses, specialities and physical attributes.

It included only a fraction of approximately 6,000–7,000 prostitutes working in London, then mostly young women, many of whom had been drawn into the sex trade by poverty. Designed for a middle-class readership, Harris's List was pocket sized, sold for around half a crown (2*s* 6*d*), and had a circulation estimated at around 8,000 in 1791.

Harris's List suggests Georgian England had a fairly liberal attitude towards prostitution; this changed in the Victorian era, when a blind eye was turned to high-class brothels, but working-class prostitution became associated with disease, intemperance and disorder. For some women, prostitution was the only or best use of their assets in difficult times. Impoverished women, who sometimes worked in seasonal or sporadic employment as tailors, ballet girls or in corset making, moved into and out of prostitution when trade was poor. The journalist Henry Mayhew discovered they did not appreciate middle-class moralising; one explained in 1861 that she was 'only a mot [prostitute] who does a little typographing by way of variety' and roundly condemned 'those who have had good nursing, and all that, and the advantages of a sound education' with the 'sledge-hammer of their denunciation'.

Furthermore, the health of men, particularly those in the armed forces, became a matter of concern. An increasing number of troops were needed to 'police' the expanding British Empire, and frequent fears of a French invasion meant that maintaining a healthy army and navy became critical. By 1864 a third of all cases of illness in the British army were as a result of venereal diseases and 290 per 1,000 of the admissions to hospital were gonorrhoea or syphilis. The government sought to address this by adopting a system already tried in various continental countries: the state regulation of prostitution in garrison towns and ports, as embodied in the Contagious Diseases (CD) Acts. Any woman suspected of being a prostitute could experience enforced examination and detention in 'lock hospitals'. The CD Acts operated initially in eleven, later eighteen, garrison towns of the United Kingdom and Ireland between 1864 and 1886; women could be rounded up, taken before a magistrate and then forcibly imprisoned. They were then subjected to fortnightly internal examinations; if found to be infected, imprisonment and treatment was initially for three months, later six and finally nine. Those prostitutes who passed

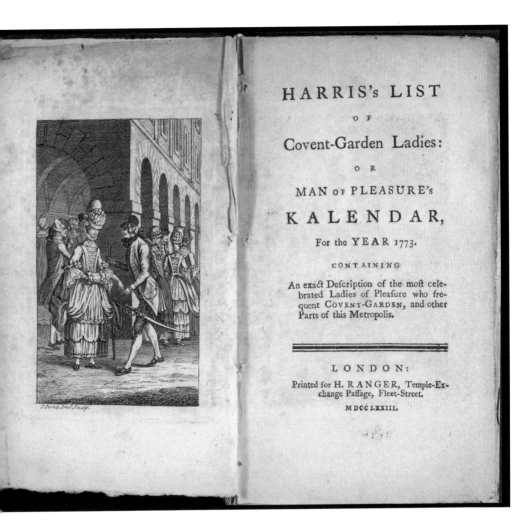

HARRIS's LIST

o f

Covent-Garden Ladies:

o r

MAN of PLEASURE's

KALENDAR,

For the YEAR 1773.

CONTAINING

An exact Defcription of the moft celebrated Ladies of Pleafure who frequent COVENT-GARDEN, and other
Parts of this Metropolis.

LONDON:

Printed for H. RANGER, Temple-Ex-
change Paffage, Fleet-Street.

M DCC LXXIII.

their examination used this as a marketing tool and described themselves as 'the Queen's women', often displaying a certificate of cleanliness over the bed.

By identifying and registering 'common prostitutes' it was hoped to combat venereal diseases among enlisted men; the legislation embodied a double standard and made no attempt to curb men's sexual activities. Working-class women out after dark or seen speaking to soldiers in the designated areas were liable to be picked up by police. Girls, sometimes as young as 13, had to submit to internal examinations regardless of evidence of good character. Any refusal to comply could lead to imprisonment with hard labour. One convicted woman summed up her feelings about the way they were being treated:

It is men, only men, from the first to the last that we have to do with! To please a man I did wrong at first, then I was flung about from man to man. Men police lay hands on us. By men we are examined, handled, doctored. In the hospital it is a man again who makes prayer and reads the Bible for us. We are had up before magistrates who are men, and we never get out of the hands of men till we die!

By 1869 there was opposition to the CD Acts, and campaigns against them led by the Ladies' National Association for the Repeal of the Contagious Diseases Acts (LNA) under the leadership of Josephine Butler. Working men, worried about the reputations of their wives and daughters, also joined the campaign, as did various religious groups; they finally succeeded in securing the repeal of the acts in 1886. During a contentious campaign Josephine Butler, who had an impeccable reputation, was subjected to abuse from many sides; Sir James Elphinstone MP declared that she was 'worse than the prostitutes' while the *Daily News* wrote that women like Mrs Butler 'have to be noticed at all costs, and take pleasure in a hobby too nasty to mention'.

> How is it that working-class prostitutes seem to be treated so much worse than their better-paid sisters?

The LNA also conducted successful campaigns against similar legislation operating across the British Empire wherever soldiers were based, including the Cape Colony in Africa, Hong Kong, New Zealand and India, where up to one third of the British army was garrisoned prior to 1914. This CD legislation was also repealed in 1888 but the practice of regulated prostitution continued semi-officially under a law allowing the hospitalisation of persons suspected of having an 'infectious disease' in India. There is no clear evidence that the CD Acts had an appreciable effect on the incidence of CD in the UK, while admissions to hospital peaked in India in 1895. Furthermore, in France during the First World War prostitutes with VD charged higher prices for their services; many men saw being hospitalised with sexually transmitted diseases as preferable to fighting on the Western Front.

Despite the glamorous and inaccurate image of prostitution in Hollywood films such as *Pretty Women* (1990) prostitution continues to attract censure, but must be considered within the context of women's employment options. As one member of the English Collective of Prostitutes recently explained on their website:

I was fed up of being a cleaner, bar maid and shop assistant, often all on the same day. Prostitution is certainly not the worst job I have ever had. I have worked on the fish market and as a cleaner where I was working for people who didn't care if we were cold or tired or how we were spoken to.

64 | Portrait of Dr James Barry
Dressing as a Man and Transgender Lives

JANIS LOMAS

The miniature portrait of James Barry, painted around 1815, shows a young man embarking on a career as an army surgeon. He had recently qualified from Edinburgh University medical school, where his slight build and short stature aroused some comment and caused him to stand out from the other graduates.

This is not surprising as, unknown to them, James Barry had been born Margaret Anne Buckley in Cork, Ireland. After graduating she spent most of her career abroad in various outposts of the British Empire and rose to become Inspector General of Military Hospitals.

James Barry probably had the most successful career of any of the women who dressed in men's clothes in the nineteenth century. Changing her outward appearance was the only way for Buckley to fulfil her ambition of a career in the army after her family had fallen on hard times. Her qualification as a doctor predated the first official female doctor to qualify in the UK, Elizabeth Garrett Anderson, by some fifty years. As James Barry she strove to improve conditions for the indigenous population and wounded soldiers in her care and performed many successful surgical operations, including the first caesarean section operation in the Empire in which both the mother and child survived. She spent her entire adult life as a man and her identity was only discovered by the maidservant who laid her out after her death.

James Barry was just one of many women who cross-dressed, who lived a transgender life. There have been examples throughout history, with some of the earliest recorded being in ancient Greece. The orator and philosopher Philostratus describes the cult of Aphrodite, in which followers staged festivals that allowed 'women to act the part of men, and men to put on women's clothing and play the woman'. Throughout the centuries, some women only dressed as the opposite sex for a short time or for a particular reason; it is estimated that between 400 and 750 women disguised themselves in male clothing and joined the army during the American Civil War. Their reasons were varied, although often their primary motivation was a fervent loyalty to one side or the other. For some it was also to be near their soldier husbands or brothers, while for others it was the excitement and desire for travel, adventure or even for the regular wages. Sarah Edmunds Seelye joined the 2nd Michigan Infantry under the name Franklin Thompson, writing: 'I could only thank God that I was free to go forward and work, and I was not obliged to stay at home and weep.'

She took part in several battles and was sent on spying missions behind enemy lines, but deserted the army, probably after contracting malaria and fearing discovery

James Barry had the most successful career of any of the women who dressed in men's clothes in the nineteenth century.

if sent to hospital. Nevertheless, she was the only woman awarded a service pension after the war when she married and brought up three children. In the First World War, Englishwoman Dorothy Lawrence was so determined to become a war reporter that she donned male clothes and enlisted to get to the front line.

There was more scope for cross-dressing in the arts and entertainment industries. In the nineteenth century the French novelist Armandine-Aurore-Lucile Dupin wrote under the pseudonym George Sand and scandalised society by smoking cigars and preferring to wear men's clothing. On the British music hall circuit there were several women who enjoyed great success by dressing as men, of whom the most famous was Vesta Tilley. She appeared on the stage from 4 years old; her father was her manager and she was soon financially supporting the whole family. Borrowing her father's clothes she began appearing on stage as a male impersonator, a dapper little man, small and slight, performing a diverse range of characters including an upper-class gentleman, an orphan boy, a clergyman, a soldier or sailor. She had thousands of male and female fans, singing to rapturous applause:

Did the transgender life of James Barry undermine binary divisions of masculinity and femininity?

Jolly good luck to the girl who loves a soldier ...
Girls, if you'd like to love a soldier you can all love me.

When she retired, an extremely wealthy woman, her husband became a Conservative Member of Parliament and she eventually became Lady de Frece, an enormous rise in status from her working-class beginnings.

In the USA, in the 1930s, the very well-known jazz musician Billy Tipton lived as a man all his adult life, had a series of relationships with women and adopted three children, no one apart from his birth family knowing that he was born female until his death in 1989.

For some women, such as James Barry, cross-dressing provided access to a well-paid career; for others it was a search for adventure and an escape from the restrictions society placed on women, and they felt more comfortable as a man. Their choice could risk legal punishment or social ostracism, but in many parts of the world these boundaries have now been broken down; clothes and gender identity are more fluid and more a matter of personal choice than they were in the past.

65 | Three-Legged Milking Stool and Yoke

Women's Work in Dairies and Farms Across
Time and Continents

MAGGIE ANDREWS

The pretty milkmaid was understood to have peasant beauty and sexual allure in eighteenth- and nineteenth-century Britain; in popular ballads she had a wholesome and vigorous sexuality.

The novelist Thomas Hardy was apparently inspired to create the heroine of his literary classic, *Tess of the d'Urbervilles* (1891), when he caught sight of the beautiful Augusta Lydia Florence Way sitting on a milking stool. Tess, the heroine of the novel, is raped and has an illegitimate child who dies; she briefly finds happiness and love as a milkmaid before her past catches up with her and the tragedy leads to her death. Milking stools helped milkmaids to get down to the level of a cow's udders to milk more easily; their three-legged design made them more stable on uneven ground. The milk was carried in buckets suspended from the shoulders by a yoke.

The day-to-day life of many milkmaids, however, involved hard work and rising early to milk cows seven days a week. This enabled milk from rural farms to be sent by train to large conurbations such as London and Manchester. Women have a long history of working in many areas of agriculture. Some work was seasonal, helping to bring in fruit, vegetable and corn harvests. Women worked on family farms or were part of a gang. The employment of men in a number of agricultural jobs came with the expectation that their wives or daughters would also undertake agricultural work without any wages of their own. In nineteenth-century Britain, this work began when girls were young. Mrs Burrows, recalling her childhood in the 1850s, noted:

> On the day that I was eight years of age, I left school and began to work fourteen hours a day in fields, with forty or fifty other children of whom even at that early age, I was the eldest. We were followed all day long by an old man carrying a long whip in hand which he did not forget to use.

A concern that women who worked in the fields urinated behind hedges or in sight of men led to growing disapproval of women's outdoor work and a reduction in some areas of women's agricultural work. There were, however, according to Harriet Martineau, approximately 64,000 dairymaids in Britain in the middle of the nineteenth century. As she pointed out:

Neither in America, nor anywhere else, would dairy work be objected to as a feminine employment, conducted within doors as it is, and requiring feminine qualities for its management; yet it is harder work, and more injurious to health than hoeing turnips or digging potatoes.

Although dairying was a skilled occupation, traditionally it was women's work and consequently had lower status than, for example, growing cereal. Dairying, however, has provided income and empowerment to women in many countries. A German military officer at the beginning of the twentieth century noted that Masai women looked after sheep, goats and calves, milked cattle mornings and evenings, shared out the milk and traded any surplus milk to supplement their income. Turkana women continue to be in charge of the milk production in contemporary Africa. The Samburu people of north-central Kenya allocate a number of cattle from her husband's herd to a woman on marriage; in the following months she may receive further gifts of calves, sheep or goats from friends.

In Britain in the early twentieth century wives, sisters and daughters on small farms kept hens or produced butter and eggs which were sold at the farm gate, the local market or to a 'higgler' who visited farms buying produce and taking them to market. Cream was churned to make butter; Maggie Joe Chapman, born in 1899, recalled how her father helped turn the handle of the churn so that her mother could keep her hands cool to make the butter. From May to October she also made cheeses which were sold to the Co-operative stores in Durham for the miners. Cheese making requires a number of skilled processes, warming the milk to separate the curds from the whey, squeezing the liquid out of the curds, pressing and drying the cheese. She recalled:

> We always pickled our cheese … You made this pickle of salt and boiling water, and it had to cool two days before it could be used. Cheeses would swim in this pickle for a day, and then you turned them over and left 'em another day and then they were ready.

Women continued to undertake dairy work in the twentieth century, although mechanisation and factory production was being steadily introduced. An advert in 1925, for example, required 'Man and wife wanted at once (not over 40) for a home farm in Herts. Man to attend small herd of registered Shorthorn and Jersey cattle, pigs and poultry, help given; wife to be a first-class dairy woman; model dairy, good cottage and garden.'

Why is it that dairy work continues to be associated with women, while other agricultural work is not?

Churning milk to make cheese was a task undertaken using a range of implements by women across the world. In 1947, Britain finally and hurriedly relinquished its colonial rule of India, which had once been seen as the jewel in the crown of the British Empire. The partition of the Indian sub-continent, into the mainly Muslim Pakistan with India remaining a secular country with a significant Hindu population, had catastrophic consequences. A million people were massacred in the ensuing violence. The partition led to 12 million people gathering up what possessions they could carry or place in bullock carts and migrating across India and Pakistan, leaving their homes. Aanchal Malhotra's great-grandmother crossed the border from Lahore to Amritsar to Delhi; she had very few possessions but one she chose to take with her was a copper vessel for churning milk. For women in rural India in the twenty-first century, dairying remains important. 75 million women – but only 15 million men – keep one or two cows, which provide food and help alleviate poverty by making a substantive contribution to their income, even in landless families. For many women dairy work is preferable to seasonal agricultural labour, such as planting, weeding and harvesting, which provides an irregular income and is not so easily integrated with other domestic responsibilities.

66 | Servant's Bells
Domestic Service: a Suitable Job for a Woman

JANIS LOMAS

In his 1902 play *The Admirable Crichton*, J.M. Barrie wrote: 'How shall we ever know that it's morning if there's no servant to open the blind?' His joke also made a point: in Victorian and Edwardian Britain, the middle and upper classes were used to having their every want fulfilled by a largely invisible resource – servants.

An army of women and men looked after the minutiae of domestic life for their employers. Servants undertook menial domestic tasks and tended to the requirements of the higher ranks of society, the middle classes and even some skilled tradesmen. From the end of the eighteenth century to the beginning of the twentieth, houses in Britain and America had mechanical bell systems or servant call bells installed. Employers pulled a knob or tassel mounted on the wall which was linked to bells in the servants' quarters or the kitchen at the bottom or the back of the house. Thus these bells not only summoned servants to do their employers' bidding but were symbols of their employers' control and dominance of servants' lives.

Having a servant conferred status on householders, and the Industrial Revolution in the late eighteenth century produced both status-conscious urban middle classes and fewer jobs for working-class women on the land or in traditional occupations such as spinning. Consequently the use of female servants was widespread by the mid-1800s in the United States, Britain and much of Europe. By 1870 over half of all women workers were domestic servants. Servants were cheap and plentiful; in 1905, a kitchen maid earned just £11 a year and on average female servants were paid around half as much as male servants. In Europe, most of these girls were native born but in the United States they were more likely to be immigrants, often Irish, with over 60 per cent of Irish immigrant women working as domestic servants. After the American Civil War, when many African-American women moved from the impoverished southern states to the urbanised north, they too provided a plentiful supply of cheap labour in white middle-class homes.

In Britain, there was a clear hierarchy of servants; the lady's maid or housekeeper in one of the great country houses was near the top, and the solitary young female maid-of-all-work at the bottom of the pecking order. Although not typical, at Eaton Hall near Chester, the Duke of Westminster employed 300 indoor and outdoor servants – among them over forty men to look after the gardens. This number of servants did not mean that the workload was reduced; the wealthy had exacting requirements that had to be met by this army of staff. At Wellbeck Abbey, where the Duke of Portland was extremely fond of having roast chicken whenever he fancied a

slice, one of his thirty-eight kitchen staff had to ensure that the spit always had one just cooked ready for whenever he fancied it. Unsurprisingly, when the 6th Marquis of Bath recalled his boyhood at Longleat, where he had his own valet to dress him from the age of 4, he said, 'You were looked after in the lap of luxury. I think the more servants you had the better.'

In contrast, when employed as a maid-of-all-work, a girl could have sole responsibility for cooking, waiting on tables, washing the dishes, all the cleaning, fire lighting and bed making, laundry and ironing, mending, and sometimes even childcare. As one young servant wrote to her parents:

> I have been so driven at work since the fires began I have had 'ardly any time for anything for myself. I am up at half past five and do not go to bed until nearly twelve at night and I feel so tired sometimes that I feel obliged to have a good cry.

By 1870 over half of all women workers in Britain were domestic servants.

For all live-in servants the hours were long, on average eleven to twelve a day, seven days a week, and a domestic servant was 'on call' twenty-four hours a day. Domestic servants traditionally got one Sunday a month and one afternoon a week off, having accomplished most of the daily chores first. Employers also exercised control over their dress, speech and contact with family and friends.

In the USA newly arrived immigrants often found the assurance of room and board a distinct advantage, but most women worked in domestic service because a lack of education, limited job opportunities or discrimination made other jobs inaccessible. However between 1890 and 1920, while the demand for domestic servants persisted, a wider array of jobs became available for women. Work in offices, shops and department stores, and even in factories, offered greater freedom and in the United States the proportion of women working in domestic service fell from over half in 1870 to less than a fifth in 1920. However, the percentage of African-American women working as domestic servants rose from 24 per cent in 1890 to 40 per cent in 1920 in the USA.

Is it surprising that in Britain and the USA women and girls rejected domestic service in the second half of the twentieth century?

Simultaneously in Britain, the proportion of live-in servants began to decline; in 1911 servants were about a quarter of all employed women but it became increasingly difficult to find women and girls prepared to enter domestic service. Labour shortages led even the upper classes to pay higher wages and discover they could no longer afford the army of staff they had previously employed. From the Second World War onwards, working-class women and girls in Britain and the USA rejected a life of servitude for better wages and more freedom elsewhere.

In contemporary Western societies the numbers of servants are once again on the increase. There is again a hierarchy among modern servants; some live-in skilled servants for the super-rich who are nannies, chefs or butlers may earn well but there are also numerous migrant workers, part-time cleaners and au pairs on minimum wages.

67 | The Typewriter
From Copy Typist to Personal Computers

JANIS LOMAS

In 1867 an American, Christopher Latham Sholes, began to construct the first typewriter that could allow a person to write quicker than handwriting. Following improvements, the first typewriter came on to the market in 1874 produced by Remington. It could only write in capital letters but it introduced the 'qwerty' keyboard still in use on many keyboards today.

Over the next twenty years further enhancements resulted in the typewriter being widely used in many offices. As the standard price was between $60 and $100, while a male clerk only earned $5 a week, it was initially out of reach for most people in their home and many small offices, but it heralded a new working environment and occupation for women; its use was to spread quickly from the USA throughout Europe.

Concerns about the 'surplus women' problem were aired in Great Britain from the 1860s onwards. These were women for whom marriage and motherhood were not available due to age, looks, poverty, predisposition or a shortage of eligible men. With increasing access to education, women railed against the limited career options available to them and began to filter slowly into jobs as shopgirls, teachers, nurses and even journalists. The invention of the typewriter opened up offices as a new, rapidly expanding area of employment for women. In 1870, there were barely 1,000 women working in offices, but by 1901 women were beginning to dominate the lowly, repetitive positions in office work, particularly typing. The music of Miss Remingon's Reverie, introduced in 1901, helped develop the regular click-clack of typing, a rhythmic approach to typing used for many years.

Why are only one in five jobs in computers undertaken by women?

Female typists (at first confusingly called typewriters) increasingly replaced boys and young men employed as copyists as they could do the job more quickly, were thought to have smaller hands and nimbler fingers, and were much cheaper. The treasury noted that 'women typists have proved themselves an efficient and economical form of labour' and rather begrudgingly added that 'copying with the aid of a machine ... is not difficult, so their pay should be "moderate"'. A typist's starting pay in a government department was just 16s a week in 1894.

Wages had not significantly improved by 1911, when one woman complained that even though she had passed the Higher Cambridge Certificate with Honours, spoke

French and German, had studied shorthand and typing, and worked in a large office for fifteen months, she was still only earning £40 a year. Nevertheless, by 1911 there were 125,000 women in such roles and fifty years later 1.8 million. Men were often deeply resentful, as the *Liverpool Echo* in 1911 noted:

> These intrepid typewriter pounders, instead of being allowed to gloat over love novels or do fancy crocheting during the time they are not 'pounding', should fill in their spare time washing out the offices and dusting same, which you will no doubt agree is more suited to their sex and maybe would give them a little practice and insight into the work they will be called up to do should they so far demean themselves as to marry one of the poor male clerks whose living they are doing their utmost to take out of his hands at the present time.

Government departments and large firms sought to prevent women and men meeting, with different entrances and meal breaks for women, and women working behind screens or in the attics so no man could see them. Any woman who married was required to leave her employment immediately, but working apparently had a beneficial effect on women's clothing. *The American Journal* commented in 1898: 'No expert can manage either the typewriter or the bicycle while she is held in a close-fitting cage of whalebone and steel.'

Office jobs were considered a genteel position and business colleges sprang up to give women the skills they needed. An experienced shorthand typist could earn £2–£3 a week and in 1911 a top secretary could earn up to £250 a year. However, hours were long and there were no promotion prospects, except as a supervisor of other women clerical workers or typists. A woman's highest aspiration might be to become a personal assistant – a sort of office wife, catering to their male bosses' every need.

In the latter part of the twentieth century, the typewriter was replaced by the personal computer; many women slowly saw their jobs in typing pools and clerical work disappear, while others were freed to work from home. Women were quite prominent in the early days of computing but now only one in five jobs is undertaken by women and these are often low-level data processing roles. In the 1980s, information technology (IT) products were marketed with men in mind, showing women struggling to use technology while images of the male nerd, hacker or gaming enthusiast became prominent. Computer companies promoting themselves through the male 'geniuses' who run them reinforced such stereotypes. The personal computer, unlike the early Remington typewriters, is affordable; few first-world homes are without at least one, and this new technology has offered women a range of new, flexible ways of working from their homes.

68 | The First World War Policewomen's Armlet

Taking a Role in Maintaining Law and Order

LISA DAVIES

In 1915 Edith Smith, a 35-year-old widow and former midwife, became the first officially appointed woman police constable in Britain. Smith, who was stationed in Grantham, Lincolnshire, was employed to address concerns arising from the billeting of soldiers in two large army camps in the town and the consequent influx of young women and prostitutes.

Smith had no handcuffs or truncheon, and her uniform consisted of a long navy skirt, severe navy tunic and a felt hat. The only identifiable police insignia was an armlet, similar to those worn by male officers. This uniform identified the wearer as a new invention, a female police patrol, the first time women had been entrusted to maintain law and order and keep the peace.

Prior to the First World War women's involvement in policing was restricted to the role of matron. These women, small in number and often the relations of male officers, were first employed in 1883 and looked after female prisoners in cells and in court, representing the first recognition that there was a role for women in policing. The very nature of policing, dealing with the violence and unpleasantness of society, was deemed to be masculine, and unsuitable for women. It was, however, felt that women could address concerns about the moral welfare of women, and particularly working-class girls, in the First World War. The National Union of Women Workers received Home Office approval for their voluntary patrols to prevent unwanted sexual activity, and the Women's Police Volunteers, led by suffragettes Nina Boyle and Margaret Damer-Dawson, became the Women's Police Service in 1916. Between them these two groups policed women both criminally and morally, near army camps, parks, cinemas and munitions factories. With the exception of Edith Smith, none of these early 'policewomen' were able to arrest offenders, there was no official police training and the Home Office was reluctant to give them official sanction, stating that 'these female patrols are for preventative purposes and do not want to be regarded as having undertaken any police duties in respect of prostitutes'.

> Is policing, dealing with the violence and unpleasantness of society, still perceived to be an unsuitable job for a woman?

These pioneering women succeeded in creating a gender-specific role in dealing with women and children and established a foothold for women in policing. The 1916 Police Act allowed women to be appointed as police constables at a time when women were not deemed 'proper persons' to serve on juries. However the

Paid Patrols : Somerset.

employment of women in the regional police forces was left to the discretion of individual chief constables, some of whom resisted for the next three decades. In other countries women were beginning to take a role in policing; Marie Owens joined the Chicago Police Department in 1891, while Vancouver and Edmonton in Canada had their first female officers in 1912, similarly to address issues around female morality. In South Australia, Kate Cocks was recruited in 1915 and uniquely received the same pay and police powers as her male colleagues. France had its first female officer the same year.

By the end of the First World War women had a role in policing. Birmingham recruited two women in 1917 and the Metropolitan Police directly recruited its own female officers in 1918. Although many forces often only had a handful of women, by 1948 only two forces out of 133 in England and Wales had failed to employ any women as police officers. Women still faced challenges; although the marriage bar was removed in 1946, cultural and social expectations meant many women continued to leave upon marriage. Policewomen worked in separate women's departments, focusing on women and children, with their own promotion structure and shift pattern; they earned 90 per cent of men's pay until 1975 when the Sex Discrimination Act was introduced, forcing all police forces to integrate women's departments into mainstream policing. Since that time women have continued to breach traditionally masculine roles and work in varied roles such as traffic officers, dog handlers and firearms officers. The increasing sensitivity to crimes directed at women in recent years has, however, once again begun to raise concerns around the roles that women should undertake and in the 1980s some countries, such as Brazil, introduced women's police stations, seen as safe havens to report gender-specific crimes.

The British public are now familiar with the sight of female police officers on patrol and in the media in fictional TV dramas such as *Cagney and Lacey* (1981–86) and *Prime Suspect* (1991–2017). Nevertheless, some still see policing as a masculine profession: in 2011 only 12 per cent of the 700,000 police officers in the USA were women. Furthermore, many women working in the police have faced discrimination, marginalisation, and the operation of a glass ceiling limiting promotion. The National Association of Women Law Enforcement Executives (NAWLEE) was set up in the USA in 1995 to assist women seeking to obtain management positions. In Britain, change is occurring; Jackie Malton, former detective chief inspector, has remarked: 'It's absolutely less sexist than when I was working in the Flying Squad in the late 80s and early 90s', when her male colleagues apparently routinely presented her with sex toys. The first female chief constable was appointed in 1995 and in 2017 the Metropolitan Police appointed its first female commissioner, Cressida Dick. These women's positions in policing have been a hundred years in the making and owe much to those early pioneering women.

69 | Nursing Qualification Certificate

Professionalising Women's Caring Role

MAGGIE ANDREWS

The certificate Mary Haywood was awarded in January 1940 recorded that she had successfully completed three years of nursing training at the children's hospital in Pendlebury. She went on to undertake further training at University College Hospital in London during the Blitz, becoming a State Registered Nurse before she joined the Royal Air Force (RAF).

In the latter years of the Second World War she cared for those whose service in the RAF had led to mental illness, marrying one of her ex-patients in 1945. At this point her career came to an end – nursing, like many other professions, operated a marriage bar at this time.

Nursing the sick has been seen as a traditional female role for hundreds of years in a multitude of societies. Wise women with knowledge passed down from their mothers and grandmothers used herbal remedies or folk medicines made from plants and natural ingredients to cure the sick or alleviate suffering. However, the rise of the medical profession in the Western world during the eighteenth and nineteenth centuries relegated women to caring for the sick while male doctors were responsible for curing them. The long white aprons and caps worn by nurses in the nineteenth century can be seen to suggest that their role is akin to that of domestic servants.

The reputation of nurses continued to deteriorate; concerns were expressed over their gambling, swearing, quarrelling and drinking – problems that hospital porters and orderlies were also accused of. The iconic image of an untrained nineteenth-century nurse was personified by Sarah Gamp, a character created by Charles Dickens in *Martin Chuzzlewit* (1843–44). This was neither fair nor accurate; Sarah Gamp was a domiciliary carer, undertaking housework and nursing care for people within their homes, while London teaching hospitals were making nursing more professional. Florence Nightingale lobbied for nursing staff to be under the control of a female matron like Mrs Wardroper, of St Thomas's Hospital. An Anglican lay sisterhood was founded at St John's House in London 'to elevate the character of the Nurses, by training them in a regular course, which shall fit them for their professional calling' in 1842 and a few years later they were providing the nurses for University College Hospital where Mary Haywood would finish her training eighty years later.

Britain, the USA and many other countries established nurse training schools to develop a female profession in the second half of the nineteenth century. In Brazil the first president created the first professional school for nurses at the National

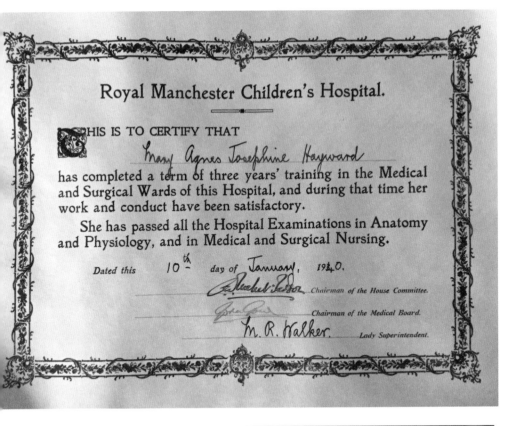

Royal Manchester Children's Hospital.

THIS IS TO CERTIFY THAT

Mary Agnes Josephine Hayward

has completed a term of three years' training in the Medical and Surgical Wards of this Hospital, and during that time her work and conduct have been satisfactory.

She has passed all the Hospital Examinations in Anatomy and Physiology, and in Medical and Surgical Nursing.

Dated this 10th day of January, 1940.

_____ Chairman of the House Committee.

_____ Chairman of the Medical Board.

M. R. Walker. Lady Superintendent.

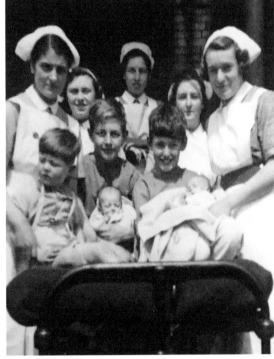

Insane Asylum, the year after the proclamation of the republic occurred in 1889. The Australian Trained Nurses Association was founded in 1899, with an examination compulsory for membership by 1906.

Textbooks such as *A Hand-Book of Nursing for Family and General Use* (1878) and *Nursing: Its Principles and Practice for Hospital and Private Use* (1893) shaped the curriculum of new nursing schools in the USA, where the American Nurses Association was set up in 1911. It was not, however, until the aftermath of the First World War in 1919 that state registration of nursing was introduced in Britain, three years after the Royal College of Nursing had been established.

The very first hospital dedicated to treating children, in Pendlebury near Manchester, had by then expanded by building wards with the vaulted ceilings and brightly painted walls advocated by Florence Nightingale; by 1921 the newly formed General Nursing Council approved the hospital's nurse training scheme. When Mary Haywood started her training in 1937, the hours that nurses worked had been reduced from sixty-three to fifty-four per week. Much free time was spent in the nursing home, where all nurses had to live. Its tight regulations governed the behaviour of some trainee nurses, reassuring their parents if, like Mary, they had left home many miles away at only 17. Much of her spare time was needed for study and in 1938 she successfully undertook her Preliminary State Examination, writing answers to questions such as 'Describe how you would make up the bed to receive a patient suffering from acute rheumatism; Give reasons for what you do', and 'Describe briefly the skull and its contents'.

How problematic is it that nursing the sick continues to be seen as a traditional female role in numerous societies?

In post-war Britain, many nurses like Mary had left the profession to start families; the National Health Service, established in 1948, was short of nurses and hence recruited thousands of them from the Caribbean and India. By the mid-1960s between 3,000 and 5,000 Jamaican nurses were working in British hospitals, where they experienced racism, often finding themselves on the least desirable shifts or doing the most unpleasant jobs.

In the twenty-first century, nursing continues to change; it has become a graduate profession. In her nursing home, Mary Haywood is now looked after by nurses who may be men or have come from any one of a multitude of different countries. For women, the certificate that confirms their professional status in nursing continues to be a source of pride and to open the door to travel.

70 | The Royal Shakespeare Theatre

Working in a Profession

LEAH SUSANS

The Royal Shakespeare Theatre, designed by Elisabeth Scott, opened in Stratford-upon-Avon in 1932. It was one of the first really iconic buildings designed by a woman. Many of the public were stunned that a woman had designed the theatre, which was considered one of the country's major tourist attractions at the time and has a proscenium-arch stage and a seating capacity of 1,400 people.

The theatre had Art Deco features, including the stairs and corridors at either side of the auditorium, and is now a Grade II listed building. Following its completion in 1932, some provocative and extreme reactions surfaced; the musician Sir Edward Elgar described the theatre as 'unspeakably ugly and wrong ... an insult to human intelligence'.

Scott gained the commission through a competition launched in 1927 to design a replacement for the Shakespeare Memorial Theatre, which had been destroyed by fire the previous year. Elisabeth Scott, who had been working for Maurice Chesterton's practice in Hempstead, London, succeeded against seventy-one other entries in the competition. Chesterton agreed to oversee her proposals; two fellow Architectural Association (AA) students, Alison Sleigh and John Chiene Shepherd, assisted in the project. Scott had previously worked in a variety of architectural firms but, on winning the competition, she formed a partnership – Chesterton, Sleigh and Shepherd – to prepare the detailed plans and supervise the construction.

Scott was one of the first women to study for the AA, which had refused to accept female students prior to 1917. Scott's design for the theatre won world recognition and after winning the competition in 1927 she was the centre of much media attention with her work becoming front-page news. Scott's achievement and her decision to employ where possible female architects to assist her on the Stratford design was instrumental in opening up the profession to women. Even though Scott was not an outspoken feminist, she challenged traditional assumptions about women and their professional status. Scott's prominence became quite inspirational. For example, Judith Ledeboer changed her career path instantly after hearing about Scott's win and became a leading post-war architect herself.

In the years that followed the theatre's opening in 1932 women continued to design iconic and controversial buildings. Norma Merrick Sklarek was a pioneering African-American architect and was the first black women to be licensed as an architect in the USA in New York in 1954. She was later also licensed in California in 1962 and remained the only licensed black woman in California until 1980. While a director at

The Architectural Association refused to accept female students prior to 1917.

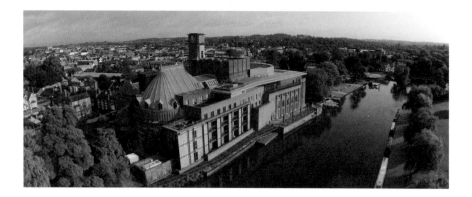

Gruen Associates, Sklarek collaborated with Cesar Pelli on a number of projects, but her race and gender often excluded her from the recognition she deserved.

Most recently the Iraqi-born British architect Zaha Hadid was the first woman to receive the Pritzer Architecture Prize in 2004. She also won the UK's most prestigious architectural award, the Stirling Prize, in 2010 and 2011. In 2015 she became the first woman to be awarded the Royal Gold Medal. *The Guardian* described her as the 'queen of the curve' who 'liberated architectural geometry, giving it a whole new expressive identity'. Her major works include the aquatic centre for the London 2012 Olympics and the Guangzhou Opera House in China. Hadid passed away in 2016; however, some of her designs have received awards posthumously, including the statuette for the 2017 Brit Awards.

Why is it that many women in demanding professions choose not to have children?

Elisabeth Scott defied expectations of women's roles in the inter-war years and established a professional career. However, even today architecture remains a difficult industry for women to break into. The results of the 2016 Women in Architecture Survey, which involved 1,152 women worldwide, revealed that more than one in five would not recommend a career in architecture. Additionally only 15 per cent of these women thought women were accepted in the industry. The survey also revealed 75 per cent of female architects do not have children, suggesting that women consider motherhood would disadvantage them in their profession. This survey suggests many women still struggle to feel equal in architecture. In the words of the successful architect Zaha Hadid: 'It is hard to believe, but it's still difficult for women to break the business barrier. Through perseverance and hard work, I've been able to do so, but it's been a long struggle.'

71 | 'Women of Britain – Come into the Factories' Poster

Dangerous War Work in the Second World War

AMY DALE

In both the world wars, when men were sent to fight, women moved into traditionally masculine occupations. This had the potential to challenge, change, re-assert or simply redefine women's roles in society. The poster entitled 'Women of Britain – Come into the Factories' (1941), by Philip Zec, was intended to both encourage women into industry and to reaffirm the importance of their wartime role.

The poster places the munitions worker centrally, her arms open and gazing upwards with pride at the fighter pilots on their way to do battle. It is she who has equipped them with planes, munitions and the tools needed to go into combat.

Traditionally, the Second World War has been held up as an emancipatory experience for women. Although many of the roles that women performed were for the duration only, traditional gender roles were questioned. This experience was not unique to British women. In Russia and the USA, women also trained as pilots; the American WAVES and British ATA were tasked with transporting aircraft while the Soviets trained their own female fighter pilots. Germany had to abandon their rhetoric of *Kinder, Küche, Kirche* (children, kitchen, church) as women were required to step out of the domestic sphere to support their nation. But the majority of women workers in the Second World War were in industry; even in predominantly rural Japan, 4 million women were mobilised to work in factories. Millions of women across the world found themselves in the labour force for the first time or breaking new ground within the armed forces.

In Britain, the National Service Act (2) of 1941 conscripted women, and for the first time over 7 million were engaged in wartime service. Single women and widows without children, aged between 19 and 43, were directed into war work, particularly industry. Nearly 2 million women manufactured the chemicals, machines and ammunition needed to form the bedrock of the fighting forces. By 1943, 57 per cent of all women in the workforce were engaged in munitions work. The work was gruelling, with long days and the constant threat of factory explosions and enemy attack. The most dangerous of all munitions work was undertaken in Royal Ordnance factories (ROF) where 70 per cent of the workforce were women. Handling high explosives and detonators led to many accidents, some fatal, and left thousands of women injured and permanently disabled. One ROF lady worker from Stoke on Trent recalled the dangerous nature of the work:

> We were in the yellow powder ... [it] went really yellow, skin and hair ... it was a very bad night one night, a real explosion ... one was blinded, one was

killed. But, they kept us away from the news as much as possible when we were working.

Others told more humorous narratives:

When I had my accident, I was a fitter and I used to look after paint machines … I went into the store … there used to be tubes that the paint came out of … through a spray gun … I unscrewed the top … switched it on … My face! It was black … and it set the moment it touched the shells … and my eyes were burning red … I went over to the girls and I said 'Oh God!' They thought I was acting … because I am a bit of a funny woman … but the ambulance came up for me … and my face was black set and the only thing you could see were my teeth.

In 1942 ROF workers were issued with a pin badge saying 'front line duty' to recognise their work. However, after the war, many munitions workers felt frustrated at what they perceived to be a lack of recognition for the harsh conditions of their wartime employment. A worker from the Swynnerton factory, who suffered a serious accident that left her both temporarily blind and unable to walk, expressed such frustration:

We don't talk about it a lot. But the feeling is still always there … I saw more in those few months than a good many people do in a lifetime. You could never describe it to anybody … the full horror of the place … but it's still the

WOMEN OF BRITAIN

COME INTO THE FACTORIES

ASK AT ANY EMPLOYMENT EXCHANGE FOR ADVICE AND FULL DETAILS

feeling underneath, especially when it's Armistice Day, of why weren't we remembered? They used to give us a badge, and it used to be a bomb and a shell, crossed. And underneath it, it said 'front line duty'. Now, we were front line duty, because without us, there wouldn't have been any war.

Some 17,000 women were disabled by their Second World War work, a significant portion of whom were employed in industry. The wartime paradox required women to perform dangerous, traditionally masculine roles, but did not give them equal rates of pay or compensation. The issue of equal pay was never remedied, but women did gain ground in other areas. The Personal Injuries (Emergency Provisions) Act 1939 established the rate to be paid to those disabled as a third less for women. In April 1943, campaigning led to equal rates of compensation for women. The Disabled Persons (Employment) Act 1945 gave preferential job opportunities to women on equal terms with men. They were recognised in their own right, and not just as the wives of injured soldiers.

Are women who work in munitions complicit in the subsequent killing?

There is little doubt that for some women, wartime employment led to an increase in confidence and heightened social and economic freedom. Many women moved away from home to work at the factories and took full advantage of their independence. One recalled: 'It was great, we used go out most nights ... I went with a soldier first, then an airman [laughing] then a Yank and then a sailor ... I thought I'd try all the services.'

But much progress was temporary. What was of greater significance is that women's wartime employment was responsible for the emerging ripples of change that would grow in the post-war period.

72 | Maria Montessori 1,000 Lira Note

Education and Teaching

JANIS LOMAS

In 1990 the Italian 1,000 lira bank note carried an image of the renowned educator Maria Montessori. Born in Italy in 1870, she became the first woman to enter an Italian medical school, qualifying as a doctor in 1896. She developed an interest in children with learning disabilities and after opening a school for them developed teaching aids and self-directed activities to support their learning through creative play.

Her success brought into mainstream schooling her idea that children had the power to educate themselves, if given the activities and materials to support their natural development. Schools using her methods sprang up all over the world and her books were translated into over twenty languages. Although the rise of fascism and the Second World War restricted her work, she continued to travel after the war; even after her death in 1952 her methods have continued to influence children's education.

Banknotes, since 1970 in the UK, have featured 'celebrated individuals that have shaped British thought, innovation, leadership, values and society', but until recently, only two women – Florence Nightingale and Elizabeth Fry – had been featured, and then only temporarily. Jane Austen has been on the £10 note since 14 September 2017, following a petition begun by Caroline Criado-Perez in 2013. Australian banknotes have five men and five women on them, but only one of the fifty-three people who have been featured on USA banknotes was a woman, Martha Washington. Maria Montessorri's place on the 1,000 lira note signalled her significance and the importance of education for women, as both students and educators.

The education of girls has proved a contentious issue. Girls from middle-class and aristocratic families in nineteenth-century Britain were initially taught at home by their mother or a governess; their education was designed to fit them for marriage and running a household. They learned skills such as playing the piano, singing, needlework, sketching and perhaps a smattering of a foreign language to ensure they would be 'an ornament' to their husband's household. Girls were informed that 'the first thing of importance is to be content to be inferior to men, inferior in mental power in the same proportion that you are inferior in bodily strength'.

Parents felt money spent on a girl's education would be wasted, as they would marry and have babies, and also that no one would want to marry a young woman thought to be clever. The anti-suffragist writer Sarah Sewell wrote in 1868 that 'women who have stored their minds with Latin and Greek seldom have much knowledge of pies and puddings'. Some doctors claimed that brain-work would

damage women's reproductive organs. Dr Henry Maudsley wrote that menstruation was a great physical drain on women's bodies, and education would place an additional 'excessive mental drain'. The consequence of educating women would be 'a puny, enfeebled and sickly race'. In reply the first female English doctor, Elizabeth Garrett Anderson, pointed out dryly that female servants were expected to carry out the same onerous duties whether menstruating or not. Despite opposition, the movement for women's education grew in the second half of the nineteenth century, fuelled by some women's desire to be economically independent and to gain access to professions such as law and medicine.

The desire for a university education for girls was partially resolved in 1869, when Emily Davies, Barbara Bodichon and Lady Stanley of Alderley founded Girton College, Cambridge; in 1878, the University of London became the first in the UK to award degrees to women. It was 1920 before Oxford University followed their lead, even though women had been permitted to study there without being full members of the university or being awarded degrees even after successfully completing courses. Indeed, when in 1897 a vote was taken over allowing women to receive degrees at Cambridge University and become full members of the university, a near-riot ensued in the city. Male undergraduates hoisted an effigy of a 'new woman' on a bicycle above one college, burned dummies of female scholars, and

threw fireworks at the windows of women's colleges. Women were finally awarded degrees at Cambridge in 1948.

Many women who gained degrees went into secondary school teaching. Sara Burstall, who became a celebrated writer on education and the second headmistress of Manchester High School for girls, recalled her first job at the North London Collegiate College in 1882:

> Apart however from income, we teachers have the additional work which is happy in itself … Indeed the first time I cashed my cheque I thought the shining sovereigns passed across the counter were magical, for I should have been glad to work for nothing.

Others were not so blasé about the need to earn a living. The status of elementary school teachers was rising as the profession began to be seen as a respectable profession for middle-class women, even as a 'vocation', and they took advantage of the new teacher training colleges set up in the latter part of the nineteenth century. Working-class girls with ability, whose families could forgo their income for a few years, were able to train on the job. From the 1870s, women teaching in elementary schools began to outnumber men. Teaching is both an extension of women's assumed role as carers and nurturers and a career, and can be combined with motherhood. Women now make up 85 per cent of all primary school teachers and 62 per cent of secondary school teachers in Britain. However, only 36 per cent of head teachers are female; one woman who was the only woman on a shortlist of nine candidates for headship suggested: 'In my own experience of applying for a head teacher role, governors overtly believed that a man would be better because he would be tougher and more respected by students.'

Why have so many feminists seen educating girls and women as so important?

Few women have reached the status and influence of Maria Montessori in the world of education, but the numerous women teachers are helping girls to achieve. In both Britain and the USA, women are now more likely go to university and complete their courses with a good degree than men. One pupil who joined Edgbaston High School for Girls in Birmingham is a reminder that education is not the right of all girls and women across the world. Malala Yousafzai came to Britain after she was shot by the Taliban in Pakistan for campaigning for girls' education. She has since received the Nobel Peace Prize at the age of 17 in 2014 for her work on women's rights and the education of girls. Across the world her work for girls continues; after visiting Kenya she explained: 'I met wonderful girls, girls who wanted to help their communities. I was with them in their school, listening to their dreams. They still have hope. They want to be doctors and teachers and engineers.'

73 | The Equal Pay Plate

The Unfinished Struggle for Equal Pay

ANNA MUGGERIDGE

This commemorative plaque, currently displayed at the People's History Museum, Manchester, celebrates the 187 female sewing machinists at Ford's Dagenham plant who went on strike in 1968 demanding equal pay for equal work.

Their actions brought the factory to a standstill and Eileen Pullen recalled:

Some of the men said: 'Good for you girl,' but others said: 'Get back to work, you're only doing it for pin money.' A lot of women jeered us. They didn't go to work and their husbands were at Ford and we'd put them out of work.

It took a further seventeen years before the Dagenham women got equal pay but their actions encouraged the Labour government to pass the Equal Pay Act in 1970, giving women the right to be paid the same wages as men for doing the same job. Theirs was, however, just one battle in the long fight over equal pay, a fight that still continues.

In the nineteenth century, many women were employed in domestic service or did home-based work in the sweated industries, where pay was terrible and conditions even worse. Where women did work in factories alongside men, they were paid less as it was assumed that women's earnings were secondary, and it was men whose pay supported the family – even though this was not necessarily the case.

Early trades unions excluded women when campaigning for better pay and conditions. In the 1880s women-only unions began to form, and in 1888, Clementina Black proposed the first ever equal pay resolution at the Trades Union Congress. The same year women workers known as 'matchgirls', who worked at the Bryant and May match factory, went on strike in protest at their terrible pay and conditions. In 1910 the successful Cradley Heath women chainmakers' strike ensured all employers complied with the minimum wage set by the Chain Trade Board in Britain. Mrs Patience Round, who was aged 79 and combined her work with care of her disabled husband, excitedly proclaimed that 'I never thought that I should live to assert the rights of women'.

During the world wars, there were a number of strikes by British women demanding equal rates of pay. Female workers on the London transport system successfully struck in 1918, demanding the same pay bonus as men. In a 1943 strike at the Rolls Royce factory in Glasgow, the majority of men walked out alongside the women, who were demanding equal pay. However, it has been suggested that they did so to protect the wages of men fighting in the armed forces who did not want to

MAY·JUNE 1968
Ford Sewing Machinists win equal pay and secure passage of the 1970 Equal Pay Act

Ford River Plant Shop Stewards Committee Dagenham

1968
SCROLL OF HONOUR

Lil O'Callaghan
Rosie Boland
Henry Friedman
Bernie Passingham
Kathy Mc Govern
Jock Mc Crae
Les Moore
Billy Mc Guire
Fred Blake
Jack Mitchell
Reg Birch
Charlie Gallagher

1984
SCROLL OF HONOUR

Kathy Mc Govern
Rita Sharpe
Bernie Passingham
Doreen Cook
Mick Murphy
Ron Todd
Henry Friedman
Derek Horne
Bob Henderson
Lil Thompson
Frances Kerwin

EQUAL PAY FOR WOMAN

END SEX DISCRIMINATION

EQUAL PAY FOR WORK OF EQUAL VALUE

WE DEMAND SKILL RECOGNITION AND UPGRADING

WE ARE FIGHTING FOR WOMENS RIGHTS

NOVEMBER-DECEMBER 1984
Ford Sewing Machinists win upgrading and skill recognition

discover at the end of the conflict that they had been replaced by cheaper women. In the post-war period, women continued to agitate for a number of workplace rights including equal pay and the right to keep their job when they married or had children. The belief that men were breadwinners, while women only worked for supplementary gain or 'pin money' persisted. Nevertheless, France passed equal pay legislation in 1946, newly independent India in 1947 and Germany in 1949. Teachers were the first group of British women to receive equal pay in 1961, followed by the civil service the following year. Women, however, were often employed in women-only roles, for example secretarial work, so their rates of pay did not increase. It took the Dagenham machinists' strike in 1968, and the efforts of the employment minister Barbara Castle, to get the Equal Pay Act passed in 1970, and finally into law in 1975, making it illegal to pay women less for doing the same job as men.

While in most countries it is now illegal to pay women less for doing the same job as men, it is not illegal to devalue feminised jobs, and thus many women still earn far less than men. The so-called 'pink jobs' – cleaning, caring and cooking – are poorly paid. What is considered to be a feminised, low-paid job shifts and changes. During the early years of computing, the 'simple' task of inputting numbers was considered ideal work for women. As computers became more complex, the prestige surrounding working with them and the salaries earned increased, and the number of women working in the field decreased. In modern-day Russia, most medical doctors are women; it is apparently a caring role to which women are supposedly uniquely suited. The rates of pay are consequently low compared with those of doctors in many other countries.

Why have women found it so difficult to earn wages equal to those of men?

Despite equal pay legislation, many women do not earn as much as men. The World Economic Forum's Gender Pay Gap Report in 2015 noted that the gender pay gap was smallest in Iceland, and largest in Yemen, with the United Kingdom in eighteenth place and the USA in twenty-fifth. In the summer of 2017, one of the largest pay-gap scandals in recent years engulfed the BBC, when it was revealed that its male presenters were paid more than women presenters of the same programmes, and that the highest-paid man earned three times as much as the highest-paid woman. In response, the BBC reiterated its pledge to close the gender pay gap by 2020 – a full half-century after the first Equal Pay Act was passed in Britain.

In addition, women are more likely to work part-time or miss promotion opportunities if they focus on raising children. Gender is not, however, the only factor influencing low wages; in 2015 calculations suggested that while white women in the USA earned 78 cents for every dollar that men earned, black and Latina women only earned 64 cents and 56 cents respectively.

Part VII
Creativity and Culture

Stereotypes of men and women often suggest that women are more creative and imaginative while men are considered to be more rational and scientific; while we would not want to endorse such assumptions about gender, the existence of such stereotypes has perhaps allowed women to find spaces within cultural and creative arts to express their identities, articulate their experiences and emotions or promote their causes, as many of the objects in this section demonstrate.

Excluded from taking their place in many branches of civil society, women have participated enthusiastically in religion, in women's organisations, in reading and in other areas of culture in imaginative ways. Black women jazz singers used their sublime talent to rise above poverty and discrimination to create a new genre of music while in 1598, the artist Artemisia Gentileschi used a biblical story to express the pain and helplessness she had suffered.

Other women have put pen to paper to protest against the restrictions placed on them, from the novels of the Brontë sisters depicting women as passionate equals to men to the more recent autobiographical work of Maya Angelou and Jung Chang which shed light on the injustices to which women were subjected, and their strength and tenacity which enabled them to survive living in oppressive circumstances. Similarly Anne Frank's diary has come to express the horror and waste of young lives during the Holocaust.

It is within culture that ideas, attitudes and prejudices about women are reinforced, challenged or reworked. Artefacts, not necessarily produced by women, have had important political roles to play. Paintings of the Ladies of Llangollen, the medallion of the anti-slavery league and the postage stamp of Mary Wollstonecraft, who critiqued women's role in society at the turn of the eighteenth and nineteenth century, have all made their mark. More recently, Marc Quinn's sculpture of Alison Lapper has challenged people's thinking about issues of disability.

Perhaps it is in the transgressive spaces that arts offer, the invitation they provide to shock and turn upside down dominant ideas, that they can make their most important contribution to challenging ideas about femininity. The artist Tracey Emin propelled women's private and intimate experiences into museums and public discourse; her sketches referring to abortion shocked and challenged people by articulating the trauma of abortion from a personal perspective, while the Greek tragedy *Medea* continues to raise issues about revenge and infanticide.

74 | *Medea* (Ancient Greek play)
Infanticide and Revenge

MAGGIE ANDREWS

Euripides's play *Medea*, produced for the first time in 431 BCE, depicts the story of a transgressive woman, a sorcerer and a heroine in ancient Greek mythology. Medea was an outsider in the city of Corinth, where she wrought revenge on her ex-husband Jason who had rejected her. She killed both their children and Jason's new bride before escaping in her chariot to start a new life in Athens.

Her image has since been depicted on vases, statues and other cultural artefacts as the iconic vengeful woman. Legally women's rights in ancient Greece seem to have been limited: they could not vote, own land or inherit property, and were not expected to keep a shop or go to the markets. As wives and daughters, as in many other societies, women's place was in the home. Indeed some have described the Greek culture, with its public whorehouses, mythology of rape and monuments featuring male genitalia, as the reign of the phallus. More complex interpretations of the era have noted there were variations between different city states and that the public and private spheres were not interpreted or divided as they are in contemporary culture; hence the public world of religion and ritual reached into the home. Some women, such as Sappho of Lesbos, became acclaimed as poets, but plays were not only performed by men but also written for men, by men. Within theatre, men authored tales of women's lives in tragedies such as *Medea,* exploring emotions and relationships, marital breakdown and stepfamilies.

While the female characters in these plays have been seen as men's fantasies, it might be more accurate to describe them as nightmares. For while the Greek tragedy plays often explore the victimisation of women, in a surprising number of them women murder men accidentally or, like Medea, quite deliberately. Furthermore, women speak proudly, determinedly, challenging the established order and criticising men. Medea demands:

> Flow backward to your sources, sacred rivers,
> And let the world's great order be reversed.
> It is the thoughts of men that are deceitful,
> Their pledges that are loose.

In the latter part of the twentieth century, when feminism argued that personal relationships and interactions were politically significant, women took an interest in staging, watching and studying *Medea* and other Greek tragedies. The plays explore women's ties to children, siblings and parents rather than romantic

It has been estimated that 200 women kill children each year in the USA.

partners; furthermore Medea's emotions, her rage and desire for vengeance are treated sympathetically, although her actions are not. As the chorus explains: 'I both wish to help you and support the normal ways of mankind, and tell you not to do this thing.'

It is the authenticity of the emotions that are expressed in the plays that speak to contemporary women. Euripides portrays Medea's rage as justified; she had given up a great deal for her husband Jason and reacted aggressively to being mistreated, used and abandoned. Her emotions override her reason as she cries: 'I know indeed what evil I intend to do, but stronger than all my afterthoughts is my fury, fury that brings upon mortals the greatest evils.'

Medea's desire to seek revenge resonates with contemporary audiences, and can be identified in many areas of popular culture, from the rape-revenge movies of the 1970s and 1980s to the tabloid and social media depictions of women who have found innovative ways to enact retribution on erring partners. There are narratives of women posting compromising images, cutting up and dumping clothes, selling houses or, like Michelle Mone, the boss of Ultimo bras, taking a key to the paintwork of their husband's car when he left her for one of her designers. Zhang Yufeng, known as the 'mistress killer', set up the Fire Phoenix Agency in 2003 to assist Chinese wives to collect evidence for divorce cases or enact violent revenge on their cheating husbands' mistresses. To some she is a celebrity heroine. Arguably, it is socially much more acceptable to attack other women than children. If Medea had killed Jason or only his new wife, she might have garnered empathy, but a woman killing her own children has enacted one of the strongest taboos, contravening assumptions about maternal love.

Are women more likely to take revenge in a non-violent way than men?

Moral panics surround infanticide, perceived to be one of the greatest social evils of Victorian England, but court records in many countries suggest it was the desperate act of the young, unmarried and financially desperate. Child murder is often now seen as a psychological issue, the perpetrator defined as mad rather than bad. This is how Medea's story is sometimes staged or reworked, in an era when children continue to be murder victims, often at the hands of their parents. The horror and importance of the play *Medea* is that it asks audiences to confront the realisation that what is assumed to be women's greatest emotion – maternal love – is not their only or even always their strongest emotion. Without support, care and the material necessities of life it is almost impossible for women to love and care for their children.

75 | Judith and Holofernes
Women Artists

JANIS LOMAS

In classical art male artists tended to depict women as objects of desire, or as mothers, servants, prostitutes, victims or virgins. Women were often not the main focus and were painted off to one side or in the background. Yet a closer examination of some paintings suggests more complexities and ambiguities in women's roles.

This painting, *Judith and Holofernes*, which now hangs in the Uffizi gallery in Florence, illustrates this and suggests the importance of art for understanding the history of women. It was painted sometime between 1614 and 1620 and its graphic detail was considered so shocking at the time that its owner, the Grand Duke Cosimo II de' Medici, hung it in a dark corner of his palace and the artist was not paid during de' Medici's lifetime.

The painting shows the biblical heroine Judith, a symbol of chastity and virtue, decapitating the Assyrian general Holofernes in order to save the people of her city, Bethulia, from the threat of the Assyrian army. According to the story, which was well known in both Renaissance and Baroque art and formed part of the Roman Catholic Old Testament, Judith travelled at great risk to Holofernes's camp. He, besotted by her beauty, allowed her to enter his tent hoping to seduce her. Instead she lulled him into a false sense of security and encouraged him to drink too much. When he passed out, Judith, her virtue intact, was able to decapitate him.

In the painting Judith and her maid Abra are portrayed as determined young women working together with rolled-up sleeves, intent upon defeating their enemy. Judith braces herself as she pushes Holofernes's head down and uses all her strength to push the sword through his neck while Abra is unflinchingly holding the struggling man down. In other depictions of this story, Judith is portrayed as shrinking back, appalled at what she is about to do, while in Gentileschi's painting the women are both fully engaged in their grisly task. Judith appears as aggressively in charge and is unfazed by the blood spurting from the neck of the decapitated man in the forefront of the picture.

What made this depiction of violent women even more scandalous was that it was painted by Artemisia Gentileschi, one of the very few women who made a living as an artist and who was by far the most successful and influential female artist of her age. She was also the first woman to be allowed to become a member of the Accademia di Arte del Disegno in Florence. The reason that Gentileschi was drawn to this subject and portrayed it in such a graphic way almost certainly lies in her own life. Her mother died when she was 12 years old and from that time on she grew up in the artist studio of her father, from whom she learned her craft. When she was

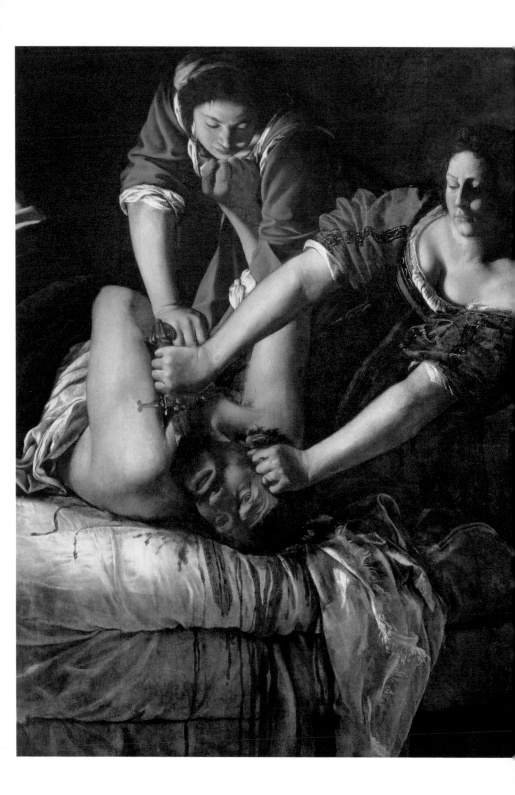

Artemisia Gentileschi was the most successful woman artist of the seventeenth century.

17 years old she was raped by the artist Agostino Tassi, a close friend of her father whom he had asked to tutor Artemisia. Under Roman law, Tassi was obligated to marry Artemisia after raping her. This Tassi refused to do, so her father took him to court in an attempt to reinstate her reputation. The trial dragged on for ten months, in the course of which she was subjected to a gynaecological examination in front of the judge and tortured to prove that she was telling the truth.

Although Tassi was found guilty and sentenced to one year's imprisonment this was never enforced and, humiliated, Artemisia was forced to leave Rome. During the trial, she described how she had tried to fight Tassi off with a knife and the betrayal she felt that her female chaperone and friend Tuzia had colluded with Tassi and ignored her cries when she called out to her for help. It seems that she is working out her anger and pain in the painting and her portrayal of Abra as working in unity with Judith is in direct contrast to the way she had been treated by Tuzia, the only female figure in her life. Many of her later paintings also convey the importance of women working together and showing solidarity with each other.

Why do women painters have a different style, focus or approach from male artists?

Male artists had been depicting brutal acts in paintings for centuries but what was almost unheard of was for a female artist to depict so violent a scene in which two women are the protagonists and a man the victim. Gentileschi's life and work has proved inspirational for generations of female artists and she portrayed historical and religious subjects in an unprecedented way at a time when those topics were considered out of the reach of women artists. In the twentieth century she became known outside the art world when she was rediscovered by feminists who were drawn to her life story as emblematic of the way women throughout the centuries have survived and even triumphed over adversity.

76 | Watercolour of the *Ladies of Llangollen*

Women's Romantic Friendships

JANIS LOMAS

This watercolour of the *Ladies of Llangollen* was painted by their friend Mary Parker, later Lady Leighton, in 1828 and portrays at the top in the centre a mourning ring with the ladies' hair entwined and their initials B and P. The ladies were unlikely rebels, coming from respectable Irish aristocratic families.

Eleanor Butler was born in 1739, the youngest daughter of the Earl of Ormonde of Kilkenny Castle. Her friend Sarah Ponsonby was sixteen years younger, an orphan in the care of her father's cousin Lady Betty Fownes and her husband William. They lived near to each other and formed a close romantic friendship from their first meeting. When Eleanor was 39 her mother, contrary to Eleanor's wishes, decided that Eleanor should become a nun, thereby cementing the family's relationship to the Catholic Church while easing the financial burden of keeping her. Sarah was also unhappy and subject to unwelcome attention from her guardian Sir William, whose wife was very ill, and who planned initially to make her his mistress, and when his wife died, to marry her. Determined to live their own lives away from family pressures, the pair made plans to elope to England and live together.

Their first attempt to run away, dressed in male clothing and carrying pistols, was unsuccessful and they were caught and brought back to Ireland, but eventually the two ladies' families relented; Eleanor and Sarah left for England in 1788, stopping on the way for a tour of North Wales. After falling in love with the countryside near Llangollen, they settled there, renting a cottage they later bought and renamed Plas Newydd (New Hall). There they lived in some style, with their devoted Irish servant Mary Carryl, along with several other servants and a gardener, for the next fifty years. The two eccentric women embellished and extended the house and made an outstanding garden. They lived an extremely secluded life, rarely spending a night away from the house. Whether the two women had a sexual relationship is unknown; they were inseparable, slept in the same bed, called each other 'My Beloved' or just 'My B' and sometimes 'My Better Half', had their hair cut short and wore riding habits and men's hats constantly. It was, however, much more common to use terms of endearments to friends and to share beds at that time.

The idea of romantic friendship was popular in late eighteenth-century intellectual circles and often seen as the ideal of a well-lived life; the couple who spent time in intellectual reading, learning languages, contemplation and improving their minds fitted this model. Their relationship seems to have been accepted, and well-known figures such as Lady Caroline Lamb, the poets William Wordsworth and

Robert Southey, the novelist Sir Walter Scott and statesmen including the Duke of Wellington all visited them.

A few perhaps thought the women's relationship was sexual, including the diarist Hester Thrale who visited and wrote to them but in her diary referred to them and their friends as 'damned Sapphists'. Anne Lister, a friend of theirs, certainly had full sexual relationships with several women. Two hundred years later, it is impossible to know the true nature of their relationship, but they certainly provide an example for women who choose a life living with a person of the same sex. The term 'Boston marriage' was coined to describe long-term relationships between two women a century later in the USA.

Is it possible to tell whether women like the Ladies of Llangollen were in a lesbian relationship or a romantic friendship?

The people of Llangollen accepted the ladies, as their presence drew an unprecedented number of visitors from far and wide to the area; even during their lifetime, souvenirs of them were produced and sold commercially. One visitor, Leman Thomas Rede, described them in 1799:

Miss Butler is tall and masculine, always wears a riding habit, hangs up her hat with the air of a sportsman, and appears in all respects like a young man, except the petticoat. Miss Ponsonby is polite and effeminate, fair and beautiful … They live in neatness, elegance and taste. Two females are their only servants. Miss Ponsonby does the honours of the house, while Miss Butler superintends the gardens and grounds.

When their servant Mary Carryl died in 1809, the ladies decided that the three of them would be buried together so they designed a three-sided, Gothic-style monument in Llangollen churchyard; Mary's side was faced with sandstone and the ladies' sides were marble. Thus in many ways they lived a conventional existence once they had escaped from lives that had become intolerable to them; their decision not to accept the roles that had been set out for them, whether it was marriage or life in a convent, was incredibly brave. They took hold of their own destiny and lived a life they chose for themselves, prioritising their female companionship over everything else. Whether their relationship was a lesbian one or not is immaterial, it was all-encompassing and liberating for them. American feminist of the 1970s Adrianne Rich, who critiqued the pressure on women to live in heterosexual relationships, wrote:

> The denial of reality and visibility to women's passion for women, women's choice of women as allies, life companions and community, the forcing of such relationships into dissimulation and their disintegration under intense pressure have meant an incalculable loss to the power of all women to change the social relations of the sexes to liberate ourselves and each other.

Nearly 200 years earlier this was not the fate of two remarkable women in a small Welsh town.

77 | Postage Stamp of Mary Wollstonecraft

The Birth of Feminism in Britain

JANIS LOMAS

Mary Wollstonecraft's *A Vindication of the Rights of Woman* was published in 1792, and came to be regarded as one of the earliest feminist treatises written; this has led to her being described as the 'forewoman of feminism'. A British postage stamp celebrating Wollstonecraft's life and work, which included philosophical works, novels and travel books, was issued in 2009, 250 years after her birth.

Wollstonecraft argued in *A Vindication of the Rights of Woman* that women were equal to men but lacked the educational opportunities to fulfil their potential. Women, she suggested, should eschew frivolity, be disciplined and both behave and be treated as rational and equal in public and private spheres. Thus women should have opportunities to participate in the political process 'instead of being arbitrarily governed without any direct share allowed'. With regard to marriage, she suggested: 'Make women rational creatures, and free citizens, and they will quickly become good wives; – that is, if men do not neglect the duties of husbands and fathers.' Although written at some speed and with some stylistic quirks, *A Vindication of the Rights of Woman* was widely read and quickly published in both France and the United States.

Mary Wollstonecraft married the anarchist philosopher William Godwin in 1797 but tragically died a few months later from septicaemia following the birth of their daughter, Mary, who later achieved fame as the writer of *Frankenstein* and wife of the poet Percy Shelley. After his wife's death Godwin published *Memoirs of the Author of A Vindication of the Rights of Woman*, a rather too honest account of Wollstonecraft's life detailing her love affairs, suicide attempts and illegitimate child. This account shocked society and tarnished her reputation. Nevertheless, Wollstonecraft's significance in the thinking of feminists can be identified in the years that followed, for example in Elizabeth Barrett Browning's seminal poem 'Aurora Leigh' (1856). The American women's rights activists Elizabeth Cady Stanton and Lucretia Mott acknowledged the effect of Wollstonecraft on their thinking when they set up the Seneca Falls Convention, generally considered the birth of the women's rights movement in the United States, in 1848. The writer George Eliot (Mary Ann Evans) also penned an essay in 1855 on the roles and rights of women after reading *A Vindication of the Rights of Woman*.

When the suffragist Millicent Garrett Fawcett wrote an introduction to the centenary edition of Wollstonecraft's book, it began to be more accepted and in the 1920s Virginia Woolf wrote an essay praising Wollstonecraft and went on to

Mary Wollstonecraft 1759–1797
Pioneering feminist

write two feminist treatises herself. *A Room of One's Own* (1929) interrogated how limitations and expectations placed on women constrained their creativity. She stressed the importance of financial independence for women, pointing out that 'a woman must have money and a room of her own if she is to write fiction'. Her *Three Guineas* (1938) was a critique of patriarchy, war and fascism. Woolf argued in this that war was a consequence of the way in which men were brought up to see violence, competition and domination as normal.

In the aftermath of the Second World War debates about men and women's roles and behaviour in society intensified. In 1949 Simone de Beauvoir's *The Second Sex* asked, 'What is a woman?' and argued that a woman is 'defined and differentiated with reference to man and not he with reference to her'. Feminist treatises differ in their thinking but share a perception that traditions, social

A Vindication of the Rights of Woman is regarded as the first feminist treatise.

expectations and the exercise of power are responsible for women's subjugation rather than nature or biology. Betty Friedan's popular book *The Feminine Mystique* (1963) is seen as a seminal text in American feminism of the 1960s and 1970s. In it, Friedan discusses 'the problem with no name', meaning the unhappiness of many women trapped into a life of domestic drudgery by the 'feminine mystique' – the idea that household duties and motherhood should be women's only role. Friedan called for a drastic rethink of what it meant to be feminine and shared with Wollstonecraft and Woolf the view that education was key for women's self-determination and autonomy.

When Germaine Greer published *The Female Eunuch* in the United Kingdom in 1970, she too called on women to reject their traditional roles in the home and explore ways to break out of the mould that society had imposed on them. She also encouraged women to question the power of traditional authority and urged women to explore their own sexuality. Her book was rapidly translated into eleven languages. However, the concerns and analysis of women's oppression explored by Greer and other white middle-class feminists have not gone unchallenged.

Do the scandals and circumstances of women's personal lives overshadow their work?

Working-class and black women have found little that addresses their needs and concerns in many of these feminist treatises. Many women's lives have been shaped not just by gender but equally by the exercise of power based on their class or race, or both. Anne Oakley's *Housewife* (1984) pointed out that many working-class women regarded feminists with deep suspicion and did not share Betty Freidan's belief that housewives lived a life of domestic drudgery, while bell hooks's *Ain't I a Woman: Black Women and Feminism* (1981) interrogated the particularity of black women's experiences of racial, sexual and class oppression in America from slavery to the end of the twentieth century. Hooks argues that black women should be at the forefront of feminist debates, for not only do they have a 'unique vision' but also 'survival skills' which are 'a form of power'. Like Mary Wollstonecraft, many feminist writers since the publication of *The Vindication of the Rights of Woman* have identified ways in which male privilege has been woven into every social, political and economic institution. They have encouraged women to rethink their lives and the way society has been organised; they have helped to bring about fundamental change in the opportunities now available for most, if not all, women.

78 | Joanna Southcott's Box
Women and Religion

MAGGIE ANDREWS

On 11 July 1927 a public meeting presided over by Professor A.M. Low was held in Hoare Memorial Hall at Church House, Westminster. The packed gathering heard a lecture on the life and writings of the 'Prophetess', Joanna Southcott, who died in 1814, and then witnessed the opening by the Bishop of Grantham of what was supposed to be her box.

Its contents had previously been X-rayed and it was shown to contain a slight bizarre collection of items including a lottery ticket dated 1795, a puzzle, a child's night-cap, a book with a metal clasp, a dice box, a rusty pistol, a coin of Cromwell, and a diary with manuscript notes. Someone at the back of the hall was heard to mutter 'a lot of fuss about nothing', while the conjecture that followed in the newspapers questioned whether this was Joanna's only box or was there another.

Joanna Southcott was born in Ottery St Mary in East Devon in 1750 to a farming couple; she worked on the farm before becoming a domestic servant and then an upholsterer. At the age of 42, according to her own account, she was 'strangely visited by day and night about what was coming upon the whole earth'. Becoming convinced that it was the Holy Spirit that had visited her she began to prophesy, apparently predicting a crop failure and France's declaration of war on Britain.

Southcott's apocalyptic prophecies about the end of the world were articulated in a profusion of writings, sixty-five published works, manuscripts and letters, which captured the mood of uncertainty in the era of the Napoleonic wars. She critiqued the wealthy and the corruption of the Church, and defended her position as a female prophet, arguing: 'Is it a new thing for a woman to deliver her people? Did not Esther do it, and Judith?' She gathered supporters in the west, south Lancashire, the West Riding of Yorkshire and Stockton-upon-Tees, mostly among the poor, who found it appealing that spiritual revelations were being visited upon a working-class woman; but she also had followers in the clergy, including the Rev. T.P. Foley. Southcott died in 1814, but not before her followers had waited for her to fulfil her promise to give birth to 'Shiloh', the Son of God. As she was at the time in her 60s, this was perhaps one prophecy too many. She left a box or boxes, which were to be opened in the presence of twenty-four bishops in a time of national emergency.

Notwithstanding Joanna's reference to prophetesses in the Old Testament and to a number of goddesses in Eastern and ancient Egyptian religions, for most of the nineteenth and twentieth centuries women made up the majority of the congregations in Christian churches in the Western world; yet positions of power and status, and membership of the clergy and ecclesiastical bodies, were almost

exclusively male. This had not always been the case; in the Middle Ages wealthy women could exert power and influence in monasteries and convents, which were not necessarily separate. Bridget of Sweden founded the Brigittines in the middle of the fourteenth century, in a double house for monks and nuns with an abbess in charge. It was not a strategy without risk; the order of the Gilbertines in the twelfth century was damaged by the scandal that surrounded their house in Yorkshire when a nun was found to be pregnant; she was forced to castrate her lover and then 'had the parts thrust into her mouth'.

Why do more women engage with religion and yet most religons are led by men?

Following the Reformation, St Paul's letter to Timothy was used as a justification to limit women's contribution to Christian churches; this admonished him to 'suffer not a woman to teach nor to usurp authority over the man, but to be in silence. For Adam was first formed then Eve.' Thus women were limited to roles administering welfare, fundraising and supporting churches, writing hymns, ministering to the poor and only teaching children in Sunday schools, although vicar's wives took on numerous subordinate roles in parishes.

Nevertheless, within some of the Protestant churches and sects such as the Southcottans, women found ways of exerting influence, preaching and making their

Across the world there is a gender gap in religious affiliation. In the USA 60 per cent of women say religion is very important in their lives compared with 47 per cent of men.

voices heard. Rosina Davies left her Welsh mining village in 1879 to develop a career as a preacher with the Salvation Army that took her to America three times. She went on to hold a number of successful missions in Rhosllanerchrugog, North Wales, in 1904. Suffragists, such as Maude Royden who preached during the First World War, saw female ordination as the next step to women's enfranchisement.

Joanna Southcott and her box became something of a cultural icon; she is referred to in the opening of Dickens's *A Tale of Two Cities* (1859) when he sets the scene for the end of the eighteenth century as the best of times and the worst of times. By 1927 Joanna's followers had been demanding that her box was opened, in letters and petitions to the clergy, adverts in newspapers, billboards and posters on the Tube. The box has been the subject of political cartoons and student 'Rag' stunts; E.P. Thompson's epic history of *The Making of the English Working Class* (1963) set out to 'rescue the deluded followers of Joanna Southcott from the condescension of posterity'. Finally, in 1969, it was referred to in a *Monty Python* television comedy sketch on the BBC. This was an indication perhaps that even in the twentieth and twenty-first centuries women's position in organised religion is surrounded by anxiety and tension despite the iconic status of Mother Teresa of Calcutta and the political engagement of nuns like Sister Joan Chittister in the USA.

79 | Statues of the Brontë sisters at Haworth Parsonage

Women's Literature

ROSE MILLER

The bronze sculpture of the Brontë sisters, from left to right Charlotte (1816–55), Emily (1818–48) and Anne (1820–49), designed by Jocelyn Horner, is situated in the garden of the Brontë Parsonage Museum in Haworth, England, where the three sisters lived with their father, a widower and vicar.

In their short lives, the sisters produced novels and poems that are considered major works of literature that have inspired other women to write. Haworth, in consequence, has become a place of pilgrimage for readers and scholars.

The Brontë authors unsettled critics and readers alike because they challenged nineteenth-century views on the behaviour of women. The passivity of Charlotte's figure in the sculpture indicates her shyness but belies a capacity for questioning boundaries that was unusual for her time. Writing after Jane Austen (1775–1817) who was celebrated for novels that were satiric social commentaries on the lives of the restrained nobility, the Brontë sisters focused instead on emotional depth, dramatic landscapes and on challenging social conventions. Charlotte is best known for the novels *Jane Eyre* (1847), *Shirley* (1849) and *Villette* (1853). *Jane Eyre* was a bestseller straight after publication and remains one of the most widely read novels in the English language, unique for its focus on the resilient individual and the assertion that a satisfying life for a woman is predicated on her equal status with men. As a governess, Jane's romance with her employer, Rochester, would have constituted a scandal in Victorian society, but Jane's spirit is not cowed by social position; she sees herself as Rochester's equal, passionately demanding of him:

> Do you think, because I am poor, obscure, plain and little, I am soulless and heartless? You think wrong! – I have as much soul as you, – and full as much heart! And if God had gifted me with some beauty and much wealth, I should have made it as hard for you to leave me, as it is now for me to leave you!

Anne Brontë penned *Agnes Grey* (1847) and *The Tenant of Wildfell Hall* (1848); Emily wrote only one novel, the masterpiece *Wuthering Heights* (1847), a passionate, stormy novel challenging ideas of Victorian morality and social class. The wild setting of the Yorkshire Moors is central to the Gothic atmosphere with the visitation of a child ghost during a snowstorm signalling how the past haunts the everyday. Additional chills are provided by the vengeful figure of Heathcliff, who combines obsessive

feeling with the discipline to plot meticulously and ruthlessly against others, fuming against Cathy who has married another:

> Why, she's a liar to the end! Where is she? Not there – not in heaven – not perished – where? Oh! you said you cared nothing for my sufferings! And I pray one prayer – I repeat it till my tongue stiffens – May she wake in torment!

Anne's closeness to Emily, from whom she hated to be parted, is evident from her attentive posture in the sculpture. Initially the sisters used the names of men; male pseudonyms increased their chances of publication because writing was not perceived as a suitable occupation for a woman in the nineteenth century. Wearing

In 2010 *Wuthering Heights* was one of the bestselling novels in Tesco in Britain.

the masks of male pseudonyms might be perceived as cultivating misplaced expectations and assumptions from readers and publishers, but it was a means of assertion, liberating the sisters from isolation and mobilising their interior lives, enabling them to expose a dehumanising social system through their novels' themes and characters. The novels of Charlotte Brontë's biographer, Elizabeth Gaskell (1810–65), *Mary Barton* (1848) and *North and South* (1855) highlighted divisions between the wealthy and the poor in industrial Manchester, suggesting a need for social reform.

Tracing the growth of a female character from childhood to maturity was an innovation and yet integral to the wider plot of *Jane Eyre*, later used by Manchester writer George Eliot in *The Mill on the Floss* (1860). However, it is important not to create false connections between those who are separated by everything but gender, who are different with reference to style, narrative voice, era, social and economic background. A common factor in the Brontës' work and that of modern women writers is the unflinching depictions of the inner lives of women and the continual surprise this generates in the response of critics. Charlotte, for example, was criticised by Eliot's partner, G.H. Lewes, for writing too dramatically. Centuries later, the aggression demonstrated by the female protagonist in Doris Lessing's *The Golden Notebook* (1962) was attacked as 'unfeminine'. What women are capable of thinking, feeling and experiencing is boldly represented by women writers while demonstrating control and inventiveness in their use of narrative structure and form. The goal of individual liberation also reveals the unpalatable truths concerning their own position and how this connects with the conditions of society.

It is appropriate that the sculpture of the sisters is in Haworth, the small Yorkshire mill town bordering the bleak and beautiful moors. Just as the town sought to adapt to the demands of the Industrial Revolution, so the sisters pushed for the right to independent careers, to challenge and transform assumptions about women and writing. It is unusual for women to have commemorative sculptures or statues and, rather than being celebrated for their achievements, they are portrayed through the ages as semi-clad or reclining, depicting sexualised, maternal or virginal images of womanhood. The idea of women as society's 'ghost writers' who do not receive sufficient civic recognition for their work can, in part, be challenged by public monuments that reveal women to be, quite literally in the case of the Brontës, the authors of their lives. In this context, the statue at Haworth possesses a symbolism of which the sisters would wholeheartedly approve.

Why might women choose to publish their novels under a male pseudonym?

80 | Am I Not a Woman and a Sister? Anti-Slavery Medallion

Campaigns to Abolish Slavery

The first medallion was made in 1787 by Josiah Wedgwood's pottery and produced in Wedgwood's famous black jasper ware on a white background. Wedgwood produced the medallion at his own expense, for the Committee, later to become the Society, for the Abolition of the Slave Trade, and it was to become the icon of the British anti-slavery movement.

In 1788, Josiah Wedgwood also sent a packet of his medallions to Benjamin Franklin, then president of the Pennsylvania Society for the Abolition of Slavery. The medallion was reproduced on snuff boxes, pendants, bracelets, coat buttons, hair ornaments, seals for sealing envelopes and all manner of pottery items. In 1828 Sophia Sturge, a member of the Female Society for Birmingham, designed the female version of the medal, 'Am I Not a Woman and a Sister', and several years later it was also adopted by the American female anti-slavery societies. The medal emphasised the essential humanity of enslaved women and the sympathy that women in the movement felt for their suffering.

It took many years for female anti-slavery groups to be accepted by the Society for the Abolition of the Slave Trade, as William Wilberforce was very much against women taking an active part in the movement; in 1788 the Abolition Society had just 206 female subscribers. These were mostly wives and daughters of Quaker, Unitarian and Evangelical businessmen, manufacturers and shopkeepers, but by the 1790s, despite their exclusion from taking a leadership role, women had found their own ways to campaign, writing poems and pamphlets; former slaves such as Phyllis Wheatley also wrote accounts of their lives. The Quaker, Unitarian and Evangelical women campaigners played an important role in boycotting plantation sugar which had been grown using slave labour. In 1807 the Abolition Act abolished the transatlantic slave trade but a child born to a slave was still a slave, and the slave trade was allowed to continue in the colonies of the British Empire.

In the 1820s women began to form their own groups to press for the complete abolition of the slave trade throughout the British Empire. This was very different from the policy of the mainstream Abolition Society, which favoured a gradual abolition. In 1824 Elizabeth Heyrick published a pamphlet arguing passionately for the immediate emancipation of all slaves in the colonies, and a boycott of sugar produced on slave plantations. She wrote: 'The West Indian planter and the people of this country stand in the same moral relation to each other as the thief and receiver of stolen goods.' She attacked the gradual abolition policy as a 'satanic policy'. William Wilberforce gave instructions that no leaders of the movement

were to speak at women's anti-slavery societies and they attempted to suppress information about the pamphlet. Wilberforce wrote: 'For ladies to meet, to publish, to go from house to house stirring up petitions – these appear to me proceedings unsuited to the female character as delineated in Scripture.'

The Female Society for Birmingham was the first women's anti-slavery group and they promoted the sugar boycott, targeting shops and shoppers, and visited 80 per cent of the houses in Birmingham asking women for their support. In 1830 they decided they would give their annual £50 donation to the national anti-slavery campaign only when they were willing to drop the word 'gradual' from their stated objective of gradual abolition. They were successful and the annual conference agreed to support the Female Society's plan for a new campaign to bring about immediate abolition. By 1831 there were seventy-three women's organisations campaigning against slavery and in 1833 the London Female Society organised a national petition against it. It was signed by 298,785 women – the largest single petition in the movement's history. The Slavery Abolition Act was passed in August 1833 with the British government paying £20 million compensation to slave owners. The Bishop of Exeter received £12,700 for the 665 slaves he owned.

Were the anti-slavery medallions degrading to black men and women?

By the 1830s thousands of American women were also involved in the movement. In 1833 Lucretia Mott and seventeen others, several of whom were African-Americans, founded the Philadelphia Female Anti-Slavery Society. They wrote articles and petitioned Congress calling for abolition, and circulated petitions door to door. Despite considerable opposition, between 1837 and 1839 American women also held three national Anti-Slavery Conventions, after the second of which Pennsylvania Hall, where the convention was held, was burned by protestors who hated the aims of the abolitionists. A New York newspaper wrote that 'females who so far forget the province of their sex as to perambulate the country' in order to attend anti-slavery meetings should be 'sent to insane asylums'.

In 1840 the World Anti-Slavery Convention was held in London, but when the women arrived they were refused permission to speak. However, it did allow an opportunity for British activists to meet the American delegates Elizabeth Cady Stanton and Lucretia Mott. Stanton later wrote that it was after this that the American women resolved to hold a convention to form a society to advocate women's rights, and in Britain, too, many of the tactics used by women in the anti-slavery movement formed the blueprint that suffragist women used when they began to campaign for the vote.

81 | Brownies' Badge for Agility

Girls' Groups and Sport

MAGGIE ANDREWS

The Agility Badge awarded to members of the Brownies portrays a girl balancing on one foot and is the most recent example of numerous badges that have been given to young girls to recognise their physical and sporting achievement through the Girl Guides.

What has become the UK's largest girls-only organisation, the Girl Guides, was established in 1910; the Brownies, for younger girls, followed in 1914. Guides were separate but complementary to the Boy Scouts, which Lieutenant General Sir Robert Baden-Powell started in 1908, to develop boys' 'character' and encourage self-reliance and responsibility.

The ten tenets of the Girl Guides' law have some similarity in tone, and include being thrifty and a friend to animals, and suggest a Guide should 'smile and sing through difficulties'. The comfortable environment offered by Girl Guides, away from the male gaze and censure, has provided opportunities for girls to gain confidence and try new activities. Oscar-winning actress Emma Thompson, who was a Girl Guide, suggested that through the movement 'girls and young women can gain the confidence to be equal partners and to make informed, responsible choices about their lives'.

The first leader of the movement, Agnes Baden-Powell (Robert's younger sister), imbued with the values of her Victorian upbringing, warned of possible damage to women's internal organs if they involved themselves in too many 'violent jerks and jars'. Nevertheless, one of the very first badges Guides could obtain was cycling; a gymnast badge soon followed. Robert Baden-Powell expected girls to be 'partners and comrades rather than dolls', and himself married the tall, sporty 23-year-old Olave St Clair Soames in 1912 when he was 55. Olave become Chief Guide for Britain in 1918 and sport, physical exercise, camping and woodcraft became core components of guiding, mirroring a growing preoccupation with women's health, diet, exercise and sport which emerged in the late nineteenth century.

Are girls more likely to engage in sport and other physical activities in girls-only groups?

Swimming was regarded as a particularly acceptable pursuit for women, despite the constricting and unwieldy costumes they had to wear. This was, in part, to avoid women drowning due to their inability to swim. The sinking of the *Princess Alice* in the Irish Sea in 1878, when only one of the 339 women on board was able to swim to safety, had received extensive media attention.

By 1925, there were 500,000 Guides and Brownies in thirty countries across the world, almost twice the number of Boy Scouts. For many girls, Guide camp provided their only holiday where they enjoyed independence, travel, camaraderie, adventure and an outdoor life for a few days. Joy Laycock, who was a Guide in Plymouth after the Second World War, recalled that her 'folks were quite put out' because having hired a car to come as visitors for a day during Guide camp, she greeted them with the news, 'I am going swimming'. The outdoor life of guiding allowed scope for swimming in rivers, lakes and sometimes swimming pools; in 1966, the girls' relay record for swimming the English Channel was broken by six Girl Guides. A 2007 survey indicated that two-thirds of Britain's most prominent women were Guides, and three-quarters of these were ex-Guides, including the author J.K. Rowling and the Labour politician Clare Short, both of whom say they benefited from their experiences in the movement.

The varied activities available to girls in the Guides and the participation in sport enable women to feel comfortable within their bodies. Clare Short, recalling her time in the Guides, noted: 'When I think now about the angst young women go through about their bodies and their clothing, looking back it seems like a lovely time of innocent pleasure.'

The Guide movement also sought to develop girls' determination, discipline and self-belief, which Nawal El Moutawakel, the first Olympic gold medallist from

Morocco, has said were important elements in her success. Athlete Dame Kelly Holmes, who won Olympic gold medals for the 800m and 1,500m track events in 2004, has suggested that as a Girl Guide she learned to 'be the best you can be'. Little wonder she has become a role model for many Guides.

For young girls and women to participate in sport, they may have to overcome practical, social, cultural and personal barriers. In many cultures past and present these barriers can seem insurmountable despite the physical and mental health benefits of sport and the scope it offers to challenge assumptions about gender. Research that looked at the Mathare Youth Sports Association in Kenya, for example, suggested that while boys articulated gendered assumptions, once they saw girls' achievements playing football these were challenged. Cultural assumptions about women have created barriers to women's participation in Olympic sports. Women's tennis was introduced into the Olympics in 1900, but wrestling and boxing had to wait until 2004 and 2012 for inclusion.

In competitive and 'professional' sports men dominate: in the organisation and management of sports, in media coverage and in terms of financial remuneration. It was not until 1981 that the International Olympic Committee (IOC), under the presidency of Juan Antonio Samaranch, appointed the first woman, Pirjo Häggmann. As late as in 2007 only 15 of the 113 active IOC members were female. The media in Britain only allocate 4 per cent of their sports coverage to women's sport, which is often broadcast on marginal rather than mainstream television channels. To some extent this explains why, in 2016, male footballer Wayne Rooney was paid £300,000 a week but the best-paid female English player, Steph Houghton, earned only £65,000 a year.

Eliminating the gender pay gap in sport, as with other areas of society, is a slow process. However, campaigns to encourage more women and girls to engage in sport continue; in Wales the Girl Guide movement has introduced the Give it A Go Sports Challenge, and an accompanying range of badges feature an engaging red Welsh dragon, while the current Guides badge for sport features a range of activities that would have been frowned upon for women in the past.

82 | *Strange Fruit* Album and Song

Giving a Voice to Black Women's Experience:
Jazz and Soul Music

JANIS LOMAS

The lyrics of blues singer Billie Holiday's 1939 recording of the song 'Strange Fruit' begin:

Southern trees bear strange fruit,
Blood on the leaves and blood at the root,
Black bodies swinging in the southern breeze,
Strange fruit hanging from the poplar trees …

The incredibly powerful words of this song describe the lynching of black men by the Ku Klux Klan. Lynching was the extrajudicial murder of innocent people by a hate-filled mob incited by the white supremacist Ku Klux Klan. It was first sung by Billie Holiday at Cafe Society, New York, the first integrated nightclub in the United States, and was originally written two years earlier as a poem by American writer, teacher and songwriter Abel Meeropol. African-American women have recorded the song many times since and in 1999 *Time* magazine named 'Strange Fruit' the 'Best Song of the Century'. Holliday sang the song with all the lights turned down and a single spotlight on her face, as the last song of her set, night after night, although it drained her emotionally. Many customers walked out when she performed it; others greeted it with wild applause. She released it on a small independent label, Commodore, as Columbia, her usual record label, were concerned the song was too contentious and Holiday herself feared retaliation whenever she sang it. It sold a million copies and has been called the first great protest song.

Billie Holiday followed a blues tradition of rising from absolute poverty to stardom. Trailblazer Ma Rainey was born to a poor family in Columbus, Georgia, in 1882. She wrote many of her own songs; some such as 'Prove it on me Blues', recorded in 1928, had lyrics that hinted at her lesbianism. She became a mentor to Bessie Smith, who had endured a sad and poverty-stricken childhood after losing both her parents by the time she was 8 years old. Ma Rainey encouraged Bessie Smith to leave Chattanooga, Tennessee, assisted with her singing technique and took her on tour singing around bars, small theatres and tent shows all over the southern states.

Have particular music genres given women's experiences a voice?

Bessie Smith signed a contract with Columbia Records in 1923. Her records were marketed and released on a label designated as being for black people; she

recorded 160 songs including 'Down Hearted Blues', which sold 2 million copies. She told a reporter, 'I've been poor and I've been rich, and rich is better.' Despite, or perhaps because of, her success, she encountered virulent racism. Columbia bought her a custom-made railway carriage, painted in distinctive colours and lettering so it also acted as an advertisement for her show, as she was not allowed to travel in 'whites only' first-class carriages. In 1927, the Ku Klux Klan tried to stop her performing at one of her tent shows but Bessie Smith confronted them, shaking her fist and swearing: 'pick up them sheets and run'. On another occasion in Mississippi shots were fired at her railway carriages, although no one was hit.

Bessie Smith was born in 1894, less than thirty years after slavery was finally abolished in the USA. Although black women had gained the vote in 1920, their communities were still hugely disadvantaged. The black American singer Josephine Baker was so disgusted with the intensity of the racism and scared by threats from the Ku Klux Klan that she fled to Paris in the 1920s. Billie Holiday encountered so many instances of racism that she refused to tour, choosing to perform in New York where she felt safest. All black people encountered racism but these high-profile black women singers were so visible they were a target for intense bigotry. They were often asked to leave through the kitchens after their performances in clubs, and hotels and restaurants would not accept them.

Discrimination was still experienced by black singers such as Ella Fitzgerald and Lena Horne, who began their careers in the 1940s. Ella overcame a terrible

In 1999 *Time* magazine named 'Strange Fruit' the 'Best Song of the Century'.

childhood, saying 'it isn't where you come from; it's where you're going that counts'. However, despite becoming one of the most famous singers in America, she was still turned away from dozens of hotels because of her colour. She sued Pan American Airlines, having booked first-class tickets, after she and her entourage were thrown off a plane and forced to spend three days waiting in Honolulu before they were allowed to fly. On another occasion she was arrested simply for playing dice with her band, retaliation for the efforts of her producer, Norman Granz, to get concerts performed in the desegregated South.

Offstage Ella avoided the limelight as much as possible, while Lena Horne was more confrontational; when a man in a Beverly Hills restaurant shouted a vile racist word at her she threw a table lamp, glasses and an ashtray at him. She was light-skinned and was asked by MGM to pretend she was South American rather than black as it would be easier to sell her films in the southern states. She refused, and said of the contradictory attitudes she encountered, 'you wouldn't be allowed to get on a particular bus, but you'd be asked to sign your autograph'.

Through their musical talent these women brought pleasure to millions, had long successful careers and helped to demonstrate that it was possible for women to forge a musical career for themselves whatever the colour of their skin. These black women refused to submit to the discrimination and prejudice they received from sections of white society. They forged a route out of poverty for themselves but also gave a voice to black women everywhere as they sang from their hearts and poured their emotions into their songs in a unique way.

83 | Anne Frank's Diary
Genocide

JADE GILKS

'If only there were no other people in the world.' These are the words of Anne Frank, written in her teenage diary, when she and her family were in hiding during the Second World War.

Anne, her family and 6 million other Jews were victims of the Nazi Holocaust, which also killed approximately 220,000 Romany, thousands of homosexuals, 250,000 physically and mentally disabled people, millions of Soviet prisoners of war and many others such as Jehovah's Witnesses. As Hitler's Nazi regime tightened its control over Germany in 1933, Anne's family and many other Jewish people sought refuge in surrounding countries. When the German army invaded Holland in 1940, their new lives in Amsterdam became difficult. Anne and her family were among eight people who went into hiding in a secret annexe at Prinsengracht 263 in Amsterdam in July 1942. They remained there for two years, during which Anne wrote the diary that made her the most high-profile victim of the Holocaust. Otto Frank, Anne's father and the only survivor from the annexe, edited and published the diary in June 1947.

The diary is not all doom and gloom; it portrays Anne Frank's coming of age as a bright, comical teenager who, like many young women, does not have the easiest relationship with her mother. The diary also discusses another significant relationship in Anne's life – that with Peter van Pels, the son of her parents' friends who also shares the annexe. She experiences many of the feelings that are familiar to teenagers wherever they live: 'Once when Father and I were talking about sex, he said I was too young to understand that kind of desire. But I thought I did understand it, and now I'm sure I do. Nothing is as dear to me now as my darling Petel!'

But Anne also deals with the terror of worrying about discovery, capture and being sent to death camps. She calls her diary Kitty, and writes to it as if it were her friend, sharing her worries, good days, bad days and what her life was like as a Jew in hiding. 'Thinking about the suffering of those you hold dear can reduce you to tears; in fact, you could spend the whole day crying.'

Anne's last entry was made on Tuesday, 1 August 1944 and her journey ended at Bergen-Belsen concentration camp where she died of a typhus epidemic in early 1945. But she lives on through the Anne Frank Museum, established in the house where she and her family hid in Amsterdam, and in memories and memorials.

Anne was only one of many young girls whose lives were destroyed by politics and prejudice. Kitty Hart Moxon, like Anne Frank, was a young Jewish girl who experienced the wrath of the Nazi regime. She and her mother had obtained

fake documents claiming they were Polish and not Jewish, but when they were betrayed they were sentenced to death. This was commuted to imprisonment in Auschwitz-Birkenau; Kitty, unlike millions of Jewish people, survived the horrors of incarceration. As the Second World War drew to a close, Kitty and her mother, and many other prisoners, were marched to other camps. Many died on these marches, but Kitty and her mother's journey ended in Salzwedel. As a survivor of the Holocaust, living with the memories, Kitty has spoken about her experience on television, to universities and schools, musing that:

> As it is barely credible to someone like myself who lives through the worst of it, perhaps I ought not to be surprised at a member of a younger generation who cannot believe it happened at all … But I did live through it; and I do know it happened.

The Holocaust was one of the worst atrocities of the twentieth century, but other genocides have taken place since. For example, it is estimated that when the Khmer Rouge seized Cambodia in 1975, over 2 million civilians were killed between 1975 and 1979, while in 100 days in 1994, 800,000 were killed in the Rwandan genocide. Young girls continue to be victims of genocide; Sophal Leng Stagg was 9 years old when she and her family were forced to leave their home in Phnom Penh in April 1975, joining millions of other Cambodians whose lives were devastated by the Khmer Rouge. She survived and later explained: 'As I lay motionless I recalled my mother's voice urging me on and not to accept death, for it was this that saved my life. The Khmer Rouge would not kill me.'

Angèle was 24 years old when she was raped several times in the Rwandan holocaust, but she continues to remember her losses: 'In April 1994, my husband and son were abducted and killed by the interahamwe. My other son was also murdered at his grandmother's house in Kibuye.' These genocides, although not forgotten, have not received the attention they should have, perhaps because they occurred outside of Europe. Sophal Leng Stagg's husband explains: 'The Cambodian holocaust, while well documented in such treatments as the movie *The Killing Fields* and in the autobiography by Dr Haing S. Ngor, has been almost totally ignored outside of Southeast Asia.'

Anne Frank is now increasingly remembered as a representative of all victims of genocides, as Otto Frank wished in 1970, when he said of visitors to the Anne Frank Museum: 'I think it is not only important that people go to the Anne Frank House to see the secret annexe, but also that they are helped to realise that people are also persecuted today because of their race, religion or political convictions.'

But Anne's life is frozen in time as a teenage girl writing a diary, not able to have a normal life, sexual encounters, a career, marriage or motherhood. All of these experiences were denied to her, like many other victims of the Holocaust and mass genocides, although she lives on through the memories fulfilling her wish when she wrote: 'I want to go on living even after my death!'

Have the experiences of Anne as a young girl made it easier for people to understand the horror of the Holocaust?

84 | Statue of Alison Lapper
Women and Disability

JANIS LOMAS

The 3.5m-high sculpture *Alison Lapper Pregnant* was made by Marc Quinn for the fourth plinth in Trafalgar Square, where it sat from 2005 until 2007. Statues of male heroes of the past surrounded it; Quinn saw his work as portraying 'a different kind of heroism' as Alison, having overcome her personal disabilities and a difficult childhood, obtained a first-class degree in Fine Arts and became an artist, using her feet to paint.

Waldemar Januszczak, writing in *The Sunday Times*, suggested the Lapper statue strikes a 'huge blow' for issues of disability and should 'be ranked as one of the most significant sculptural moments in Britain's post-war art history'. Alison Lapper has also expressed her hope that the statue will make a difference, pointing out: 'It puts disability and femininity and motherhood on the map. It's time to challenge people's perceptions of these things. I'm hopeful it can make a difference.'

Alison Lapper's statue is one example of how the world's disabled women are becoming more visible and more assertive, but as Elena Kochoska points out, 'women bear a double burden because of their gender and disability'. They continue to be marginalised by gender and disability. A disabled woman is twice as likely to suffer verbal and physical abuse, more likely to live in poverty and often perceived to be a burden on society. She is also more likely to have her sexual and reproductive rights violated than an able-bodied woman. When Lapper became pregnant, alongside many supportive, positive reactions there were also critics of her decision to have a baby. Alison heard one woman, in a supermarket, ask her friend: 'Do you think people like that should be allowed to have children?' The threat of having her son Parys taken into care was in the background as he was growing up. She has endured three investigations by social services 'assessing' if she was coping and was an 'adequate mother'.

In 2012 a huge inflatable recreation of the sculpture was the centrepiece of the London Paralympic Games. Although generally well received, the work was not without its critics. It was re-erected on the island of San Giorgio Maggiore in the Venetian lagoon as part of the Venice Bianniale art exhibition. Despite the figure having been compared to a modern-day Madonna, the Catholic Church's representative for cultural heritage felt it was 'out of place' and he was 'perplexed' by the decision to place it near a church.

Disability has always proved challenging – for those affected, for some of the public and for governments. In Britain during the Middle Ages, those disabled by illness or disease were either seen as deserving little sympathy as they were being punished for their sins, or, more charitably, considered nearer to God because their sufferings would be rewarded in the next life. With a limited range of work available

to them, many disabled women struggled to support themselves and resorted to begging, or charity from their community or churches. Wealthy benefactors set up hospitals and almshouses, and in the nineteenth century large institutions increased rapidly although many disabled people continued to be cared for by their families.

In the late nineteenth century attitudes to disability began to be influenced by the eugenics movement in many countries. Supporters of eugenics seized upon a crude Darwinian distortion of the notion of natural selection and 'the survival of the fittest' to suggest that anyone who was disabled or 'deficient' threatened the health of the nation. Although sterilisation programmes were never legalised in the UK, in the USA marriage of those considered 'feeble-minded, epileptic, and the mentally ill' was forbidden in 1896. Between 1907 and 1939, 30,000 Americans were compulsorily sterilised; half the procedures took place in California. In 1930 Julian Huxley, chairman of the British Eugenics Society, wrote: 'What are we going to do? Every defective man, woman and child is a burden. Every defective is an extra body for the nation to feed and clothe, but produces little or nothing in return.'

When Adolf Hitler came to power in Germany in 1933, a sterilisation policy and later a systematic extermination programme resulted in 400,000 mentally and physically disabled people being sterilised and around 275,000 murdered. Disabled women and girls are still being sterilised in many countries including Mexico and Ukraine.

Since the 1980s routine ultrasound scanning of pregnant mothers has detected many severe abnormalities in babies prior to birth; recently, blood tests and more sophisticated scanning techniques have allowed chromosomal abnormalities such as Down's syndrome to be detected, enabling women to abort disabled babies. Some countries, such as Iceland and Denmark, are now envisioning eliminating Down's syndrome entirely. Iceland has not had a single child with Down's syndrome born in the last five years – all have been aborted. In 2014, 98 per cent of Danish babies with Down's syndrome were aborted; in the UK 90 per cent of those whose test results indicated a chance of Down's syndrome chose to have an abortion. Not all women take the test, even though arguably it is women who do the lion's share of caring for children with disabilities. *The American Journal of Modern Genetics* survey in 2011 found just 4 per cent of parents of a child with Down's syndrome regretted having them, and only 4 per cent of individuals with Down's 'expressed sadness about their lives'. Yet concern has been expressed that societies will be unwilling to spend the money needed to enable those with Down's syndrome and other disabilities to participate in a diverse and varied society, if the cheaper option of termination is available.

Why are women more likely to become disabled than men?

Estimates suggest that one in five women will experience some form of disability in their lifetime, and many more will be the carers of those experiencing disability; disability rights must therefore be an issue for all women. However, as Liz Carr, a disabled actress and wheelchair user, said when talking about the future for disabled people: 'What chance do people who don't have a voice, who don't have support and the resources have, when people label their lives as not having any quality or not worth living?'

85 | *I Know Why the Caged Bird Sings*

The Revolution in Publishing

MAGGIE ANDREWS AND JANIS LOMAS

I Know Why the Caged Bird Sings, Maya Angelou's account of growing up as a black girl in Stamps, Arkansas, in the 1930s and 1940s, changed publishing history. It was an immediate bestseller, proving to publishers that not only did black women's lives matter but their stories were commercially viable.

The book describes Angelou's own experience of abandonment by her parents, rape by her mother's boyfriend and his subsequent murder, the trauma of which resulted in five years of mutism. The book ends with the birth of her own son, Guy, when she was 16 years old.

This narrative of one girl's life is a prism to discuss how racism and segregation permeated every aspect of the society in the rural American South. Within the book, the heroine regains her voice when introduced to books and poems by an inspirational teacher. *I Know Why the Caged Bird Sings* gave women who had previously been marginalised a voice and paved the way for other black women writers such as Alice Walker, Toni Morrison and Ntozake Shange in the years that followed. In 2011 *Time* magazine included the book in a list of the 100 best and most influential books written in English since 1923.

In Angelou's autobiographical text it is the black community, and women in particular, who are singled out for discrimination and blind hatred. The misery of black women's lives before the civil rights movement is shown in graphic detail, as Angelou writes: 'The Black female is assaulted in her tender years by all those common forces of nature at the same time she is caught in the tripartite crossfire of masculine prejudice, white illogical hate and Black lack of power.'

The book and Maya Angelou's life demonstrate the strength of the women who survive despite overwhelming odds against them. Maya Angelou was an author, poet, songwriter, playwright, dancer, stage and screen producer, director, performer, singer, and civil rights activist who in 1959 became the northern co-ordinator for the Southern Christian Leadership Conference after a request from Dr Martin Luther King. Her tenacity is expressed in her 1978 poem 'Still I Rise'.

Since the publication of *I Know Why the Caged Bird Sings*, a multiplicity of women's experiences have been shared across the world through literature and autobiography. Laura Esquivel's novel *Like Water for Chocolate* (1989), about the youngest daughter of a family who cares for her mother and reserves her passion for her cooking, gave a voice to Mexican feminism. In 1991 Jung Chang's book *Wild Swans,* which portrays the deprivations, injustice and cruelty inflicted on a family

by the heartless Maoist regime, became the biggest grossing non-fiction paperback in publishing history. The true story of three generations of Chinese women during one of the most tempestuous periods of change in China's history was translated into over thirty languages and sold 13 million copies.

Unlike Maya Angelou, Jung Chang had a loving family life. When Jung's grandmother is asked if she would be happy marrying a poor man, she replies: 'If you have love, even plain cold water is sweet.' The book is in three parts, each the biography of an admirable, strong woman: Jung's grandmother, mother and herself, whose lives were torn apart as Mao Zedong and the Chinese Communist Party dominated every detail of their lives. Chang describes the claustrophobic control exerted by the regime in their slogan: 'Father is close, Mother is close, but neither is as close as Chairman Mao.'

In Jung Chang's family history the regime in which the family is caught up crushes the spirit and idealism of her father and millions of others but the women continue to fight against oppression. Her parents 'had regarded the restrictions on women as precisely the sort of thing a Communist revolution should put an end to. But now oppression of women joined hands with political repression, and served resentment and petty jealousy.'

For Jung Chang, learning English at university opened up the world for her: 'I managed to borrow some English language textbooks ... These contained extracts from writers like Jane Austen, Charles Dickens, and Oscar Wilde, and stories from European and American history. They were a joy to read.'

I Know Why the Caged Bird Sings was a bestseller for two years.

Chinese novels were rarely read in the West and the history described in *Wild Swans* is largely undocumented from women's perspective; but it, too, prompted other books including Anhua Gao's *To the Edge of the Sky* (2000), an autobiographical account of her family's life from 1926 until they fled to the West in the 1990s. *Wild Swans* and Jung Chang's biography of Chairman Mao are still banned in mainland China although she says: '*Wild Swans* is even more relevant now ... My generation knew what Mao's China was like – the new generation have no idea ... Politics is still dangerous, history is dangerous.'

In recent years a diverse range of women's writing has been hugely influential, communicating the perspectives of ordinary women surviving in difficult circumstances, stories which have resonated with readers all over the world. This literature has made the personal political by using their experiences and those of their closest family to shine a light on injustices against women. These books also convey a belief that education and the power of books can transform women's lives and bring a sort of freedom, even in the most desperate of situations. As Maya Angelou described when writing about discovering books: 'I had given up some youth for knowledge, but my gain was more valuable than the loss.'

Does autobiographical writing have the potential to broaden ideas about who and what struggles the women's movement should focus on?

86 | *A Week from Hell*, 1995 by Tracey Emin

Abortion

A Week from Hell, 1995, is a series of drawings by British artist Tracey Emin, exhibited at the Minky Manky South London gallery in 1995, which refer to events in the artist's life including a split from her boyfriend, serious dental work and an abortion which all took place within a traumatic seven-day period the year before.

Abortion is surrounded by shame and taboo; these drawings, her video entitled *How it Feels* (1996) and many interviews Emin has given challenge this. Avoiding presenting abortion as a mundane surgical procedure, she explained in May 2009: 'I know abortion is different for every woman, but I suffered the most disgusting amount of guilt – when, actually, all I had done was make the right decision.'

Her 1990 abortion of twins was, however, a life-changing event; she has described coming round from the anaesthetic and deciding 'that all the art I'd ever made was a real big bunch of crap and had to be destroyed immediately'. She did not paint for the next two years but her autobiographical and confessional art laid bare her life and emotions in a range of media including sculpture, letters, appliquéd blankets and watercolours. Her most iconic and controversial installations include *Everyone I Have Ever Slept With 1963–1995*, 1995, and *My Bed*, 1998, which featured an unmade bed, replete with empty vodka bottles, semen-stained sheets, used condoms and blood-stained underwear. Such work, like her pieces on abortion, propelled women's intimate or sexual experiences from the private sphere, where they are often shrouded by shame, into the heart of the established polite society – art galleries. As she argued: 'Being an artist isn't just about making nice things, or people patting you on the back; it's some kind of communication, a message.'

The Portuguese artist Paula Rego also produced a series of ten pictures of women undergoing abortions between July 1998 and February 1999, in response to a referendum that rejected the liberalisation of Portugal's restricted abortion laws. Despite such artists' work, and that of many television and documentary makers and campaigns by women's groups, abortion remains illegal in some countries such as Chile, Nicaragua and Vatican City. The circumstances under which abortions are permitted are varied in some countries and very restricted in others. In 2015 a 10-year-old girl who had been raped by her stepfather was denied an abortion in Paraguay, as the pregnancy was not considered to be threatening her life – the only circumstances which allow such a procedure in the country.

The illegality and unreliability of the wide variety of actions undertaken to terminate pregnancies, and the significant number of pregnancies that spontaneously abort, make it both controversial and difficult to judge how common

From the book of Hell 34   Tracey Emin 16

abortion has been in the past. One British mother facing another pregnancy she could not afford in 1915 explained that, when offered help, she 'took their strong concoctions to purge me of the little life that might be mine. They failed as such things generally do and a third baby came.'

Her attempt to abort had no detrimental effects, but many women were not so lucky; they relied on the services of untrained people seeking to induce a miscarriage, often by inserting instruments in less-than-sterile domestic environments. The BBC play

Up the Junction (1965), directed by Ken Loach, reminded the viewer, as main protagonist Rube visited an abortionist, that there were at least thirty-five deaths per year from backstreet abortionists in Britain. The same year the TV documentary *A Law for the Rich* portrayed a working-class married women with ten children who felt she would go mad if she had another child. She could not afford £20 for an illegal abortion; two years later legal changes would have enabled her to have a safe abortion on the National Health Service.

> Are the current abortion figures an indication that birth control has yet to be really effective?

There were a number of campaigns across the world in the 1960s and 1970s to make safe, legal abortion available to women. The Supreme Court judgement known

There were 185,824 abortions performed on women and girls in England and Wales in 2015.

as Roe versus Wade opened the way for legal abortions in the USA in 1973. Two year later, France legalised abortions in the first twelve weeks of pregnancy. The motivations of campaigners were varied; in Britain their primary concern was to end the danger to women's life and health from backstreet abortions, while the Roman Catholic Church argued that all human life was sacred whatever the circumstances of conception. For some feminists access to abortion and birth control were a fundamental right for women, important to prevent them being forced into motherhood. They adopted the slogan 'A Woman's Right to Choose'; in so doing they sidelined debates about the circumstances within which women make choices about continuing their pregnancies: poverty, abusive relationships, health issues, youth and adverse events surrounding conception.

Making abortion accessible to women remains controversial and contested; the operation of laws is subject to regional variation even within countries such as USA and Australia. In Cameroon, legal abortions are limited but can be performed if two doctors approve and a woman has been raped. Rural women, for whom access to two doctors is very difficult, often resort to illegal abortions. For women in Cameroon and many other countries, it is the economic resources at their disposal that will influence how safe their abortion will be. Recent decisions by the President of the USA to deny government funding to any charitable groups and NGOs which provide abortions in other countries may exacerbate this situation.

Part VIII
Women's Place in the Public World

The objects that chart women's place in the public world are varied. Women's influence is sometimes subtle or behind the scenes; perhaps this is why they have less in the way of statues and blue plaques, and they are less likely to have huge buildings constructed in their honour or to write diaries. Conceivably this makes the objects that signify women's powerful roles – such as Hatshepsut's temple – all the more significant. Many women have encountered formidable legal, cultural and social obstacles preventing them from playing a role in the public world; nevertheless the stories behind some of the objects indicate the struggles undertaken by women determined to be regarded as citizens, leaders and warriors. For example, the suffrage petition delivered by women in New Zealand led them to become the very first group of women to get the vote in 1893.

From Boudicca, who in 61 CE opposed the Roman occupation of Britain, to the women protestors at Greenham Common opposing nuclear weapons in the 1980s, women who embraced a cause they believed in passionately have struggled when the odds were stacked against them; women have chosen a variety of different methods to pursue their cause. While Joan of Arc and Boudicca went into battle seeking to beat men at their own game, so to speak, others like

Rosa Parks chose passive resistance and civil disobedience. Many women paid a high price for their entry in the public sphere, and their attempt to exert power in their communities or in the world of politics and warfare led to death: for witches, for Boudicca, Joan of Arc and Mary, Queen of Scots, who found herself pitched against her cousin Elizabeth. One queen held on to her power at the expense of the other, perhaps aware her own survival relied upon being seen to be as determined, as ruthless and as unforgiving as any man ruling in Tudor England would have been.

Many of the objects in this section explore women who responded to injustice and oppression in unexpected situations. The Second World War gave Irena Sendlerowa a choice and an opportunity. She could either keep quiet and ignore the misery and death around her, or make a stand against the Nazi regime occupying Poland. However, by the 1970s and '80s both Margaret Thatcher and Barbara Castle were part of small number of female politicians who made their mark and proved that women could hold positions of power, even if in so doing they did not or could not necessarily do much to forward the causes of other women.

87 | Hatshepsut's Temple, Djeser-djeseru

A Female Pharaoh as an Early Woman in Power

JANIS LOMAS

This beautiful temple dedicated to the god Amon was built as the funerary shrine for one of the very few women who ruled ancient Egypt as pharaoh. Hatshepsut was born around 1508 BCE, the daughter of Pharaoh Tuthmosis I. Her father died when she was around 12 years old and her half-brother Tuthmosis II became pharaoh.

In order to strengthen his position he married Hatshepsut; they had a daughter but no son, although Tuthmosis II did have a son by one of his lesser wives. After reigning for perhaps around three years Tuthmosis died, leaving Hatshepsut a young widow. Before his death he had decreed that Hatshepsut was to act as regent until his infant son, also called Tuthmosis, was old enough to become pharaoh.

For the first few years of her reign Hatshepsut did indeed rule as regent, with the understanding that Tuthmosis would be taking over from her when he matured, but gradually she took on more of the ceremonial and religious duties of a king, and seven years into her reign she declared that the gods had decreed that she should be pharaoh. Unusually, she did not assassinate her stepson, who remained at court in the background and was never formally deposed; it was, however, clear that Hatshepsut was the ruler in power.

A female pharaoh was unprecedented, so although she had previously been shown in statues as an idealised feminine young woman she now began to be depicted in the traditional king's kilt and crown, along with a fake beard and a male body, as a way of asserting her authority and mandate to rule. Her temple and the two great obelisks she commissioned were also designed to show her power, supremacy and that she was worthy to be a pharaoh and take her place in the afterlife in the Valley of the Kings.

Hatshepsut seems to have had influential supporters, the most important of whom was called Senenmut. He had risen from a fairly lowly background to become royal steward and seems to have had great influence with Hatshepsut. He supervised the building of her temple, and there appears to have been gossip about their relationship at the time. When the temple was under construction the workmen used to rest out of the burning sun in a rough cave cut out of the cliffs above the temple, and they drew graffiti on the cave walls. One of these shows a woman wearing a pharaoh's headdress having sex with a man, and some historians have speculated that this is evidence that Senenmut was Hatshepsut's lover. He was certainly very close to her, and is depicted on the wall of the inner sanctum of her private chapel within the temple. He seems never to have married, which was

unusual for someone in the Egyptian court at that time, and there is a statue showing Hatshepsut's daughter on his knee. However, there is no evidence that they were lovers. Perhaps the crude graffiti of Hatshepsut having sex was meant to suggest that a man, probably Senenmut, was really the power behind the throne and may be an example of misogyny 3,500 years ago. Hatshepsut ruled very effectively for around fifteen to twenty years, leading campaigns into other countries and making trading alliances which brought prosperity and peace throughout her kingdom, but perhaps there was resentment of a woman with such power and a feeling that as she was so successful she must have had a man making the decisions for her.

After her death, Tuthmosis III finally became pharaoh, and he systematically began to erase all traces of his stepmother's rule. Arguably, Tuthmosis III erased all records of Hatshepsut so that her reign could be incorporated into his, making him the greatest pharaoh and the Tuthmosis dynasty an unbroken line of male pharaohs. Statues of Hatshepsut were smashed or defiled, and her existence as pharaoh was virtually unknown for over 3,000 years until the modern era when archaeologists began to reconstruct her temple and statues, found her tomb and read the hieroglyphs that had survived.

Why were there no more female pharaohs for 1,500 years after Hatshepsut?

Women in ancient Egypt had the right to go to court, to own property, make contracts and earn the same as men, suggesting that it was the most egalitarian kingdom in the ancient world. It seems likely there were a few other female rulers before Hatshepsut, and exceptional women did hold positions of authority after her reign, although none became pharaohs. It was to take another 1,500 years until around 30 BCE for the next great female pharaoh to emerge: Cleopatra, the last female ruler before Egypt became a province of the Roman Empire. The exceptional nature of these women who, despite all odds, both achieved and kept great power meant that they were subject to criticism, distrust and even hatred, but this makes their achievements even more remarkable.

88 | Boudicca

A Rebellious Queen

JANIS LOMAS

This sculpture of Boudicca (called Boadicea at the time of construction) and her daughters by Thomas Thorneycroft was commissioned in the 1850s and finally erected in 1902 near to Westminster Bridge and the Houses of Parliament in London.

Queen Boudicca is shown standing in her chariot pulled by two rearing horses, while her two daughters are bare-breasted kneeling behind her. They are all three shown as athletic, muscular women with Boudicca holding a spear aloft urging her unseen army forwards into battle. The chariot is light, with long knives protruding from the wheels ready to cut down enemy warriors or their horses in the charge. The blades on the chariot are mythical; much of the detail of Boudicca's rebellion is supposition, with few surviving sources detailing these particular events in the period.

The Roman invasion of Britain begun in 43 CE and Boudicca became queen of the Iceni tribe after the death of her husband, King Prasutagus, in 60 CE. The Iceni had co-operated with the Romans, and the great wealth Prasutagus had accumulated during his lifetime was divided on his death: half to the emperor and half to his wife, Boudicca, in trust for his daughters. Unfortunately Rome was not satisfied with only half of the Iceni treasure and records suggest that 'kingdom and household alike were plundered like prizes of war'. Boudicca was flogged and her two young daughters were raped.

Boudicca's consequent rebellion was joined by other tribes – some suggest as many as 120,000, indicating widespread British discontent with Roman rule. The uprising sacked Camulodunum (Colchester); the town was totally overrun and the Roman population massacred. Londinium (London) was deserted by the Romans who left the inhabitants to their fate. Boudicca's rebel army showed no mercy and the massacres and tortures, even of women and children, were pitiless.

The Iceni swept on to Verulamium (St Albans), a town inhabited by Britons sympathetic to the Roman invaders, where once again the rebel army succeeded in burning and plundering the town. At one final battle, probably in the West Midlands, the Romans defeated the rebellion and exacted a terrible revenge. Without the benefit of surprise the Iceni were no match for the experienced Roman soldiers. The British fought without body armour and the Romans each had helmets, two javelins, a short sword and a dagger, and were disciplined fighters. The British suffered terrible casualties and the Romans tortured and killed them with as much ferocity

> Why are women often used as mythic symbol of nations?

The proof for Boudicca's rebellion is based on some
archaeological evidence and two Roman accounts, one
written long afterwards.

as the British had shown previously. Boudicca is thought to have taken poison and probably poisoned her daughters after the defeat to avoid capture. Nevertheless, her attempt to overthrow the vastly superior Roman forces has ensured her immortality and conferred on her a mythic status. The positioning of her statue near to the Houses of Parliament adds to Boudicca's iconic status, as the embodiment of the Warrior Queen defending Britons from tyranny.

Boudicca is endowed with something of the same propaganda appeal as the other female personifications of a nation or its people used in this way in several countries. Britannia is the female personification of the British Isles, first depicted as a goddess and portrayed on coins since the first century CE. She has been used as a symbol of British imperial power and unity, and appeared on pennies from 1797 and the 50p piece until 2008. Marianne is used as the symbol of France, seen all over the country in statues in town halls, and on coins, stamps and banknotes, propagating the *liberté*, *egalité* and *fraternité* ideals of the French republic. In the USA the Statue of Liberty, or Libertas, the Roman goddess of freedom as she is meant to represent, is a symbol of freedom from British rule and the subsequent US Declaration of Independence. While Boudicca was an actual person, unlike Britannia, Libertas or Marianne, they are all in their own ways idealised figures, mythic symbols of womanhood and the manifestations of the ideals of the nation they have been used to represent.

89 | Joan of Arc's Ring

Fighting and Dying for a Belief

NICOLA CONNELLY

Joan of Arc (Jeanne d'Arc), the Maid of Orléans (1412–31), supposedly wore a fifth-century gold-plated silver ring she was given by her parents on the occasion of her first communion.

France's best-known martyr and patron saint was a young peasant girl who led the French army for a year against the English during the Hundred Years War (1337–1453). When captured she was accused of over seventy crimes including heresy, witchcraft, inciting idolatry and dressing as a man, disregarding her femininity and place in society against the teachings of the Church of France; she was found guilty and burned at the stake. Her greatest crime was perhaps transgression of the almost universal cultural assumption that men go to war to protect women, who remain at home. The transcripts of her trials refer to and describe her ring which was then transferred into the possession of Cardinal Henry Beaufort, who took it back to England, where it stayed until 2016, when the Puy Du Fou Foundation purchased it at auction for $425,000 and it was finally returned to France.

Joan of Arc was born into a poor tenant farming family in Domrémy, France, in 1412. At the age of 13 she claimed to have heard voices from God telling her to fulfil a prophecy of a virgin destined to save France from the English and the Burgundians. In the fifteenth century, a young French peasant girl was expected to be pious and chaste, help at home, learn to weave and sew, and to be obedient to her parents before marrying and to her husband thereafter. A girl of Joan's status and age successfully leading the French army into battle against the English was unprecedented. Nevertheless, Joan went to the Dauphin Charles and promised to see him crowned at Reims – something which happened after she led the French army to relieve the besieged town of Orléans, and following a decisive victory over the English.

Why is Joan of Arc a heroic martyr to some and a delusional young girl to others?

Joan's success was short-lived; the Burgundians captured her and put her on trial, and she was burned at the stake in Rouen in May 1431. Artefacts pertaining to Joan were destroyed with her – an unsuccessful attempt to prevent people turning her into a martyr. Her ring is possibly the only relic to survive, alongside the transcripts from the trials. Joan was officially beatified in 1909 and eventually canonised in 1920, but she had been revered as a martyr for centuries before. Today she is the patron saint of France, and also the patroness of soldiers. Reportedly many Allied troops carried Joan's image into battle with them during the First World War.

When captured, Joan of Arc was accused of over seventy
crimes including heresy and witchcraft.

90 | The Death Warrant of Mary, Queen of Scots

Intrigue, Plotting and Rivalry Between Tudor Queens

LINDA PIKE

The death warrant of the Catholic Mary, Queen of Scots, signed by the Protestant English Queen Elizabeth I, is one of the most significant documents of the Tudor period. It was the culmination of religious animosity between two queens, cousins who never met, although Mary was held under house arrest in England for twenty years.

The original warrant disappeared following her execution and the principal clerk, Robert Beale, made this copy for court records to the Privy Council. Elizabeth, who became queen at 25, in 1559, was in a vulnerable position with enemies plotting against her, especially when wars between Catholics and Protestants were occurring in Europe. Mary became a focus for Catholic opponents to the new Protestant Church of England formed by Elizabeth's father, Henry VIII. In a period of dramatic plotting and paranoia, the warrant alluded to Elizabeth's life being in danger and fear of Catholic conspiracies.

Mary, Queen of Scots, who like Elizabeth was also related to Margaret Tudor and Henry VII, became Queen of Scotland at 6 days old following the death of her father, James V of Scotland. She spent much of her childhood in France and married Francis, the eldest son of the French king Henry II, returning to Scotland after his death in 1560, where she married her cousin Henry Stuart (Lord Darnley) on 29 July 1565. He was also Margaret Tudor's grandson.

Was it Mary, Queen of Scots's unfortunate choice of husbands as much as intrigue and politics that led to the loss of her kingdom?

Elizabeth was reluctant to marry a Protestant who would become king, as it would reduce her power; she needed an heir but refused to name Mary as her heir because it would return Catholicism to England. Mary, however, had other ideas. Mary's husband, Darnley, was a jealous and violent drunk who killed Mary's secretary, David Rizzio, in front of his pregnant wife; their son James was born on 19 June 1566, thus providing an heir for both Scotland and England. Mary then became romantically entangled with another violent and jealous lover, James Hepburn, Earl of Bothwell, who murdered Darnley in Edinburgh. Her marriage to Bothwell, on 24 April 1567, implicated her in Darnley's murder and damaged her reputation. In portraits, Mary was depicted as a mermaid, a symbol of prostitutes and adultery, and imprisoned in Castle Kinross, Loch Leven, where she miscarried Bothwell's child. She unwillingly abdicated the Scottish throne in favour

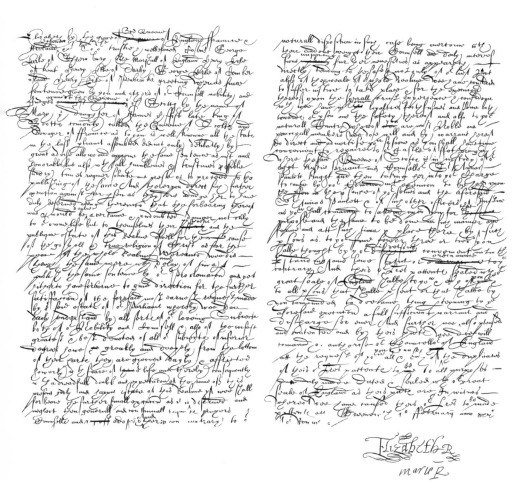

of James and fled to England in the misguided belief that Elizabeth would welcome her cousin and give her sanctuary.

For Elizabeth, Mary's arrival in England was problematic; she could not restore the unpopular Catholic monarch to a Protestant Scotland, and her royal heritage meant that she was a legitimate heir to the English throne. Elizabeth's problem was exacerbated when Pope Pius V issued a papal bull encouraging Catholics to rebel and put Mary on the English throne; Mary now became an inspirational figurehead to Catholics in England and Europe. While imprisoned, Mary received smuggled letters from Catholic supporters, including Anthony Babington, which appeared to describe plans to kill Elizabeth and have Mary become queen. These were written in code and transported in beer barrels during the summer of 1586.

However, this was a plot invented by Elizabeth's Protestant spymaster, Sir Francis Walsingham. Mary was tried for treason alongside others of her supporters, and was sentenced to death on 4 December 1586 after Elizabeth had initially prevaricated over signing a death warrant for Mary and condemning to death an anointed monarch. The warrant was eventually signed on 1 February 1587, but Elizabeth ordered her secretary William Davison not to seal it until further ordered or if Spain attacked. However, Elizabeth's wishes were defied and Mary was executed inside the great hall at Fotheringhay Castle early on 8 February 1587. Mary went to the block dressed in black, which she removed to reveal a red shift dress, the colour of martyrdom. Unfortunately, the executioner made three attempts at severing her head, revealing that her auburn hair was a wig, while some onlookers maintained they could see her lips move in prayer afterwards. As was the custom, a death mask was made and her Skye terrier, concealed in Mary's underskirts, came out and pined for its mistress. Once Elizabeth discovered Mary had been executed, she had mixed emotions and her motives and involvement in Mary's death remain an area of speculation. Davison, who is often regarded as a scapegoat, was sent to the Tower.

Mary's son, King James VI of Scotland, became James I of England after Elizabeth's death and so began the Stuart era. The intertwined lives of Elizabeth and Mary, two seemingly powerful queens, suggest the tenuous and insecure hold that women had on power in this era. Even for these royal women, marriage, religion and male conspirators created many difficulties and a culture in which for one woman maintaining power involved signing another's death warrant.

91 | The *Malleus Maleficarum*
Witchcraft, Persecution and Power

CHARLOTTE SENDALL

The *Malleus Maleficarum* (1487) served as a manual for the inquisitions that defined, pursued and accused women of witchcraft in the sixteenth and seventeenth centuries in Europe. The book was first published by Heinrich Kramer, a Dominican theologian and inquisitor, with James Sprenger later identified as a contributing author.

It was composed of three distinct chapters, all of which centred upon witchcraft or witch trials. The first chapter disputed the idea that witchcraft was non-existent, silencing the argument that witchcraft was purely a superstition. The second chapter discussed the role of the devil within witchcraft, describing his ability to influence women. The final chapter described how women's instability, weakness and erotic manners were core reasons that they become witches.

The arguments in the *Malleus Maleficarum* helped to justify what some might see as the misogynist hunting of women as witches, but perhaps also indicated a deep-seated anxiety about women and their position in society. The *Malleus Maleficarum* was not the only publication to articulate concerns about witchcraft, but the image of women it identified was one of the most significant. Recent historians suggest that as many as 75 per cent to 85 per cent of those accused in the early modern witch trials were women. Inquisitors considered that witchcraft was based on lust and women's sexual weakness and their apparent greater susceptibility to the devil.

The years that followed saw a range of very different types of witch trials in many parts of Europe and America, although there were few in Spain, Italy, Russia or the Dutch Netherlands. The *Malleus Maleficarum* appeared to have stimulated a global panic, multiplying the number of trials and increasing fear and panic over witchcraft, particularly in countries where the authority of state or Church was not so strong. In fifteenth- and sixteenth-century France prosecutions of witches were restricted in the cities, but in the small towns and villages of the outlying regions, under local government control, women were more prone to accusations of witchcraft. In addition, rumour and gossip spread quickly in smaller communities, fuelling prosecutions.

In Britain there had not been more than a handful of witch trials between the Norman Conquest in 1066 and the Reformation in the sixteenth century, but from then until the mid-seventeenth century things escalated; in Essex witches were accused of causing the death of 233 people and the illness of 108. Initially, trials commonly involved the prosecution of individual witches who were often alienated from their communities. Some have suggested that women harnessed their reputation as a witch to exert power over their neighbours. Most of the alleged

Ex Libris MALLEI *Congregationis*

MALEFICARVM
TRACTATVS ALIQVOT

TAM VETERVM, QVAM
Recentiorum in vnum corpus coaceruati,

Missionis *Cadurcensis*

ARTIS MAGICÆ STVPENDOS AFFECTVS,
Lamiarum Pythonicos contractus, impia dogmata, spurcitias,
fascinationes, veneficiáque demonstrantis,

Catalogo *Inscriptus*

TOMI SECVNDI PARS PRIOR,

Cum INDICIBVS Auctorum & rerum vtilissimis;

Hac postremâ editione castigata, & ab innumeris mendis repurgata.

*Vir siue mulier, in quibus Pythonicus, siue diuinationis fuerit spiritus, morte
moriatur. Leuitici cap. 20.*

LVGDVNI,
Sumptibus CLAVDII BOVRGEAT, sub signo Mercurij
Galli.

M. DC. LXIX.
CVM PRIVILEGIO REGIS.

Estimates suggest that between 50,000 and 200,000 people died as a result of the witch trials in Europe in the sixteenth and seventeenth centuries.

victims were poor, and blamed witches for death, disease and natural disasters with no identifiable cause. In 1612, however, witch hunts reached a high point when a group of seventeen people were tried for witchcraft in the area around Pendle Hill in Lancashire. One of the accused, Elizabeth Southerns, had been known in the local area as a witch. The contemporaneous account of the trial written by Thomas Potts claims she described meeting:

> In the said Forrest of Pendle, a spirit or devil in the shape of a boy, the one half of his coat black, and the other brown, who bade her stay, saying to her, that if she would give him her soul, she should have anything that she would request.
>
> And further she confesseth, and sayth, the speediest way to take a man's life away by witchcraft, is to make a picture of clay, like unto the shape of the person whom they mean to kill, and dry it thoroughly. And when they would have them to be ill in any one place more then another; then take a thorn or pin, and prick it in that part of the picture you would so have to be ill. And when you would have any part of the body to consume away, then take that part of the picture, and burn it.

In a society of superstition and fear, narratives of encounters with the devil and spectral evidence – testimony from a witness based on beliefs and dreams against the accused – played a crucial role in prosecutions. The use of torture was often key to obtaining confessions and accusations of such activities.

Between 1692 and 1693 more than 200 people were accused of witchcraft, the 'Devil's magic', in the colonial town of Salem, Massachusetts, America. The trials, which ended with twenty people being executed, have become an emblem of paranoia and injustice. The credibility of witchcraft had already started to decline at the end of the seventeenth century, and the number of trials decreased. However, the belief still continued in some societies and cultures; in 1895, Bridget Cleary was beaten and burned to death in Ireland by her husband as he suspected that fairies had taken his wife and replaced her with a witch. The last woman to be tried as a witch in Britain was Helen Ducan, who was a Scottish medium practising in Portsmouth during the Second World War. At a séance she held in November 1941, she claimed to have materialised a spirit which told her HMS *Barham* had sunk. This had not as yet been reported in the newspapers but it was common knowledge among the families of the ship's crew. The authorities were concerned that she was

Why were the vast majority of those accused of witchcraft women?

revealing classified information and exploiting the bereaved, which ultimately led to her arrest.

Witchcraft and trials still occur in the twenty-first century in some parts of the world; reports show women in Zambia being accused of witchcraft following the spread of HIV and AIDS. More recently, Nigerian children have been accused of witchcraft, and consequently poisoned and abused, while Zimbabwe only lifted its ban on prosecuting people for witchcraft in 2006. The idea and image of a frightening old woman with evil powers continues in fairy stories, horror films such as *The Witch: A Prime Evil Folk Tale* (2016) or children's literature such as Roald Dahl's *The Witches* (1983). A more romanticised pseudo-feminist version of witches as powerful young women was suggested in *Sabrina the Teenage Witch* (1996–2003) and *Charmed* (1998–2006), leading writer Hazel Cills to suggest that:

I think a lot of feminists, like myself, have witchcraft for a few reasons ... One, it's a woman using powers to change a world that doesn't like her in the first place. A witch tale is a feminist fantasy because it's about having a physical, mystical power that can create real, dangerous change in a world that would rather take power away from them.

92 | New Zealand Women's Suffrage Petition 1893

The First Successful Women's
Suffrage Campaign

LEAH SUSANS

The petition for women's suffrage presented to the New Zealand Parliament on 11 August 1893 has been remembered as a landmark for women's history. New Zealand was at the heart of women's suffrage, the first self-governing country in the world to award all women the right to vote in parliamentary elections later that year.

In the late nineteenth century women's suffrage became an important political issue across the world and in New Zealand public opinion began to change after suffrage campaigning led by Kate Sheppard. In 1878, 1879 and 1887 bills or amendments extending the vote to women only narrowly failed to pass in parliament; a petition circulated in 1892 did not have much success, but what Kate Sheppard described as 'a monster petition' in 1893 was significant. Petition sheets had circulated throughout New Zealand and were returned to Christchurch where Kate Sheppard pasted each sheet end on end and rolled it around a section of a broom handle. This final roll contained 23,853 signatures, with a further 7,000 signatures added before it was presented to parliament. The original petition comprised more than 500 individual sheets, which were signed in various parts of the country. These were then glued together to form a single roll that stretched for more than 270m and was eventually made up of 546 sheets of paper. It is thought that other women may have signed smaller regional petitions, which may not have survived, to form the formal petition submitted to parliament. The total number of signatures represented a quarter of the adults of voting age of the female population in New Zealand.

Support for women's suffrage came from men as well as women, including leading male politicians Robert Stout, William Fox, John Balance and Sir John Hall, an MP and suffrage supporter, who brought the petition to parliament and unrolled it down the central aisle of the debating chamber until it hit the end wall with a thud. Governor Lord Glasgow gave royal assent to the electoral bill on 19 September 1893, giving all women over the age of 21 the vote. It was not long before women took to the polls and voted for the first time in the election held on 28 November 1893. This election saw a high female turnout, with 65 per cent of women exercising their new right.

The petition has been on the UNESCO Memory of the World register since 1997. It is held at the Archives in Wellington, New Zealand on display in the Constitution Room, with a plaque commemorating the achievement. Alongside it there is also

To the Honourable the Speaker and Members of the House of Representatives in Parliament assembled.

THE Petition of the undersigned Women, of the age of twenty-one years and upwards, resident in the Colony of New Zealand, humbly sheweth :—

THAT large numbers of Women in the Colony have for several years petitioned Parliament to extend the franchise to them.

THAT the justice of the claim, and the expediency of granting it, was, during the last Session of Parliament, affirmed by both Houses; but, that for reasons not affecting the principle of Women's Franchise, its exercise has not yet been provided for.

THAT if such provision is not made before the next General Election, your petitioners will, for several years, be denied the enjoyment of what has been admitted by Parliament to be a just right, and will suffer a grievous wrong.

THEY therefore earnestly pray your Honourable House to adopt such measures as will enable Women to record their votes for Members of the House of Representatives at the ensuing General Election.

THEY further pray that your Honourable House will pass no Electoral Bill which shall fail to secure to Women this privilege.

And your petitioners, as in duty bound, will ever pray, &c.

NAME.	ADDRESS.
Mary J. Carpenter	Yaldhurst
Anna Gilberthorpe	Yaldhurst
Susann Clarkson	Hornby
Julia F. Shelton	Hornby
Jane F. Smithie	Templeton
Isabella Chaplin	Templeton
Mary Hansen	Templeton
Louise Rosendale	Templeton
Priscilla Marshall	Templeton
Margaret Watson	Templeton
Ester Haarte	Templeton
Jessie Budwell	Templeton
Julia Majors	Templeton
Mary Fiffs	Templeton
Ethel	Riccarton
Emma Lambert	Hornby
K. W. Sheppard	Riccarton
Te Wallis	"
	"
J. Carleton	
M. Gulley	Lyttelton
S. W. Hewinson	Fendalton
C. Hepburn	Riccarton
L. Hepburn	
E. A. Verral	Fendalton
F. Earle	Fendalton
T. Selwyn	Fendalton
	Fendalton
M. H. Dennistoun	Fendalton

THEY therefore earnestly pray your Honou... to record their votes for Members of the House of Representatives at the ensuing General Election.

the facsimile of the first sheet bearing the signature of Kate Sheppard. In recent years, Sheppard's valuable contribution to New Zealand's history has been acknowledged on its $10 note.

There is significant variation in women's progress towards political citizenship across the world; Australia gave women the vote in 1902 and Finland in 1906. Finland, Norway, Denmark, Iceland, then the Russian Republic and Canada all enfranchised women before Great Britain gave some women the vote in 1918, or the USA 19th Amendment to the constitution enfranchised women in the USA. France did not enfranchise women until 1944 and in Switzerland women only gained the right to vote in federal elections in 1971. It was not until very recently that some Middle Eastern countries awarded women voting rights: Kuwait in 2005, United Arab Emirates in 2006 and only as recently as 2011 in Saudi Arabia. New Zealand's achievement, as one suffrage campaigner from Australia explained, 'gave new hope and life to all women struggling for emancipation'. But for many women it was a long and difficult fight to obtain voting rights and political power.

Not only was New Zealand the first country to grant women the right to vote in 1893, but the same year it also saw Elizabeth Yates become the mayor of Onehunga, the first time such a post had been held by a woman anywhere in the British Empire. Women did not, however, gain the right to stand for parliament in New Zealand until 1919. Getting women to take a significant role in law making is an ongoing struggle. In 1907 Finland elected the very first female MPs in the world. Even in 2014 only 31 of the 100 MPs in the New Zealand parliament were women. In Britain the following year, 191 women were elected as MPs in the 2015 General Election, 29 per cent of all MPs, and in 2016 only 105 women gained seats in the United States Congress, making up just 19.6 per cent of the 535 members.

> Why has there been such a wide variation in when different countries enfranchised women?

93 | Force-Feeding Equipment

Suffragette Activists and Their Treatment in Jail

JANIS LOMAS

In Great Britain, when the Women's Social and Political Union (WSPU) activists, usually known as the suffragettes, were first incarcerated in 1904 they were usually imprisoned in the First Division, the section of the jail reserved for political prisoners; however, the government refused to grant them political prisoner status.

This status was important to suffragettes as it meant that they were kept segregated from other prisoners and had several privileges not allowed to women in the general prison population. Suffragettes felt that as their protest was political, they should all be granted that status. As time went on, fewer and fewer suffragette prisoners were sentenced to the First Division.

In 1909, Marion Dunlop was arrested for using indelible ink to stamp 'Votes for women' on a wall inside the Houses of Parliament; for this she was sentenced to one month's imprisonment. Refused the First Division treatment she felt she was entitled to, she went on hunger strike. This had not been official WSPU policy but her actions were hailed as a victory by suffragettes, as after going without food for ninety-one hours she was released. This led Christabel and Emmeline Pankhurst, the leaders of the suffragettes, to believe that refusing food was a non-violent way of defeating the government; by hunger striking they could force the authorities to release suffragette prisoners.

The government, unfortunately, had no intention of giving in to the suffragettes' demands or allowing them to avoid fulfilling their sentence, so they began forcibly feeding them. This involved inserting a rubber tube 45cm down the throat or via one nostril, into the stomach. Once in place, a thin gruel or a beef extract drink was poured through a funnel into the tube. This usually caused gagging and often, once the tube was removed, the woman vomited. This process was frequently repeated three times a day. Physical after-effects of the feeding were often bruising of the face, nose and throat, damage to teeth, nausea, vomiting, stomach cramps and diarrhoea. Prior to the suffrage campaigns, doctors in asylums and hospitals used tube-feeding to save lives with compliant patients. It was a much more dangerous proposition to insert a tube down the throat of a struggling woman and risk blocking a patient's airway by inserting the tube into the lungs rather than the stomach. Lilian Lenton, a 21-year-old suffragette, was force fed but the feeding tube entered her lungs. The doctors, not realising the tube was in her lungs rather than her stomach, poured gruel down it, giving her pleurisy and pneumonia. She was lucky to survive and only lived because she was young and fit. The prison released her quickly, anxious to avoid her dying while in custody. Ethel Moorhead, the first woman in Scotland to be

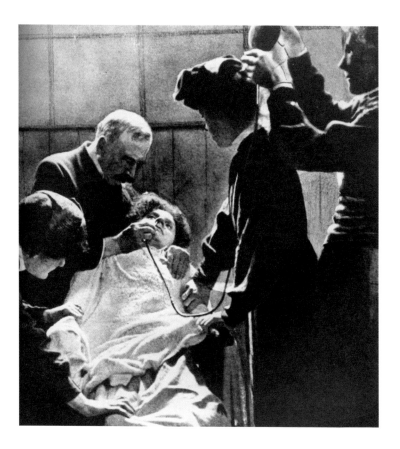

forcibly fed, also developed pneumonia after fluid was poured into her lungs while she endured forced feeding.

Suffrage prisoners came from all social classes, but once in prison they were treated very differently as Constance Lytton, the daughter of one of the most aristocratic families in England, demonstrated. Her father had been Viceroy of India, one of her brothers sat in the House of Lords and another was an MP. Having been born with a serious heart condition, Constance was a cosseted invalid until she joined the WSPU in 1908. She was imprisoned four times but in 1909, when she went on hunger strike, she was released after three days without being forcibly fed, as the prison doctor said her heart was too damaged to endure forced feeding. Her request to be treated as an ordinary inmate was refused by the governor. In 1910, determined to expose the preferential treatment she received compared with 'ordinary' prisoners she dressed herself in working women's clothes, cut her hair and, calling herself Jane Warton, got herself arrested in Liverpool, where she was unknown. After refusing food and drink she was soon forcibly fed without being medically examined. She endured forced feeding another seven times before her mother tracked her down and secured her release. Her treatment in prison caused her to have a stroke soon after and she died in 1923, but she never regretted her actions and said that she felt more alive at that time than at any other time in her life.

Between 1909 and 1914, 165 women and three male suffrage supporters were forcibly fed in ten prisons in the UK.

A struggling variety artiste and suffragette, Kitty Marion took part in stone throwing and many arson attacks between 1909 and 1913. During her last period of imprisonment she was force-fed three times daily for five weeks and five days, which resulted in a weight loss of 2st 8lb. In all, she endured forcible feeding no fewer than 232 times. While in prison, acts of camaraderie helped to keep up suffragette prisoners' spirits and resolve and women found ways to continue campaigning. Supporters in a house near Holloway sang 'The March of the Women' and the 'Marseillaise' at full voice to prisoners, especially at night when the women were at their lowest ebb.

In 1912, a study was published in the medical journal *The Lancet* which detailed stories of ninety suffragettes who had suffered damage to their cardiovascular, gastrointestinal and nervous systems after forced feeding; as suffragettes became progressively weaker, the government became concerned that a woman would die in prison. They therefore introduced the Temporary Discharge for Ill-Health Act, which became known as the Cat and Mouse Act, with the government as the cat ready to pounce on the prisoner 'mice'. This meant that hunger-striking prisoners were left to starve in prison until their health was seriously threatened; they were then released and subsequently re-arrested when they had recovered their strength. Emmeline Pankhurst went on numerous hunger strikes in this period and was released and re-arrested over and over, leading to severe damage to her health, while less well-known suffragettes went into hiding to evade being re-arrested.

Is it against a protestor's human rights to force-feed them?

In the years 1909–14, 165 women and three male suffrage supporters were forcibly fed in ten prisons in the UK. Many of them suffered lifelong problems afterwards, but it did give publicity to the cause of women's suffrage around the world. Although a majority of the general public and Prime Minister Asquith were not sympathetic to many of the militant actions the women undertook, leading to newspaper headlines such as 'Let Them Starve', force feeding did arouse sympathy for the pain and sacrifice the women were enduring, with Church leaders and many politicians denouncing force feeding and protesting that it was inhumane to treat women in this way. Since 1975, the use of force feeding has been prohibited under the Declaration of Tokyo of the World Medical Association and is considered torture unless there is consent by the patient or a genuine medical reason to do so. Nevertheless, it has been used by many countries, most notably by the United States in Guantanamo Bay.

94 | Fianna Éireann Gal Gréine (Sunburst) Flag Belonging to Constance Markievicz

Irish Nationalism and Feminism

MAGGIE ANDREWS

The Fianna Éireann Gal Gréine flag was designed by Countess Constance Markievicz for the Irish Republican Brotherhood, with a pike, the traditional weapon of the United Irishmen, and a bright yellow sun on a green background; the ancient motto embroidered in yellow metallic thread read '*Glaine ár gcroí, Neart ár ngéag, Agus beart de réir ár mbriathar*', which translates as 'The purity of our hearts, the strength of our limbs, our commitment to our vow'.

Constance Markievicz was a feminist, socialist and artist, an ardent supporter of the Irish independence movement, and remains the most well known of the 200 women who took part in the Easter Rising against British imperial rule which took place in Dublin on Easter Monday 1916. The republican revolutionaries planned to occupy strategic buildings within the city and Markievicz was both a sniper and second-in-command of the group, which took over and held St Stephen's Green for several days. After heavy retaliation from the British, with approximately 1,000 dead in the city, the republicans surrendered. Many of the ringleaders were court-martialled and shot; Constance, as a woman, was spared. As a Dublin newspaper reported:

> Countess Constance Markieviez, who has received a sentence of penal servitude for life, was one of the most active of the rebel leaders in Dublin. Dressed as a man, entirely in green – green tunic, green hat with a green feather in it, green trousers puttees and boots – she was finally surrounded with a body of 120 rebels, who were in possession of the Royal College of Surgeons. As she surrendered to the British officer she kissed her revolver before handing it to him.

Constance's imprisonment was short – she was released in 1917 – but her house had been ransacked by British soldiers and the Fianna Éireann Gal Gréine was seized as a war trophy. It remained in Britain until it was returned to Ireland, on loan, as part of the centenary of the 1916 Easter Rising.

Constance did not perhaps have a typical background for a revolutionary. She was born in 1868, one of five children of the wealthy Protestant Irish landowning Gore-Booth family. Her childhood was spent at Lissadell House, County Sligo, where she gained a reputation as an expert and daredevil rider. She trained at the Slade School

of Art and went to live as an artist in Paris, where she met her Polish husband, Count Casimir Markievicz. After their marriage they lived in Ireland where their daughter Maeve was born in 1901. In the years that followed Constance became increasingly politicised, in the suffrage movement, in trade union politics and in Irish nationalism, while her daughter spent most of her time with her grandmother. Constance explained that she believed in 'Sinn Fein and in the liberty and justice for women and for countries. Fair play for everybody all round is what I want.'

Women supported the republican movement by making speeches, garnering support, writing articles, conveying plans and orders, nursing the sick and making flags. Constance designed the blue flag with a golden sun emerging from the bottom corner, which is still part of the iconography of the Irish Republican movement.

Constance Markievicz was spared the death penalty for her involvement in the Easter Rising because she was a woman.

One of Constance's most significant contributions to the republican cause was her founding of the republican Boy Scouts, Na Fianna Éireann, with Bulmer Hobson, a northern Quaker. The organisation was a response to Baden-Powell's Boy Scout movement, seen by Constance as imperialist and excessively pro-English, which had been founded the year before; the republican youth movement aim was to be the 'training of the youth of Ireland, mentally and physically, to achieve this object by teaching scouting and military exercises, Irish history, and the Irish language'.

As well as engaging in camp-craft and scouting, Constance prepared the boys to fight for their country's independence. They were involved in gun running in 1914. Con Colbert, one of a hundred boys at the very first meeting of the Fianna in 1909, was one of many young lads who took part in the Easter Rising 1916, a role for which he was executed. To the boys of the Fianna, Constance must have seemed an exotic figure, tall, unconventional in her dress, with a cigarette hanging out of her mouth and a little dog at her heels; she was a skilled shot and supported the use of military force to win independence. She was also committed to encouraging women to join unions. She made inspirational speeches, some in support of the workers involved in the fierce industrial dispute in 1913, which began with a tram-workers' strike and led to lockouts and riots. She also engaged in the traditionally female areas of welfare politics. A Dublin newspaper later recalled how 'she revealed during these riots the human side of her complex nature by labouring indefatigably to provide a soup kitchen for a thousand poor children who were perilously close to starvation'.

> Are women necessarily going to play very different roles in nationalist politics to men?

Such actions endeared her to the working-class women of Dublin. This and her reputation as a hero of the 1916 rising enabled her to win a decisive victory to be elected MP for St Patrick's Division in Dublin in December 1918. She was the first women to be elected to the British parliament, although at the time she was a prisoner in Holloway prison. When released the following March, she apparently paid a quick visit to see her name on a peg in the House of Commons cloakroom before returning to a tumultuous welcome in Ireland. In the years that followed, until her death in 1927, Constance remained embroiled in Irish politics and the bitter civil war that ensued after the Irish Free State was set up in 1922. As a committed Irish republican she never took her seat in the British House of Commons; her commitment to the nationalist cause came before her feminism. Her choices were those other women fighting in nationalist movements have all too often felt compelled to make.

95 | Irena Sendlerowa's Jars
Women's Humanitarian Resistance

JANIS LOMAS

Irena Sendlerowa used jars to record the names of the Jewish children she helped smuggle out of the Warsaw Ghetto in which the occupying German Nazi regime incarcerated Jews between 1940 and 1943. Irena wrote details of children's Jewish names and their new name on strips of tissue paper in jars, buried under an apple tree in her co-worker's garden. Every month the jars were dug up and new names were added.

She kept the records, although it was extremely risky, because she felt it was important that the children knew who they really were and hoped they would be reunited with their birth families at a later date. Irena and her network of helpers saved 2,500 Jewish children, providing false papers and the money to support them, eventually using currency supplied by the Polish underground movement dedicated to rescuing Jews from the Holocaust. She was one of many women who have responded with bravery and compassion to the humanitarian crisis created by conflicts, women like Eglantyne Jebb, who set up the Save the Children Fund in 1919 when she found that children in Germany were starving as a result of Allied blockades.

Irena was not herself Jewish; she was a Polish Catholic social worker, which enabled her to get papers to enter the ghetto. She was appalled by the persecution of the Jewish population under the Nazi regime, especially when they were rounded up and forced to enter a small, designated part of the city behind a 10ft wall with broken glass on top, which became known as the Warsaw Ghetto. In a final malicious gesture the Nazis chose Yom Kippur, the holiest day of the Jewish year, to move the 400,000 Jewish men, women and children into the ghetto, allowing them to take only belongings they could carry; what was left behind was confiscated by the Germans. The ghetto was congested; seven or eight people shared one room. The overcrowding made epidemics such as typhus inevitable. People starved to death; while rations for the occupying German force were 2,613 calories per day, they were 699 for non-Jewish Poles and a miniscule 184 calories for Jews. Decrees posted all over Warsaw stipulated that the punishment for helping people escape or helping them in the ghetto was the death penalty.

Irena, however, redoubled her efforts to save the children and found various ingenious ways to smuggle them out of the ghetto. At first she was able to bribe a guard to allow her to take them out through a secret back door at the courthouse, but when this route was discovered and closed she used the sewers and underground passages under the ghetto. Children were hidden under blood-stained bandages and

stretchers in ambulances that were allowed to remove the dead and dying when
epidemics raged. Babies were also hidden in ventilated boxes under the floor as
the Nazis, afraid of contagion, did not usually search too closely. She also put the
children into a sack or a suitcase and pushed them out on a trolley. One emaciated
child was smuggled out by putting his feet into a man's boots and holding on to his
belt as the brave Jewish man walked out with his long coat buttoned over both of
them to his forced labour work party. In 1943, despite determined resistance from
Jewish fighters inside the ghetto, the Nazis started to empty it, sending 5,000–8,000
people a day to the Treblinka death camp, where they were murdered.

Five months after the ghetto was emptied Irena was arrested,
but despite being tortured by the Gestapo for three months
she refused to give away her network. She escaped on the
morning of her execution as the Polish underground

**Why do you think
Irene Sendlerowa's
achievement has
been overlooked in
comparison with that
of Oskar Schindler?**

bribed the executioner. After the war she dug up the jars
and tried to unite the children with their families, but it
proved impossible; most parents had died in Treblinka. In
1948 Irena was again imprisoned, this time by the Polish
communist government because of her opposition to their
Stalinist regime. This was also the reason her exploits during
the war remained largely unrecognised.

In recent years four Kansas schoolgirls discovered a brief outline of
Irena's story online and wrote a play, *Life in a Jar*, which has brought Irena's story to
a wide audience. Since that time the Irena Sendler Foundation has been established
(she is known as Sendler in America) and many school and prison projects have been
working to publicise her wartime bravery. Irena Sendlerowa's humanitarian work
was finally recognised in 1965 when she was given the title of 'Righteous Among
the Nations' by the Yad Vashem organisation in Jerusalem, and in 1991 made an
honorary citizen of Israel. Finally, in 2003, she was honoured in her homeland, given
Poland's highest distinction, the Order of the White Eagle. In 2007, a year before her
death, she was nominated for the Nobel Peace Prize. Irena Sendlerowa remained
extremely modest and dismissive of her achievements, saying only that: 'I could
have done more. This regret will follow me to my death.'

96 | Rosa Parks's Mugshot

Women's Involvement in the American Civil
Rights Movement

JANIS LOMAS

**In Montgomery, Alabama, on 1 December 1955 a black American woman called Rosa
Parks was returning home by bus after a long day's work. The bus was crowded and as
usual the first half of the bus was reserved for white people, while black people like
Parks were only allowed to sit at the back; this was in accordance with the strict racial
segregation laws that operated in the American South at the time.**

On this occasion all the seats in the white section were being used. Parks had seated
herself in the front row of the 'coloured' section but when a white man got on to
the bus the driver asked all the black passengers on her row to move back to make
an extra white row to allow the white man to sit. Three black passengers complied
but Parks refused to move. She wrote later in her autobiography: 'People always say
that I didn't give up my seat because I was tired, but that isn't true. I was not tired
physically ... No, the only tired I was, was tired of giving in.'

The white bus driver, who had already treated her badly on previous occasions,
called the police; two police officers attended and arrested Rosa Parks, as the mugshot
overleaf shows. She was released on bail later that evening, by which time news of her
arrest had spread and Edgar Daniel Nixon, the president of the Montgomery chapter
of the National Association for the Advancement of Coloured People (NAACP) was
waiting for her with a proposal. She already knew Nixon, as both Rosa and her husband
Raymond were members of the NAACP and Rosa had been secretary for some years.
She had already been an activist since the 1940s; Nixon had been hoping for years that
he could find a black person brave enough to test the validity of Alabama's segregation
laws. Nixon persuaded Rosa, with the support of her mother and husband, to do this.
The NAACP circulated 35,000 flyers asking the black population to boycott the buses
for one day on the day of Rosa's trial.

On 5 December the trial took place and Rosa was found guilty of violating the
segregation laws; she was given a suspended sentence and fined $10, with $4
court costs. The boycott was a great success, and on the strength of this a new
organisation was formed called the Montgomery Improvement Association (MIA).
A 26-year-old pastor, the Reverend Martin Luther King, was elected its president.
He later wrote that on that day, as he saw empty bus after empty bus drive down his
road, he realised that 'the once dormant and quiescent Negro community was now
fully awake'.

That night a vote was taken to continue the boycott. The boycott had a massive
effect on the bus companies and on shops in Montgomery as the black community

The arrest of Rosa Parks sparked the bus boycott that succeeded in achieving desegregated buses and helped galvanise the Civil Rights Movement in the USA in the 1950s.

was a major source of revenue. Taxis and private cars were organised to get people to work. During the boycott churches were burned and a bomb was placed at Martin Luther King's home while Parks was threatened, lost her job and received hate mail. The boycott was to continue for over a year and finally the Federal Court voted by two to one that segregation on buses was unconstitutional.

Rosa Parks certainly suffered repercussions for her actions. Both she and her husband were unable to find work in Montgomery and after two years of hate mail and death threats her family moved to Detroit. Not all the criticism she received was from white Southerners; she was very demoralised by the attitudes of some black people, many of whom did not support her stirring up racial hatred and challenging the status quo. In one piece of writing, she explained how this made her feel: 'completely alone and desolate as if I was descending in a black and bottomless chasm'.

She hoped that Detroit would prove to be an easier place to live, especially as her brother and cousins already lived there, but she continued to be targeted, despite which she persisted in working for racial, social, criminal and global justice in the decades to come. Rosa Parks's actions and the Montgomery bus boycott that followed are widely regarded as the earliest mass protest on behalf of civil rights in the US, setting the stage for additional large-scale actions outside the court system to bring about fair treatment for African-Americans. It also led to the emergence of Martin Luther King as a prominent national leader of the civil rights movement.

> Perhaps the passive but determined resistance of Rosa Parks is the best way to achieve civil rights?

Rosa Parks's action brought national and international attention to the civil rights struggles occurring in the US, as more than 100 reporters visited Montgomery during the boycott to profile the effort and its leaders. Rosa, while shying away from the spotlight throughout her life, remains an esteemed figure in the history of American civil rights activism. In 1999 the US Congress awarded her its highest honour, the Congressional Gold Medal, making her the first woman and only the second African-American to be awarded the honour since it began in 1852. She remained modest about her actions, saying: 'I was fortunate God provided me with the strength I needed at the precise time conditions were ripe for change. I am thankful every day that he gave me the strength not to move.'

The bravery of Rosa Parks and her refusal to be brought low by injustice and fear has proved to be a symbol of the strength of passive resistance following in the honourable tradition of Mahatma Gandhi and as an inspiration to other women such as those who protested against the siting of nuclear weapons at Greenham Common in the 1980s and '90s.

97 | Barbara Castle's Diaries

Women's Diaries

PAULA BARTLEY

In 1964 Harold Wilson, the newly elected Labour Party Prime Minister of Britain, called Barbara Castle to 10 Downing Street and appointed her Minister of Overseas Development, head of a newly created government department with a seat in the Cabinet. She was the only woman in the British Cabinet, and only the fourth female Cabinet minister ever to be appointed.

Over the next twelve years she held four Cabinet posts: Minister for Overseas Development, Minister for Transport, Minister for Employment and Productivity, and Minister for Health and Social Services. In 1979, just after the Conservatives were elected and Margaret Thatcher became the first female Prime Minister, Barbara Castle published the diaries that she had kept throughout her time as a Cabinet minister: *The Castle Diaries*. She went to school in Bradford, which she claimed 'had a very formative influence' on her and so she chose to house the original unedited versions of her diaries at the University of Bradford.

Keeping a diary is usually associated in people's minds with the private recording of personal reflections, maybe of innermost thoughts and feelings, of hopes and dreams, of worries and concerns; diaries, particularly those written in the romantic tradition, are never meant to be read. *The Castle Diaries* include a personal perspective on public events, such as her first attendance at a state banquet, in this case for President Frei of Chile:

> The setting was pure Ruritania: gold plate, knee breeched gentlemen advancing in an organised phalanx to serve the courses ... The best pea green soup I have ever tasted ... Then I was called to sit next to the Queen, giving my usual half-bow because I won't curtsey. The Queen talked to me very sensibly about my visit to Africa ... Then a flunkey came and whispered in her ear and she excused herself, saying laughing that 'Poor Charles' was doing his O-levels the next day and needed a bit of reassurance.

Political diaries are special. In these the writer provides a first-hand testimony of public events and usually has publication in mind. Political diaries tend to feature a certain forthright quality in their discussion of government policies, yet they bring a refreshing informality of style and expression to bear on events which otherwise would be shrouded in heavy official language. Political diaries written by women are rare because few women, apart from queens, have ever held high political office. Both Queen Victoria of Britain and Queen Charlotte of Sweden wrote diaries, which

illuminate national and international events from a woman's perspective. Barbara Castle's diaries, typed up from her shorthand notes, are distinctive, not just because they broaden and enrich the reader's understanding of the period but because they discuss Cabinet meetings from an altogether unusual perspective: that of an immensely capable left-wing politician – and a woman.

Barbara Castle wanted to end poverty both in Britain and the wider world. Her diaries show how she tried to bridge the disparity between the rich and poor nations of the world by declaring that all British loans to the poorest developing countries would be interest-free. As Minister for Transport (1965–68) she designed an affordable public transport system and improved road safety by enforcing a 70mph speed limit, making it compulsory for all new cars to have seat belts and introducing the breathalyser for drivers suspecting of drinking too much alcohol.

As Secretary of State for Employment (1968–74) Castle tried to curb the power of the trade unions. This alienated her from the left, led to a split in the Labour Cabinet and brought the government to the brink of catastrophe. Her introduction of the Equal Pay Act in 1970 went some way to restore her reputation as a left-wing politician. As Minister for Health and Social Services, Castle introduced child benefits payable to mothers. Barbara Castle was a powerful woman and the most important British female politician but, as she notes in her diary, she still faced

In 1964, Barbara Castle was the only woman in the British Cabinet, and only the fourth female Cabinet minister ever to be appointed.

sexual harassment from the Minister of Health, the Foreign Secretary and even the Prime Minister.

Barbara Castle does write about her feelings, about her hopes and fears, her delights and disappointments, and she does share her plans and her intentions and the political motivations to make changes and improvements. Castle has made a choice how to present herself; there are editorial decisions on every page about how she wanted to come across to her readers, only letting them see those aspects of her character that portray her in the best possible light: hardworking and committed. She relates how on one occasion that she 'Set alarm for 2 am to finish a speech [on Road Safety Bill], overslept and didn't wake till 4:45am. Panic rush to get it finished before I had to leave for a meeting.' On another occasion she records: 'A nightmarish day with more work to cram in than even a 24 hour day could accommodate.'

Are the diaries written by a female politician different from those of male politicians?

Her diary captures all the drama, the determination and commitment in the face of opposition, the joys of success and the moments of despair, which accompanied her struggle to improve industrial relations in Britain, and why agents for change provoke opposition and challenge. Perhaps most importantly, *The Castle Diaries* provide the most compelling reassurance that, given the will, the motivation and the commitment, power in politics is not only available to women, but theirs for the taking.

98 | Greenham Common Fence
Women Peace Protestors

MAGGIE ANDREWS

The fence around the USA army base at Greenham Common in Berkshire, England became the focus of women's peace activism in the 1980s. The Women for Life on Earth march, which arrived at Greenham in September 1981, included women of all ages, some with their children in pushchairs, who had made their way from Wales to protest against the storage of cruise missiles on UK soil.

Four women chained themselves to the military base's perimeter fence; in the many months of protest that followed, a high-security fence was constructed which women adorned with items of significance to them, or surrounded, cut and broke through. Determined to maintain their protest, some women lived in tents near the base, supported by others who visited occasionally bringing supplies and joining mass demonstrations. Lynn Rishworth recalled the moment when she knew that thousands of women had surrounded the 9-mile perimeter fence in 1983:

> Our sisters across the Common whooped back to us and we knew that we'd done it – there were enough of us to encircle the entire Base ... Women were still coming. Lines formed behind lines and we were all full of such joy and a sense of our own strength in unity.

The protests were non-violent, inventive and sometimes funny; there were teddy-bear picnics and dancing around nuclear silos when women cut the fence and entered the military base. The women in return suffered brutality, imprisonment and evictions from their camps. Little wonder that the Greenham camp has come to symbolise women's determined, powerful protest both against the weapons of war and those forms of aggressive machismo that sanction the use of such weapons.

Greenham Common camp was made up of women who left their homes to fight for peace, a women-only protest which assumed women's attitudes to violence and war were fundamentally different from those of men. This was not a new idea; at the very beginning of the twentieth century, Olive Schreiner suggested that women's maternal role shaped their response to the Boer War battlefields. She argued:

> There is, perhaps, no woman, whether she have borne children, or be merely potentially a child bearer, who could look down upon a battlefield covered with slain, but the thought would rise in her, 'So many mothers' sons! So many bodies brought into the world to lie there! So many months of weariness and pain while bones and muscles were shaped within!'

Schreiner, like many feminists, linked war and masculinity, and thought that if women had political power they would develop different ways of settling human differences with greater value placed on human life. With this in mind 1,200 women from twelve countries including Germany, Britain, USA and France, gathered in the Hague, Netherlands for an International Congress in April 1915. Against a backdrop of the First World War in her opening address Alletta Jacobs explained:

> With mourning hearts we stand united here. We grieve for many brave young men who have lost their lives on the battlefield before attaining their full manhood; we mourn with the poor mothers bereft of their sons; with the thousands of young widows and fatherless children, and we feel that we can no longer endure in this twentieth century of civilisation that government should tolerate brute force as the only solution of international disputes.

Jacobs was expressing women's shared experience of grief, their private and emotional response to the consequences of national politics, in a conflict which made food a weapon of war and in which women and children were bombed in their own homes.

Women's desire to protect children motivated the First Declaration of the Peace People in Northern Ireland, which rejected the 'use of the bomb and the bullet and all the techniques of violence' in Northern Ireland in the 1970s. Violence, bombing and civil unrest were a familiar element of life in the province when in August 1976 four children were hit and killed by a car driven by an IRA fugitive fatally shot by the British authorities. Their aunt Mairead Maguire and local resident Betty Williams set up a movement, which marched, petitioned and campaigned for peace. When their efforts were rewarded with the Nobel Peace Prize, Williams explained that she had felt 'a deep sense of frustration at the mindless stupidity of the continuing violence' and that 'as far as we are concerned, every single death in the last eight years, and every death in every war that was ever fought represents life needlessly wasted, a mother's labour spurned'.

The Nobel Peace Prize was also awarded to Rigoberta Menchú Tum, a Mayan Indian from Guatemala, Central America, in 1992 'in recognition of her work for social justice and ethno-cultural reconciliation based on respect for the rights of indigenous peoples'.

Do women respond to war differently from men?

With a growing awareness of the degree to which women were both victims of war and campaigners for peace, on 31 October 2000 the United Nations Security Council Resolution 1325 on Women, Peace and Security called for the full integration of women in all efforts regarding conflict resolution and post-conflict implementation. Just twelve years later the wives of UN ambassadors from Britain and Germany urged Asma al-Assad, the wife of Syria's president, to stop her husband's violent responses to Syrian rebels. Their online appeal explained: 'We strongly believe in Asma's responsibility as a woman, as a wife and as a mother. As the vocal female Arab leader that she used to be, as a champion of female equality, she cannot hide behind her husband.'

Like the women at Greenham Common and many others throughout the twentieth century and into the twenty-first century, these women strove for peace.

99 | Women Against Pit Closures Banner

Women's Activism in the Trade Union Movement

MAGGIE ANDREWS

In March 1984 the chairman of the Coal Board's announcement that twenty uneconomic pits would close led to a long and bitter industrial dispute involving the majority of Britain's 187,000 miners. The proposed closures involved 20,000 redundancies, the decimation of communities and the beginning of the end for the mining industry.

Legislation passed in 1842 had prevented women in Britain working down mines but nevertheless they played a crucial role in the 1984 miners' strike. Miners' wives scrimped, saved and helped each other manage, as they had during the 1926 strike. In north Staffordshire Brenda Proctor, who called a meeting at the club of her local pit, recalled: 'women turned up in droves wanting to help ... It wasn't all about soup kitchens and food parcels – though that was important. We wanted to tell people why we were on strike.'

Wives, sisters and daughters formed the Women Against Pit Closure Group (WAPC); 5,000 women attended a rally in Barnsley in May and in the months that followed women ran soup kitchens, created leaflets and badges and, like their suffragette forerunners, they embroidered banners to promote their cause. They also raised funds, held sit-ins in mineshafts, addressed rallies across the UK and Europe, sent miners' pit lamps across the country to inspire support, joined and were arrested on picket lines and chained themselves to colliery gates. Iris Preston, who kept a record of her involvement in the strike, recorded: 'I had responsibilities not just as a housewife and working mother but to workers everywhere, it is now time to stand up and be counted.'

Proctor became chair of the WAPC, which gained associate membership of the National Union of Mineworkers in December 1984. Women's relationship with the trade union movement across the world has, however, not always been so positive. Many unions were set up to look after the working lives of skilled, often white, men who sometimes saw women workers as undermining their position or in competition for their jobs. Consequently many women joined gender-specific trade unions, formed as early as the 1870s in Australia while the National Women's Trade Union League of America (NWTUL) was founded in Boston in 1903 and the National Federation of Women Workers (NFWW) started in Britain in 1906 by Mary Macarthur.

Women's trade union membership has been perhaps strongest in industries associated with garment manufacture or spinning and weaving cloth. One of the

first strikes of women workers was in Pawtucket, Rhode Island, USA, where in May 1824, 102 women workers left their looms in response to a wage cut. In November 1909 the Shirtwaist strike in New York City, which was led by the NWTUL, initially gained only a reluctant response from male union leaders. Their concern that 'women could not be trusted with a strike' was proved wrong when 20,000 striking garment workers, predominantly women, saw through the dispute to achieve an improvement in their wages, working conditions and hours, adding to the credibility for the NWTUL.

In 1914 in Britain, 90 per cent of all trade unionists were men and the conditions of many areas of women's work – domestic, isolated, part-time or piece work, where they were often susceptible to intimidation – made it hard to combine union activities with family responsibility for most women. Trade unions attempted to engage more women by including more social activities and outings in their programmes. The National Union of General Workers found in 1923 that an evening of dancing appealed to school cleaners and other isolated workers in the East End. Singing and refreshments were often combined with lectures to encourage women to engage with politics.

There are examples of women working closely with trade unions on social legislation, for example when landlords sought to increase rents in Glasgow by 25 per cent in 1915. Some 25,000 families refused to pay rent increases; they were supported by trade unionists in local shipyards and munitions factories, which prevented some evictions and led to government legislation to control rents.

In 1914 in Britain, 90 per cent of all trade unionists were men.

However, the 1984 miners' strike was not so successful; it ended on 3 March 1985, allowing pit closures and the dismantling of the British coal industry to proceed unhindered. By the end of 2015 there were no deep-shaft coalmines in Britain. The WAPC supported other industrial disputes, including the Wapping printers, women cleaners at Chesterfield hospital and the Liverpool dockers. Some women, including Brenda Proctor, continued campaigning work and political activities; she became a local councillor and gained a degree in industrial relations at Keele University. Others from the WAPC struggled with debt, drudgery and the destruction of their communities and families.

In the years that followed the miners' strike in Britain, trade union membership and power has decreased and, by the time Frances O'Grady became the first female general secretary of the Trades Union Congress in 2012, there were more women than men in the unions. O'Grady championed part-time workers and the low-paid, and had argued for a minimum wage as early as the 1980s. Not all trade unions, however, have a culture or attitudes which allow women to progress; Mexican trade unionist Martha Heredia has pointed out that in Latin America the number of women in leadership positions in the trade union movement in no way reflects the make-up of the labour force. She argues that 'it is very complicated to be a woman and a trade unionist in an environment where misogyny is embedded, and where there are doubts that we have the same commitment, willingness and capacity, even if there are no longer doubts that we have the same skills'.

Perhaps more industrial conflict than we realise has, like the 1984 miners' strike, needed wives playing a supporting and hidden role.

Like the women in the miners' strike, she has drawn attention to the complex juggling of commitments that women face as mothers and wives, and in many cases breadwinners, workers and labour or political activists.

100 | Margaret Thatcher's Statue in the House of Commons

Women Prime Ministers

MAGGIE ANDREWS

The bronze statue of Margaret Thatcher in the Members' Lobby of the British House of Commons, unveiled in February 2007 and designed by Antony Dufort, depicts Britain's first female Prime Minister with her right hand raised, making a point during a debate.

Margaret Thatcher won three general elections and was in office for eleven and a half years, the longest continuous term of any twentieth-century British politician, yet much media commentary focused on the absence in the statue of her trademark handbag. Contemporary plans for a new statue in Parliament Square are embroiled in controversy over a similar omission. Thatcher's handbag, used in preference to a briefcase, was both a symbol of her femininity and a metaphorical 'weapon'. Newspapers during her premiership talked of 'handbag diplomacy', and of her handbagging her opponents, also indicative of discomfort over women wielding political power.

More than seventy countries have now had a female president or prime minister, including India, where Indira Gandhi was prime minister from 1966 to 1977, and for a further four years from 1980 before she was assassinated. Golda Meir served as the prime minister of Israel from 1969 to 1974. Many women leaders have, however, remained in power for less than a year; in 1997 Rosalía Arteaga Serrano was the acting president of Ecuado for only for two days. But in Iceland Vigdís Finnbogadóttir, the world's first democratically elected female president, served from 1980 to 1996.

Women still struggle to win presidential elections. In 2016, despite gaining 2.5 million more votes than her rival Donald Trump, Hillary Clinton failed to become the first female President of the United States. Women have more success getting the top job when the population votes for political parties who then appoint the leader; this was Margaret Thatcher's route to power.

The first female head of government for a major Western democracy was born Margaret Roberts on 13 October 1925 in the small market town of Grantham, Lincolnshire, where her father owned a grocer's shop and was a Methodist preacher and local politician. Unusually for a woman in this era, she studied Chemistry at Somerville College at Oxford University (1943–47), and was president of the Students' Conservative Association. She trained as a barrister while seeking to develop a political career and married Denis Thatcher, an executive in the oil industry, in 1951; she gave birth to twins, Carol and Mark, two years later. When she became the Conservative Member of Parliament for Finchley in 1959, there were

only twenty-five women MPs alongside 605 men in the House of Commons. In 1974, in the wake of their election defeat, the Conservative Party sought a new leader to make them look modern. Margaret Thatcher, one of only nine female MPs in the party, surprised many by becoming party leader and Leader of Her Majesty's Opposition in parliament.

Thatcher's campaign to build support in her party and the country emphasised her femininity and 'ordinariness', claiming: 'I sort of regard myself as a very normal ordinary person, with all the right, instinctive antennae.' She brandished a dustpan and brush at the Conservative Party Women's Conference, announcing she would sweep the ruling Labour Party out of Britain. But it was a femininity that was strident with strong right-wing convictions, harnessed to past war leaders such as the 'Iron Duke' who gained victory in the Battle of Waterloo. She explained to her local Conservative Association in Finchley in 1976:

> I stand before you tonight in my Red Star chiffon evening gown (laughter, applause), my face softly made up and my fair hair gently waved (laughter), the Iron Lady of the Western world. A cold war warrior, an Amazon philistine, even a Peking plotter. Well am I any of these things? ... Yes, I am an iron lady, after all, it wasn't a bad thing to be an iron duke, yes if that's how they wish to interpret my defence of values and freedoms fundamental to our way of life.

After four years as leader of the opposition she won election victory on 4 May 1979; her premiership sought to cut welfare provision and encourage individuals and family responsibility policies, which did little for women. She promoted Britain as a property-owning democracy, selling off council houses and privatising public utilities including gas, water and electricity; and yet as unemployment mushroomed, public spending increased. She did not shrink from a fight and led the country into the Falklands War in 1982 and conflict with political partners in the European Union; she oversaw divisive battles with the trades union movement, particularly in the coal and steel industries. Perhaps best described as a drawbridge feminist, almost no women were promoted within her government, yet she did shift and stretch ideas about women's ability to wield political power.

Why do women still only make up a minority of national political leaders and elected representatives?

In life and death Margaret Thatcher was hugely controversial. On 3 July 2002, Paul Kelleher used a cricket bat to decapitate an 8ft marble statue of her, commissioned by the Speakers' Advisory Committee, on display at Guildhall Art Gallery, London. When the police arrested him he announced, 'I think it looks better like that.' The statue was not repaired; instead the much tougher bronze statue now standing in the members' lobby was commissioned. When Margaret Thatcher died on 8 April 2013, a social media campaign propelled the song 'Ding Dong! The Witch Is Dead' into the charts – a very gendered response to a very controversial female politician.

Select Bibliography

This book has drawn upon the scholarship and research of numerous historians and commentators on women's history.

Books

Addams, Jane, et al., *Women at The Hague: The International Congress of Women and its Results* (University of Illinois Press, 2003).

Andrews, Maggie, *Lest We Forget? Cultures of Remembrance* (The History Press, 2011).

—, *Women and the Media: Feminism and Femininity in Britain, 1900 to the Present* (Routledge, 2014).

—, *The Acceptable Face of Feminism* (Lawrence and Wishart, 2015).

Arrington, Lauren, *Revolutionary Lives: Constance and Casimir Markievicz* (Princeton University Press, 2015).

Beddoe, Deirdre, *Welsh Convict Women: A Study of Women Transported from Wales to Australia, 1787–1852* (Virago, 1979).

Bourke, Joanna, *Rape: A History from 1860 to the Present Day* (Virago, 2007).

Carlyle, Jane, *Welsh Letters and Memorials of Jane Welsh Carlyle* (Cambridge University Press, 2011).

Castle, Barbara, *The Castle Diaries 1964–1976* (Macmillan, 1993).

Craigmayle, A., *A Vicarage in the Blitz: The Wartime Letters of Molly Rich 1940–1944* (Balloon View Publishing Ltd, 2013).

Dallas, Sandra, *Prayers for Sale* (St Martin's Griffin, 2011).

du Preez, Michael & Dronfield, Jeremy, *Dr James Barry: A Woman Ahead of her Time* (Oneworld Publications, 2017).

Duncan, J. & Derrett, M., *Prophecy in the Cotswolds 1803–1947: Joanna Southcott and Spiritual Reform* (P.I. Drinkwater, 1994).

Epstein, Randi Hunter, *Get Me Out: A History of Childbirth from the Garden of Eden to the Sperm Bank* (W.W. Norton & Co., 2011).

Greer, Germaine, *Sex and Destiny: Politics of Human Fertility* (Macmillan, 1985).

Hall, Lesley, *Outspoken Women: An Anthology of Women's Writing on Sex, 1870–1969* (Routledge, 2005).

Hall, Stuart (ed.), *Representation: Cultural Representations and Signifying Practices*, Vol. 2 (Sage, 1997).

Haverty, Anne M., *Constance Markievicz: Irish Revolutionary* (The Lilliput Press Ltd, 2016).

Hibbert, Christopher, *Queen Victoria in her Letters and Journals* (Sutton Publishing, 2000).

Horn, Pamela, *Behind the Counter: Shop Lives from Market Stall to Supermarket* (Sutton Publishing, 2004).

Howell, Georgina, *Queen of the Desert: The Extraordinary Life of Gertrude Bell* (Pan, 2015).

Isba, Anne, *The Excellent Mrs Fry* (Continuum, 2010).

Jackson, Louise A., *Women Police: Gender, Welfare and Surveillance in the Twentieth Century* (Manchester University Press, 2012).

Kramarae, Cheris, *Technology and Women's Voices: Keeping in Touch* (Routledge, 1988).

Last, Nella & Malcolmson, Patricia E., *Nella Last's Peace: The Post-war Diaries of Housewife, 49* (Profile Books, 2008).

le Faye, Deirdre (ed.), *Jane Austen's Letters* (Oxford University Press, 2014).

Lister, Anne, Whitbread, Helena (ed.), *The Secret Diaries of Miss Anne Lister* (Virago Modern Classics, 2010).

Llewelyn Davies, Margaret, *Life as we Have Known It* (W.W. Norton & Co., 1975).

Maines, Rachel P., *The Technology of Orgasm: 'Hysteria', the Vibrator, and Women's Sexual Satisfaction* (JHU Press, 2001).

Mayhew, Henry, *London Labour and the London Poor* (Classics of World Literature, 2008).

Parker, Rozsika, *The Subversive Stitch: Embroidery and the Making of the Feminine* (IB Tauris & Co. Ltd, 2012).

Prince, Mary, Salih, Sara (ed.), *The History of Mary Prince: A West Indian Slave* (Penguin Classics, 2000).

Pruitt, Elinore, *Letters of a Woman Homesteader* (Echo Library, 2006).

Quant, Mary, *My Autobiography* (Headline, 2012).

Sambrook, Pamela A., *The Country House Servant* (Sutton Publishing, 2002).

Sand, George, *Story of my Life: The Autobiography of George Sand*, trans. Thelma Jurgrau (University of New York Press, 1991).

Stanley, Liz, *The Life and Death of Emily Wilding Davison* (Virago, 1998).

Steinbach, Susie, *Women in England 1760–1914: A Social History* (W&N, 2004).

Stuart Mackenzie, Amanda, *Consuelo and Alva Vanderbilt: The Story of a Mother and a Daughter in the 'Gilded Age'* (Harper Perennial, reprint edition, 2007).

Tillyard, Stella, *Aristocrats: Caroline, Emily, Louisa, and Sarah Lennox, 1740–1832* (Farrar Straus Giroux, reprint edition, 1995).

Walkowitz, Judith, *Prostitution and Victorian Society: Women, Class, and the State* (Cambridge University Press, 1980).

Willard, Francis, E., *A Wheel Within a Wheel* (Jungle, 2007).

Williams, A. Susan, *Women and Childbirth in the Twentieth Century: History of the National Birthday Trust Fund, 1928–93* (Sutton Publishing, 1997).

Journal Articles

Amussen, Susan Dwyer, 'Punishment, Discipline, and Power: The Social Meanings of Violence in Early Modern England', *Journal of British Studies* (1995): 34.1 1–34.

Boose, Lynda E., 'Scolding Brides and Bridling Scolds: Taming the Woman's Unruly Member', *Shakespeare Quarterly* (1991): 42.2 179–213.

Briggs, L., Fonseca, C., Cardarello, A., Marre, D., Collard, C. & Yngvesson, B., 'Feminism and Transnational Adoption: Poverty, Precarity, and the Politics of Raising (Other People's?) Children', *Feminist Theory* (2012): 13.1 81–100.

Cavender Wilson, Angela, *American Indian Quarterly* (1996).

Clark, Gillian & Bright, Janette, 'The Foundling Hospital and its Token System', *Family & Community History* (2015): 18:1 53–68.

Clarsen, Georgine, 'A Fine University for Women Engineers: A Scottish Munitions Factory in World War One', *Women's History Review* (2003): 12.3 333–56.

Cook, Hera, 'The English Sexual Revolution: Technology and Social Change', *History Workshop Journal* (Oxford University Press, 2005): 59.1.

Davin, Anna, 'Imperialism and Motherhood', *History Workshop Journal* (Editorial Collective, Ruskin College, 1978).

Dredge, Sarah, 'Opportunism and Accommodation: The English Woman's Journal and the British Mid-Nineteenth-Century Women's Movement', *Women's Studies* (2005): 34 133–57.

Evans Clements, Barbara, 'Working-Class and Peasant Women in the Russian Revolution, 1917–1923', *Signs* (winter 1982): 8.2 215–35.

Kelch-Oliver, Karia, 'The Experiences of African-American Grandmothers in Grandparent-headed Families', *The Family Journal* (2011): 19.1 73–82.

Kurosu, Satomi, 'Divorce in Early Modern Rural Japan: Household and Individual Life Course in Northeastern Villages, 1716–1870', *Journal of Family History* (2011): 36.2 118–41.

Leeson, Peter, et al. 'Wife Sales', *Review of Behavioural Economics* (2014): 1 349–79.

Sheehan, Elizabeth, 'Victorian Clitoridectomy: Isaac Baker Brown and his Harmless Operative Procedure', *Medical Anthropology Newsletter* (1981): 12.4 9–15.

Thompson, E.P. & Samuel, Raphael, 'Theory and Evidence', *History Workshop Journal* (Oxford University Press, 1993): 35 274–76.

Woodeson, Alison, 'The First Women Police: A Force for Equality or Infringement?', *Women's History Review* (1993): 2.2 217–32.

Unpublished PhD Thesis

Throsby, Karen. '"Calling it a Day"': The Decision to End IVF Treatment' (Gender Institute, London School of Economics, submitted for PhD April 2002).

Websites & Online Newspapers

aanchalmalhotra.com/work/remnants-of-a-separation/

alexanderpalace.org/palace/mariabio.html

americanhistory.si.edu/collections/search/object/nmah_1147476

anb.org/articles/15/15-00663.html?from=../11/11-00095.html&from_nm=Bradwell%2C%20Myra%20Colby

annefrank.org/en/

architectsjournal.co.uk/news/who-was-elisabeth-scott/8691468.article

autolife.umd.umich.edu/Gender/Walsh/G_Overview2.htm

badseysociety.uk/sladden-archive

barrowford.org/page10.html

bartleby.com/71/1124.html

bbc.co.uk/history/ww2peopleswar/

bbc.co.uk/news/magazine-17511491

bbc.co.uk/news/magazine-23432653

bbc.co.uk/news/uk-scotland-35414177

bl.uk/spare-rib

civilwar.org/learn/articles/female-soldiers-civil-war

cmft.nhs.uk/media/485016/history%20of%20rmch.pdf

collectorsweekly.com/articles/how-a-makeup-mogul-liberated-women-by-putting-them-in-a-pretty-new-cage/

cosmopolitan.com/uk/beauty-hair/news/a49659/cosmetic-procedures-down-in-the-uk-and-relatable-social-media-stars-could-be-the-reason-why/

cypnow.co.uk/cyp/news/1046902/grandparents-put-themselves-at-risk-while-caring-for-grandchildren

dailymail.co.uk/news/article-1226583/Pram-maker-Maclaren-recalls-1m-models-after-children-sever-fingers.html

dailymail.co.uk/news/article-1318242/Welcome-sandwich-generation-Grandparents-looking-grandchildren-AND-elderly-parents.html

discovery.nationalarchives.gov.uk/details/r/4c032411-dbdd-4030-b31f-789a537d4dd4

dofeve.org/about-us.html

everydayfeminism.com/2016/07/makeup-isnt-anti-feminist/

fhwa.dot.gov/ohim/wmntrans2.pdf

futurelearn.com/courses/empire/0/steps/2566

genevahistoricalsociety.com/medicine/neither-shall-there-by-any-more-pain/

grandmotherscampaign.org

grassrootsonline.org/who-we-are/partner/world-march-of-women-wmw/

gsma.com/mobilefordevelopment/programme/connected-women/closing-the-
    indian-social-media-gender-gap

gsma.com/mobilefordevelopment/wp-content/uploads/2013/01/GSMA_Women_
    and_Mobile-A_Global_Opportunity.pdf

gsma.com/mobilefordevelopment/wp-content/uploads/2013/02/
    GSMA-mWomen-Visa_Unlocking-the-Potential_Feb-2013.pdf

hansard.millbanksystems.com

histoiresordinaires.fr/Grabbing-life-with-no-regrets-Alison-Lapper-artist_a1600.
    html

history.com/this-day-in-history/mary-anderson-patents-windshield-wiper

historywebsite.co.uk/articles/GeorgePeck2/PawnBroking.htm

home.barclaycard/about-us/our-story-so-far.html

independent.co.uk/news/world/asia/pakistan-honour-killing-mother-parveen-
    bibi-death-sentence-burning-daughter-alive-zeenat-rafiq-a7530706.html

independent.co.uk/news/world/middle-east/video-un-wives-call-on-asma-assad-
    to-intervene-in-syria-crisis-7657831.html

independent.co.uk/voices/no-i-wont-wear-the-poppy-hijab-to-prove-im-not-an-
    extremist-a6720901.html

ladiesofllangollen.wordpress.com/a-plas-newydd-timeline/1799-1804/

margaretthatcher.org/document/102947

materialfeminista.milharal.org/files/2012/10/Political-Lesbianism-The-Case-
    Against-Heterosexuality-LRFG.pdf

medicinenet.com/script/main/art.asp?articlekey=10226

metro.co.uk/2014/09/05/joan-rivers-dies-watch-how-plastic-surgery-
    transformed-comedienne-over-50-years-4858191/

mikerendell.com/stroll-on-a-perambulation-through-history/

msmagazine.com/blog/2012/02/18/black-herstory-haunted-by-margaret-garner/

mum.org/southall.htm

mystealthyfreedom.net

nationalhumanitiescenter.org/pds/gilded/empire/text1/turner.pdf

nga.gov.au/rajahquilt/

northamptonmuseums.wordpress.com/2013/09/16/interview-with-shoe-designer-
    joanne-stoker/

nysais.org/uploaded/Conference_Documents/Educating_Girls/Empowering_Girls_
    through_embroidery.pdf

oldbaileyonline.org

oldpolicecellsmuseum.org.uk/page_id_512_path_0p303p304p183p311p.aspx

onthegotours.com/blog/2017/03/worlds-greatest-female-travellers/

ourhatfield.org.uk/content/topics/organizations/girl_guides/guiding-memories

outreach.un.org/ngorelations/content/interview-fighting-girls-education-un-
    advocate-malala-yousafzai-finds-her-purpose

prostitutescollective.net

queenvictoriasjournals.org/home.do

readingmuseum.org.uk

retiredcaribbeannurses.org.uk/page/catalogue)

savemysweden.com/hijab-resistance-feminism-trump/

sdsc.edu/ScienceWomen/anning.html

smh.com.au/lifestyle/news-and-views/news-features/women-with-children-
    biggest-financial-losers-of-divorce-report-20161212-gt92op.html

smithsonianmag.com/smithsonian-institution/the-history-behind-a-slaves-bill-of-sale-132233201/?no-ist

standard.co.uk/news/london/nicola-thorp-actress-in-high-heels-dress-code-row-celebrates-after-firm-backs-down-a3246206.html

strangehistory.net/2013/07/26/women-and-trains/

sussexliving.com/washday-past-present/

tailoredtrades.exeter.ac.uk/exhibitions/sweatedindustries/

teachers.org.uk/files/Chainmakers-A4-24pp.pdf

telegraph.co.uk/culture/tvandradio/6027583/100-years-of-the-Girl-Guides-interview.html

telegraph.co.uk/news/worldnews/barackobama/11766721/Barack-Obama-touches-bones-of-humankinds-ancient-ancestor-Lucy.html

telegraph.co.uk/women/family/8-women-talk-honestly-about-the-gruelling-reality-of-ivf---and-t/

telegraph.co.uk/women/politics/rape-murder-and-abuse-the-penalty-for-being-a-gay-woman-today/

telegraph.co.uk/women/womens-business/10011974/Zaha-Hadid-interview-Women-are-always-told-they-wont-make-it.html

thedreamstress.com/2011/04/queen-victorias-wedding-dress-the-one-that-started-it-all/

thefashionhistorian.com/2011/08/charles-frederick-worth-and-mary-curzon.html

theguardian.com/artanddesign/2002/nov/30/art.artsfeatures

theguardian.com/artanddesign/2009/may/25/tracey-emin-drawing-art

theguardian.com/artanddesign/2013/sep/08/zaha-hadid-serpentine-sackler-profile

theguardian.com/commentisfree/2006/oct/26/comment.politics1

theguardian.com/film/2015/aug/28/witches-evil-outcasts-feminist-heroes-pop-culture

theguardian.com/global-development/2016/jun/30/slavery-exploitation-worst-offender-lists-biased-towards-rich-countries-wont-help

theguardian.com/lifeandstyle/2014/apr/07/women-miners-strike-1984-wives-picket-lines

theguardian.com/lifeandstyle/2016/apr/10/sara-pascoe-boob-jobs-self-harm-animal-cosmetic-surgery

theguardian.com/politics/2013/jun/06/dagenham-sewing-machinists-strike

theguardian.com/politics/2015/aug/26/women-only-carriages-train-passengers-react-to-jeremy-corbyn-idea

theguardian.com/us-news/2015/jul/27/obama-ethiopia-lucy-fossil

theguardian.com/women-in-leadership/2015/feb/11/lack-of-female-headteachers-gender-diversity-education

theguardian.com/world/2015/dec/19/my-baby-refugee-mothers-hardest-journey-calais-jungle

theguardian.com/world/2017/apr/05/victims-should-marry-their-rapists-malaysian-mp-tells-parliament

thelancet.com/pdfs/journals/lancet/PIIS0140-6736(14)60634-6.pdf

traidcraft.co.uk/blog-entry/rozinas-story

ttin.uk/memories-of-greenham

usatoday.com/story/news/nation-now/2017/03/15/hijab-becomes-symbol-resistance-feminism-age-trump/98475212/

users.uoa.gr/~cdokou/RichCompulsoryHeterosexuality.pdf

waronwant.org/resources/baby-killer

womanandhersphere.com/tag/suffrage-banners/

Image Credits

© Anne Frank Fonds, Basel, Switzerland: p. 285

Archive Holdings Inc.: p. 188

Archives New Zealand: p. 314

Arclight/Alamy Stock Photo: p. 50

Authors' collection: pp. 84, 88, 165, 239 (all), 263, 264

Badsey Society: p. 200 (both)

CBW/Alamy Stock Photo: p. 291

City of Westminster Archive Centre, London, UK/Bridgeman Images: p. 28

Collection of the Smithsonian National Museum of African American History and Culture. Gift of Candace Greene: p. 218

Coram in the care of the Foundling Museum, London/Bridgeman Images: pp. 20, 23

DeAgostini/Getty Images: p. 57

Dunster Castle, Somerset/National Trust Photographic Library/Nadia Mackenzie/Bridgeman Images: p. 230

Edwin Remsberg/Alamy Stock Photo: p. 282 (left)

Falkensteinfoto/Alamy Stock Photo: p. 307

Flickr Commons/IWM: p. 244

Fotolibra/David Grimwade: p. 182

Frances E. Willard Memorial Library and Archives: p. 204

From *The Week of Hell '94*, 1995 © Tracey Emin. All rights reserved, DACS 2017. Image © Tate, London 2017: p. 294

Gibbs, Gardner and Company; American Anti-Slavery Society (American) 'Am I Not A Woman And A Sister' Anti-Slavery Hard Times Token, 1838. Copper. Purchased with the Abbie Bosworth Williams (Class of 1927) Fund Mount Holyoke College Art Museum, South Hadley, Massachusetts. Photograph by Laura Shea, 2015.9: p. 276 (bottom)

Gill Thorn: p. 41

Girl Guiding: p. 279

Good Vibrations Antique Vibrator Museum: p. 31

Goodwood House: p. 69

Hemis/Alamy Stock Photo: p. 215

History Collection 2016/Alamy Stock Photo: p. 75

Hulton Archive/Stringer: p. 249

Image Courtesy of The Advertising Archives: p. 211

Interfoto/Alamy Stock Photo: p. 310

Istockphoto/Afanasia: p. 34

Istockphoto/Branislavp: p. 174

Istockphoto/ConstantinosZ: p. 112

Istockphoto/georgeclerk: p. 93

Istockphoto/Marabird: p. 11

Istockphoto/mladn61: p. 197

Istockphoto/shawshot: p. 133

© IWM (Art.IWM PST 5184): p. 245

© IWM (Q 108500): p. 236

Jean-Sebastien Evrard/AFP/Getty Images: p. 305 (top)

© John Frost Newspapers/Mary Evans Picture Library: p. 179

Jonathan Walford/Fashion History Museum, Cambridge, Canada: p. 162

Kedleston Hall, Derbyshire, UK/National Trust Photographic Library/Andreas von Einsiedel/Bridgeman Images: p. 158

LBBD, Valence House Museum: p. 252

Library of Congress: pp. 85, 208, 282 (right),

Lisa Ryder/Alamy Stock Photo: p. 338

Loop Images Ltd/Alamy Stock Photo: p. 273

LSE Library: p. 194 (both)

Mary Evans/The National Archives, London: p. 91

© Mary Evans Picture Library: pp. 35, 121, 257, 270

Metropolitan Museum of Art: p. 149

Museo di Capodimonte, Naples, Italy/Bridgeman Images: p. 260

© Museum of London: p. 98

Musée Curie (Coll. ACJC): p. 114 (top)

NARA: p. 233 (bottom)

National Air and Space Museum / Gift of the Franklin Institute: p. 207

National Gallery of Australia, Canberra/Gift of Les Hollings and the Australian Textiles Fund, 1989/Bridgeman Images: p. 191

© National Museums Northern Ireland/Mary Evans: p. 60

Patrick Kovarik/Afp/Getty Images: p. 14

Paul Fearn/Alamy Stock Photo: p. 221

Photo12/UIG via Getty Images: p. 185

Photograph reproduced with the kind permission of Northampton Museums and Art Gallery: p. 144

Photo © Wedgwood Museum/WWRD: p. 276 (top)

Pictorial Press Ltd/Alamy Stock Photo: p. 135

Pictorial Press Ltd/Alamy Stock Photo: p. 317

Private Collection/Photo © Philip Mould Ltd, London/Bridgeman Images: p. 153

Private Collection/The Stapleton Collection/Bridgeman Images: p. 66

Public domain: pp. 72, 73, 124 (bottom), 126 (bottom), 156 (both), 267, 305 (bottom), 312

Rooful Ali/Aliway.co.uk: p. 143

Royal Collection Trust/© HM Queen Elizabeth II 2017: p. 320

Sallie McNamara: p. 332 (right)

Samir Hussein/Pool/WireImage: p. 63 (right)

Schlesinger Library/Flickr Commons: p. 8

Index

You may also enjoy …

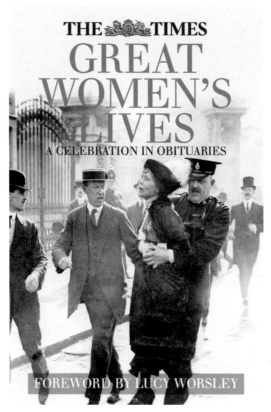

978 0 7509 6056 4

Great Women's Lives – the latest in *The Times*'
series of anthologies of its obituaries – focuses
on almost two centuries of ground-breaking
achievements by more than a hundred
women from around the world.

You may also enjoy …

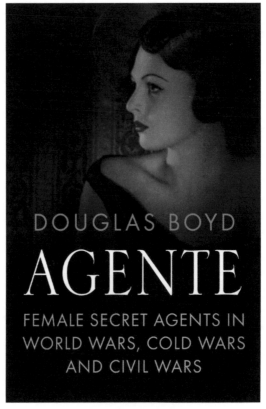

978 0 7509 6694 8

'Full of all sorts of trickery and treachery, double and even triple crossing, daring escapades and escapes, and death in the experiences of these women.' – A.A. Nofi for Strategypage.com